Frindall's Score Book

AUSTRALIA v ENGLAND
1978-79

MACDONALD AND JANE'S · LONDON

To Ray Robinson

and to many other friends in Australia for their hospitality and many kindnesses, and to my great uncle David and great aunt Eadith McNeill whom I met for the first time.

Copyright © Bill Frindall 1979

ISBN 0 354 08543 3

First published in 1979 by
Macdonald and Jane's Publishers Ltd
Paulton House
8 Shepherdess Walk
London N1 7LW

Made and printed in Great Britain by C. Nicholls & Company Ltd, The Philips Park Press, Manchester M11 4AU

CONTENTS

ACKNOWLEDGEMENTS

The author and publishers would like to thank the following for permission to reproduce the illustrations included in this book:

Patrick Eagar for figures 2, 3, 13, 14, 15, 16, 17, 18, 19, 20, 21, 22, 23, 24, 25, 26, 28, 29, 30, 31, 32, 33, 34, 35, 36, 37, 38, 48, 54, 55; *The Advocate* (Tasmania) for figure 1; Bryan Charlton for figures 39, 40, 41, 42, 43, 44, 45, 46, 47; Jim Fenwick and *The Courier-Mail* (Brisbane) for figure 12; Ron McKenzie for figures 4, 5, 7, 11; Garry Sparke for figures 6, 8, 9, 10, 27, 49, 50, 51, 52; *Sydney Morning Herald* for figure 53.

THANK YOU

This book would not have been possible without the generous help of many people. Besides recording my immense gratitude to Alan Smith for commissioning the volume and allowing me to fly my embryo arthritis away from a particularly vicious English winter, my special thanks are due to Patrick Eagar for his splendid artistry with several lenses, to the TCCB and Australian Board of Control for arranging Press Box accommodation at all matches, to Ray Robinson for his mammoth hospitality during my visits to Sydney, to Allan Leeson of *The Advocate* for introducing me to Tasmania, to Debbie Brown for holding fort and not forth whilst I was enjoying myself, to Chris and Jane Warne for housing Bonkers (my delinquent cat), to Jacky Frindall for more literary assistance, and to Isobel Smythe-Wood for putting everything in its proper order, for not smudging the inks and for never harassing me.

Bill Frindall, March 1979

1

THE FRINDALL SCORING METHOD

My scoring method is based on a system which most probably originated in Australia and was the brainchild of W. H. Ferguson, the internationally famous scorer. 'Fergie' (1880–1957) scored in 208 Test matches spread over all the Test-playing countries and officiated on no fewer than 43 tours. When continuous ball-by-ball radio commentaries were introduced, my BBC predecessors found the orthodox scoring system totally inadequate for the commentators' needs and adapted the Australian method. I revised their system and redesigned the sheets when I began scoring and supplying statistics for the BBC's *Test Match Special* commentaries in 1966. These sheets are reproduced in this volume and are those used by all scorers at BBC radio and television commentaries.

The method follows the basic conventions of the standard system as described in *Cricket Umpiring and Scoring*, a textbook for umpires and scorers compiled by R. S. Rait Kerr, who was secretary of the MCC from 1936 until 1952.

During BBC commentaries my system involves the use of three types of scoresheet: ball-by-ball record of play – *Sheet 1*; innings scorecard – *Sheet 2*; cumulative record of bowling analyses and extras – *Sheet 3*. As *Sheet 3* is essentially a commentator's aid which extracts data already recorded on *Sheet 1*, it has not been included in the match records of the six Tests. A sample has been included in this explanatory chapter just for general interest.

If you study the completed sample of each sheet you will find that the method accommodates many more details of the play than the conventional system and yet is still simple to follow.

Sheet 1, the ball-by-ball record of play, forms the basis of the scoring method but, unlike the other two sheets, it is not used by the commentators. It contains three sections: one for the bowlers, one for the batsmen, and one for recording the totals at the end of each over (or at the fall of a wicket, interval or stoppage of play for rain). Each line across these columns records one over; the time when the bowler starts an over is entered in the first column.

The sample *Sheet 1* shows the start of the Fourth Test at Sydney. You will see that there are two bowling columns (one for each end of the ground) and two batting columns which list the batsmen in the positions (left or right) in which their scores are shown on the scoreboard. Elaborate Australian scoreboards give the complete batting order of the innings in progress and list the two not out batsmen one above the other. My sheets were designed for use in England where only the Trent Bridge board follows the Australian style. In this volume the left/right separation serves only to identify the batsmen in End-of-over Totals columns.

My sheet shows that umpire Bailhache is standing at the Paddington (Press Box/Commentary Box) End, while umpire French is at the Randwick End with his back to the famous Hill. England, having won

AUSTRALIA v ENGLAND — 4th Test

at Sydney

ENGLAND 1st INNINGS — 1st DAY

Umpires: BAILHACHE (Paddington End), FRENCH (Randwick End)

Batsmen: BOYCOTT (cap), BREARLEY (Helmet cap)

Hot (33°C), no wind, very humid

TIME	BOWLER (Paddington)	O.	BOWLER (Randwick)	O.	SCORING (Left)	BALLS	6s/4s	SCORING (Right)	BALLS	6s/4s	NOTES	O.	RUNS	W.	L BAT	R BAT	EXTRAS
11.00	HOGG	1			+.+.↑..	8					W W M1	1	2				2
07			DYMOCK	1	.	9		L....L3 .1	7		ATTENDANCE (1st) 20,824	2	3			1	
12	"	2						1↑1•x .1	15		*Hit on chest M2	3					
18			"	2	BE 2.......	17						4	5		2		
22	"	3						...P⊙...2.1	24		NB NB/1	5	7			2	3
28	3-2-1-0(-)		"	3				EP	32		YARDLEY sub for HOGG M3 (5 overs)(23min)	6					
32	HURST	1			..3x2 2.1	23		8 2.	34			7	12		5	4	
37			"	4	↑..x7P 2.1	31						8	14		7		
41½	"	2						E2P 2.	42			9	16			6	
46			"	5	...9 1	35		.⊙•...	47		*Appeal ct wkt NB NB/2	10	18		8		4
51			"	3	↑.E W	40	-					10(5)	18	1	8	6	4
54					RANDALL cap										0		
56	"	3			.W↑8	2	-					10(7)	18	2	0	6	4
57	DRINKS														0		
12.01	"	3			GOOCH (Helmet cap) :	1					M4 1HR→	11					
03			"	6				...P9 2....	55			12	20		8		
08			"	4	..LB.⊙..	8		.8 .1	57		LB NB NB/3	13	23		9	6	
13	4-1-8-2(-)		"	7	P..	10		...P4 .1	63		Round wkt	14	24		10		
18	HOGG	4			...3 3	15		4.4 .1 9	67		NB/4 over wkt	15	31		3	14	
26			"	8				P .3 4	72			16	34			17	
30	"	5	8-1-12-0(-)					.⊙....W	80	-	NB NB/5	16(7)	35	3	3	17	7
36					GOWER (Helmet cap)(LHB)											0	
38	"	5						L	1		M5	17					
39	5-3-8-1(-)		HIGGS	1	L.P7P 3	24		.7 .1	3		Ball turning	18	39		6	1	
45	HURST	5			...x7 .1	30		4.4 21	5			19	43		7	4	
51			"	2	..8 4	38	1					20	47		11		
55	6-1-16-3(-)	6	2-0-8-0(1)		..7 1	41	1	.1 2 7xG W	10	-	Round wkt to LHB 2HR→	21	51	4	12	7	7
1.02	LUNCH							BOTHAM (Helmet cap)			M5 NB/5		LUNCH				
1.43			HIGGS	3	7 1	42		.......P	7			22	52		13	0	
46½	HOGG	6			YP..2.⊙. 7	51					NB NB/6	23	55		15		8
53			"	4	...1	54		...3⊙ 1	12		*Yallop misfielded	24	56			1	
57	"	7			.6 1	56		↑9% ... 8E 2.1	18		*nearly played on	25	60		16	4	
2.02			"	5	....	64						M6	26					
06	"	8			..9 6 .1	68		B 7..7.1	22		B Round wkt	27	65		18	6	9
13	8-3-18-1(-)		"	6				x	30		M7	28					
17	HURST	7			....	76					M8	29					
22			"	7	....W	81	1	6 1	31			29(6)	66	5	18	7	9
24	DRINKS				MILLER (Helmet cap)						Batsmen crossed				0		
28	7-2-16-3(-)		7-2-11-1(1)	7	-	-		..	33	-	M8 NB/6	30	66	5	0	7	9

the toss, elected to bat and I enter Boycott and Brearley's names in the batting columns. As batsmen wore such a variety of headgear in this series I thought it worth noting this alongside their names at the start of their innings. If they changed it during their innings, I recorded this fact in the Notes column. This data did prove useful and was the basis of an article by Ray Robinson.

Hogg is about to bowl the first ball of the match from the Paddington End and I enter his name on the next line of the appropriate column. I put a '1' in the square alongside it to show that it is his first over. When umpire Bailhache calls 'play', I enter the time in the first column and start my three stop watches: one for each batsman and one for the England innings as a whole.

I am now ready to record the first ball which is bowled to Boycott and called a 'wide'. This is recorded in that batsman's column as '+' just as in the traditional system. Four wides would be shown as '#'. The wide is also marked as 'W' in the Notes column, which serves to record details of all extras (or 'sundries' as they are called by Australians). Hogg gives me further practice at scoring a wide with his next delivery and I repeat the entire process. At this stage I am becoming a little alarmed as Boycott's scoring space has been planned with an eight-ball over in mind. I have filled a quarter of it before a legitimate ball has been bowled. Fortunately Hogg does not have to resort to blinkers and I do not have to devise a two-storey scoring space for his over.

Hogg's third legitimate ball is a bouncer which I show by putting a small arrow pointing upwards above the dot indicating that ball. Two balls later Boycott plays and misses and I record this error by putting a small 'X' above that dot. The last three balls produce no action worthy of note and are shown just as dots.

The completed over is a maiden despite the wides and I rule a line under the dots to mark that fact. I enter 'M1' in the Notes section to show that it is the first maiden of the innings and to facilitate a check with the bowling figures. I enter '8' in Boycott's Balls Received column; the wides are not included because the batsman cannot score off them. The End-of-over Totals require entries only when they have changed during that particular over, so I enter '1' in the 'O' (Over) column, '2' in the Runs (England Total) section, and '2' under Extras.

Dymock is about to begin the second over of the match and I note the time and enter his name in the other bowling column. It is Brearley's turn to take strike and the scoring is done in his column until he becomes the non-striker. He is struck on the pads by the second and sixth balls; the Australian appeals for lbw are turned down by umpire French and are shown as small 'Ls' above the appropriate dots on my sheet. If there had been no appeal the hit on the pad would have been recorded as 'P'.

Brearley hits the next ball into the covers and the batsmen cross for a single. I record this with a '1' to show the run and add a small '3' above it to show in which area of the field that run was scored. This is a cryptic form of charting the scoring strokes of each batsman's innings and it is based on the following key (which is reversed for left-handed batsmen):

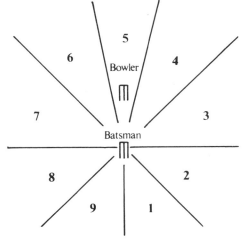

This method is only approximate but it does show if a batsman has a favourite scoring area, and also if a bowler is prone to conceding runs to a particular stroke. It is also possible to construct a scoring chart of a batsman's innings from the little numerals. After Vivian Richards had scored 232 against England at Nottingham in 1976, the England captain asked me for a set of charts showing the batsman's scoring strokes against each of the six bowlers used against him. I was able to construct these from my sheets and I also separated the 313 balls received by Richards to show his scoring rate against each bowler. After this Sydney Test, Dudley Doust, co-author with Mike Brearley of *The Ashes Retained* (Hodder & Stoughton Ltd, 1979), requested a similar breakdown of Randall's 150 to use as discussion material in his interviews with the Australian bowlers involved.

Dymock bowled the eighth ball of his first over to Boycott who failed to score off it. Before the next over I amend any totals which have changed: the Balls columns of both batsmen and the totals for Overs, Runs, and R Bat (Brearley) are the only ones which require updating.

I record the time at which Hogg starts his next over; as he bowled the previous over from that end it is not necessary to write his name – ditto marks ',,' will suffice, and a '2' in the next space denotes his second over of the innings. The first ball, a bouncer, hits Brearley on the chest and I mark the dot with an arrow and a blue dot to link that ball with my note of the incident. The over, another maiden, includes a further bouncer and a beaten stroke 'X'. At its completion only two totals require updating and the maiden is marked 'M2' in the Notes column.

And so the process continues. You will find that it quickly becomes a routine and you will devise your own sequence of recording and checking.

The first ball of Dymock's second over is edged by Boycott for two runs just backward of square-leg and I add a small '8E' above the '2', 'E' signifying the edged stroke. For routine scoring such elaborate refinements are obviously unnecessary, but for Test Match broadcasts

I need to record many minor details to be able to answer the commentators' questions. 'How many times has Boycott played and missed against Hogg?' or 'How many of Boycott's runs have come from edged strokes?' are legitimate queries in a continuous broadcast of a day's cricket.

Reduced to its bare essentials, the system requires only one digit to record each scoring stroke. Less recording is necessary while the over is in progress than with the standard scoring method. Instead of marking each run in the batting, bowling and tally sections of the normal scorebook, my method requires just the one entry. It is also immediately possible to tell exactly what has happened to each ball; who bowled it to whom, from which end, at what time, and how the batsman reacted. Unless a wicket falls, all the totalling is done at the end of the over while the fielders are changing positions and when there is no action to record.

The fourth ball of Hogg's third over is called a 'no ball' by umpire Bailhache and is recorded as 'O', just as in the standard system of scoring. If the no ball had been hit for four runs, it would have been shown as '④' in the batsman's column – similarly with any other number of runs scored off a no ball. A no ball counts as a ball received because, unlike a wide, the batsman can score off it.

Like other extras, no balls are itemised in the Notes column (NB) and a tally is kept of them immediately alongside: 'NB/1' denotes the first no ball call of the innings. This is to facilitate a check of the number of balls received by each batsman. I usually do this during drinks intervals and at the end of each session of play. The total number of overs is multiplied by eight and the number of no balls called is added to that total. This is then compared with the total number of balls received by the dismissed and not out batsmen. At the lunch interval, 21 overs have been bowled, including 5 no balls: $21 \times 8 + 5$ no balls = 173; (Boycott) 40 + Randall (2) + Brearley (80) + Gower (10) + Gooch (41) = 173.

After three overs, Hogg is taken off and his analysis (3 overs, 2 maidens, 1 run, 0 wickets) is recorded in his bowling column on the line below his last over. Any boundaries scored off him are shown in brackets after his analysis; '(–)' denotes that no boundaries were conceded by Hogg in his opening spell. Had he been hit for 5 fours and a six, it would have been shown as '(5/1)'. Hurst's name is entered on the line below Hogg's analysis. I enter the bowling analyses only at the end of each bowling spell or at the end of each session of play.

I use the Notes column to record the weather at the start of each day's play, the daily attendance figures, substitution of fielders, dropped catches, unsuccessful appeals for catches, injuries, bowlers changing from round to over the wicket, and any exceptional piece of fielding or unusual incident. Even the most obscure and apparently useless piece of data can prove invaluable.

Boycott edges the fifth ball of Hurst's third over and is caught by Border at second slip. The fall of a wicket produces a pressure point in any scoring system but practice will soon help you evolve the best action sequence and you will normally have two minutes in which to complete it before the new batsman starts his innings.

First, I stop the watch recording Boycott's batting time. It shows 54 minutes and this is recorded on *Sheet 2*, together with the other essential statistics: 'ct Border b Hurst 8', the fall of the wicket '1–18', boundaries '0', balls received '40', and a note of how he was out 'Edged forward defensive stroke to 2nd slip (dived in front of 1st slip)'. A red 'W' with an 'E' above it is entered in Boycott's batting column on *Sheet 1* to show which ball took his wicket. All the totals are completed in the End-of-over Totals section, Boycott's column in that section and his own batting column are ruled off in red and his Balls Received and '6s/4s' columns are carried down. The time of Boycott's dismissal (11.54 am) is entered on both sheets.

The name of the new batsman (Randall) is entered on the next line of the vacant batting column and Hurst's over is continued on the line below that, together with the time at which he restarts it. That time is also entered alongside Randall's name on *Sheet 2* and the stopwatch is set at zero and restarted. Two balls later Randall is brilliantly caught at backward square-leg and I repeat the entire procedure.

At this point a drinks interval is taken and noted. I always note the time of the start and finish of such intervals but, by tradition, this counts as playing time and cannot be deducted from the individual batting times. This has always seemed nonsensical and has convinced me that the only accurate and logical measurement of the duration of an innings is the number of balls received. This scoring system makes such a calculation extremely simple.

After Hurst has completed his over it is 12.02 pm and the England innings has been in progress for 62 minutes. Although strictly speaking 10.7 overs were bowled in the exact hour, it is simpler to wait till the end of the over before noting '1 HR' in the Notes column and recording 11 overs/18 runs in the appropriate section on *Sheet 2*.

At lunch, as at the end of any session or at a stoppage for rain or bad light, the three watches are stopped and all the totals on *Sheet 1* are carried down. The lunch score and not out batsmen's details are entered in the largest box on *Sheet 2*.

Before we leave *Sheet 1*, here is a list of the symbols which I use in the batting columns:

B	Bye	P	Hit on pad – no appeal
E	Edged stroke	S	Sharp (quick) run
EP	Edged ball into pads	X	Played and missed
F	Full toss	Y	Yorker
G	Hit on glove	↑	Bouncer
L	Hit on pad – lbw appeal	↓	Shooter
LB	Leg bye	⌒	Bowler used shortened run-up

The last of the above symbols was introduced in this Fourth Test when Hogg, suffering from heat exhaustion, frequently bowled (like Keith Miller) off only five or six paces.

Sheet 2, the Innings Scorecard, is the commentator's main source of reference. It records the starting and finishing times of each batsman's innings and its length in balls and minutes, his score, his number of boundaries, the total at which his wicket fell, and how and why he was out.

The lower part of the sheet shows the final bowling analyses, the hourly run and over rates, the time taken for each fifty runs scored by the team, the full details of each wicket partnership, the total and individual scores at the end of each session of play, details of when a new ball was taken, and notes of any records set during the innings.

Coloured inks are used to highlight the more important entries and to make it easier for the commentator to select essential items from a sheet containing so much data. Names and run totals are shown in blue, as is the close of play or 'stumps' score. Red is used for hundred partnerships, lunch and tea totals, and any other data of special interest.

Sheet 3, the Cumulative Record of Bowling Analyses and Extras, is essential only to radio and television commentators. It is illustrated here but has not been included in the scoresheets of the Test matches which follow.

Entries are made only at the end of each over or at the completion of a session of play. A red line is ruled under a bowler's figures when he is taken off. Intervals, close of play ('stumps'), and interruptions for rain and bad light are also shown, thus enabling the commentator to calculate quickly the length of each individual bowling spell. The number of boundaries conceded by each bowler is shown cumulatively.

Extras are recorded in separate columns on the right-hand side of the sheet. No balls and wides are also recorded against the name of each bowler.

This sheet facilitates a number of cross-checks. The total of the overs bowled by each bowler should equal the number bowled so far in the innings (5 + 8 + 6 + 2 = 21 at lunch). The total of maidens, runs, wickets, no balls and boundaries can be checked in the same way.

During the Third Test between England and West Indies in 1976, *The Sun* newspaper held a competition in which entrants were asked to score fifty consecutive overs of that Test match using my scoring method. The only guidance they had was an illustration of part of a *Sheet 1* accompanied by a very brief explanation of the system. Most of the 350 entries were of a very high standard and many of them came from the 12 to 16 age group. So, if you are studying this method for the first time, take heart — it is very much simpler than it appears at first sight.

ENGLAND 1st Innings v AUSTRALIA 4th Test

at Sydney Cricket Ground on January 6, 7, 8, 10, 11, 1979

Toss: ENGLAND

IN	OUT	MINS	No.	BATSMAN	HOW OUT	BOWLER	RUNS	WKT	TOTAL	6s	4s	BALLS	NOTES ON DISMISSAL
11·00	11·54	54	1	BOYCOTT	C⁺ BORDER	HURST	8	1	18	· ·	· ·	40	Edged forward defensive stroke to 2nd slip (dived in front of 1st slip)
11·00	12·36	96	2	BREARLEY*	BOWLED	HOGG	17	3	35	· ·	· ·	80	Missed walking defensive onside push at ball which took off stump.
11·56	11·57	1	3	RANDALL	C⁺ WOOD	HURST	0	2	18	· ·	· ·	2	Hooked short ball hard; backward short square leg (brilliant catch)
12·01	2·24	102	4	GOOCH	C⁺ TOOHEY	HIGGS	18	5	66	· ·	· 1	81	Pulled short ball to deep mid-wicket (magnificent falling catch)
12·38	1·02	24	5	GOWER	C⁺ MACLEAN	HURST	7	4	51	· ·	· ·	10	Failed to avoid ball which lifted sharply and hit gloves.
1·43	4·20	138	6	BOTHAM	C⁺ YALLOP	HOGG	59	9	141	· ·	· 7	108	Edged attempted hook at bouncer to substitute 'keeper.
2·28	2·32	4	7	MILLER	C⁺ MACLEAN	HURST	4	6	70	· ·	· 1	5	Edged firm-footed push at ball leaving him.
2·34	3·07	33	8	TAYLOR†	C⁺ BORDER	HIGGS	10	7	94	· ·	· 1	28	Followed leg-break – edged to gully.
3·09	3·18	9	9	EMBUREY	C⁺ WOOD	HIGGS	0	8	98	· ·	· ·	11	Pushed to forward short leg – two-handed catch to his left.
3·20	(4·41)	62	10	WILLIS	NOT OUT		7			· ·	· ·	43	
4·22	4·41	19	11	HENDRICK	BOWLED	HURST	10	10	152	· ·	· ·	24	Yorked (middle and leg stumps hit).

* CAPTAIN   † WICKET-KEEPER

EXTRAS	b 1	lb 1	w 2	nb 8	12

0⁶ 10⁴ **432 balls** (Including 10 no balls)

TOTAL (OFF 52·6 OVERS IN 281 MINUTES) **152**

11 OVERS 2 BALLS/HOUR
2·88 RUNS/OVER
35 RUNS/100 BALLS

BOWLER	O	M	R	W	nb/w		HRS	OVERS	RUNS		RUNS	MINS	OVERS	LAST 50 (in mins)
HOGG	11	3	36	2	5/2	1	11	18		50	120	20·6	120
DYMOCK	13	1	34	0	4	2	10	33		100	223	40·3	103
HURST	10·6	2	28	5	1/-	3	11	22		150	271	50·2	48
HIGGS	18	4	42	3	-	4	13	46					
Extras			12										
	52·6	10	152	10									

LUNCH: 51-4   Gooch 12* (41b, 61 min)
OFF 21 OVERS IN 122 MINUTES

TEA: 119-8   Botham 40* (89b, 120 min)   Willis 4* (23b, 23 min)
OFF 45 OVERS IN 242 MINUTES

YALLOP deputised as wicket-keeper for last 93 minutes (18·6 overs) of innings and 'caught BOTHAM in that position. MACLEAN left field at 3·49 pm suffering from heat exhaustion and effects of blow to left eye (6 stitches) received in nets on Jan. 4.

ENGLAND'S TOTAL OF 152 WAS THEIR LOWEST IN A FIRST INNINGS AT SYDNEY SINCE 1894-95.

WKT	PARTNERSHIP		RUNS	MINS
1st	Boycott	Brearley	18	54
2nd	Brearley	Randall	0	1
3rd	Brearley	Gooch	17	35
4th	Gooch	Gower	16	24
5th	Gooch	Botham	15	41
6th	Botham	Miller	4	4
7th	Botham	Taylor	24	33
8th	Botham	Emburey	4	9
9th	Botham	Willis	43	41
10th	Willis	Hendrick	11	19
			152	

Sheet 2

AUSTRALIA Bowling   4th Test   ENGLAND 1st Innings

HOGG					DYMOCK					HURST					HIGGS				
NB III		WIDES 11			NB IIII		WIDES			NB I		WIDES			NB		WIDES		
O	M	R	W	4s	O	M	R	W	4s	O	M	R	W	4s	O	M	R	W	4s
1	1	0	0		1	0	1	0		1	0	5	0		1	0	4	0	
2	2	0	0		2	0	3	0		2	0	7	0		2	0	8	0	1
3	2	1	0	-	3	1	3	0		3	1	7	2			LUNCH			
4	2	8	0		4	1	5	0		4	1	8	2	-	3	0	9	0	
5	3	8	1	-	5	1	6	0		5	1	12	2		4	0	10	0	
	LUNCH				6	1	8	0		6	1	16	3		5	1	10	0	
6	3	10	1		7	1	9	0			LUNCH				6	2	10	0	
7	3	14	1		8	1	12	0	-	7	2	16	3		7	2	11	1	
8	3	18	1	-		LUNCH				8	2	23	4	1	8	3	11	1	
	TEA				9	1	16	0		9	2	26	4		9	4	11	1	
9	3	26	1	2	10	1	17	0		10	2	28	4	1	10	4	16	1	2
10	3	33	2	3	11	1	21	0	1		TEA				11	4	22	2	3
11	3	36	2	3	12	1	32	0	3	10⁶	2	28	5	1	12	4	25	3	
					13	1	34	0	3						13	4	26	3	
						TEA									14	4	28	3	1
																TEA			
															15	4	34	3	
															16	4	38	3	
															17	4	41	3	
															18	4	42	3	3

EXTRAS				
B	LB	W	NB	TOTAL
			1	1
		2		2
			1	3
		2		4
			3	6
			4	7
		5		8
1				9
			6	10
			7	11
			8	12

Sheet 3

13

THE ASHES RETAINED

Before the tour began most pundits would have backed England to retain the Ashes fairly comfortably, despite a large question-mark over the early batting. That they won by such an unprecedented and overwhelming margin, owed much to the revised nature of Australian pitches. When England's bowlers, particularly the off-spinners and the admirable Hendrick, found pitches as responsive as those at home, the disparity in the experience of the two sides was inevitably accentuated. Australia thus found themselves up against an attack of world-class accuracy operating in helpful conditions, which was directed by the most able of tacticians, and supported by, arguably, the best wicket-keeping/fielding combination ever to visit their country. For those who think that an Australian team selected from all its current professionals would have fared rather differently, I would remind you that most of those who have rendered themselves ineligible for Test cricket were members of the team which came a very poor second in 1977.

England were handsomely served by Alec Bedser and his fellow selectors. They kept faith with Brearley despite an abysmal season with the bat. He inspired a supreme level of self-confidence in his players and was the architect of several recoveries, none more astonishing than that in the Fourth Test. They gave Randall a summer away from the limelight in which to regain his confidence and brought him back to play four major innings in the series. Miller, by no means an automatic selection, developed most on the tour and, besides playing a number of vital support innings, took more wickets in the rubber (23) than any previous English off-spinner had managed in Australia.

Australia were poorly served by their selectors, none of whom had played first-class cricket for 16 years. They replaced Simpson a year too early with a man totally inexperienced in captaincy when they had a ready-made replacement in the highly successful Western Australian captain, John Inverarity. They picked only one specialist opening batsman for the first Test and failed to choose the best wicket-keeper for the first four matches. Perhaps even more disastrously they cast aside Border and Darling when those two young players were showing every sign of coming to terms with Test cricket. Their significant triumph was the opening bowling pair of Hurst and Hogg. Hurst bowled magnificently on occasions and his endurance in the long hot second innings at Adelaide was an amazing exhibition. The incredible success of Hogg, an unknown 27-year-old who had been unable to gain a cap for his native State or hold a regular place in the team of his adopted one, was totally unpredictable. Even after the first sight of him in the opening first-class match, one correspondent had written 'You can forget about Hogg'. That young scribe's foolishness was underlined 41 times.

Australian cricket will soon recover if the selectors and public have a little more patience. For the moment let us offer the warmest congratulations to Mike Brearley and his team on a most splendid victory and savour again those glad tidings that made bearable the siege of Britain in 1978–79.

2 The 1978–79 England touring team in Australia – *Back row (l–r):* D. W. Randall, C. T. Radley, J. K. Lever, G. Miller, I. T. Botham, P. H. Edmonds, M. Hendrick, J. E. Emburey, G. A. Gooch, D. I. Gower, R. W. Tolchard, G. G. A. Saulez *(scorer)*. *Front row (l–r):* B. W. Thomas *(physiotherapist)*, G. Boycott, R. G. D. Willis *(vice-captain)*, J. M. Brearley *(captain)*, D. J. Insole *(manager)*, R. W. Taylor, C. M. Old, K. F. Barrington *(assistant manager)*.

3 Australia at Sydney, fourth Test – *Back row (l–r):* W. M. Darling, G. Dymock, A. G. Hurst, P. M. Toohey, B. Yardley *(12th man)*, J. D. Higgs, A. R. Border. *Front row (l–r):* G. M. Wood, J. A. Maclean *(vice-captain)*, G. N. Yallop *(captain)*, R. M. Hogg, K. J. Hughes.

THE FIRST TEST AT BRISBANE

England ended their long period of non-success at The Gabba by completing a most professional victory with seven wickets and half a day to spare. Eight matches had passed since 1936 when Allen and Voce bowled out Australia on a rain-affected pitch for their lowest home score this century (58). The ground is now the best-appointed in Australia and has been completely rebuilt during the last decade. It boasts a sumptuous boundaryside Cricketers' Club and a new press box with a perfect view through smoked glass.

The damp pitch, aided by a canopy of cloud and an over-grassed outfield, encouraged the Kookaburra ball to seam and swing throughout the first day; never did it favour the batsman. Those responsible for its preparation predicted early 'life' and advised bowling first. Not surprisingly, England's new ball specialists frequently appeared unplayable; Bill O'Reilly had never seen anyone swing a ball in Australia as much as Botham did, and Willis eagerly ignored the pain from blistered feet to bowl most overs in the match.

Wood gave England a vital and immediate advantage by indulging in his own peculiar form of Russian roulette from the very first ball. That initial success inspired a fifth-ball encore and the loping Gower needed no further practice at racing in and scoring a direct underarm hit.

The batting of both teams confirmed a shortage of match practice (English teams which were shipped to Fremantle enjoyed two extra first-class games). Even so, Australia's final total was probably par against that bowling in those conditions. Ken Barrington predicted that they would not

4 Woolloongabba
Ground, Brisbane

be dismissed so cheaply again and he was almost right. Yallop and Hughes showed splendid application and self-discipline in grafting the match into the last day and opening up an outside chance of victory. Oddly their partnership of 170, the highest of the rubber, exactly equalled England's lead and their ultimate target.

Randall, perhaps lucky to return to Test cricket whilst in form and with scores of 63, 110, 66 and 47 immediately behind him, was a worthy 'Man of the Match'; his first innings 75 was played when the pitch still held its early devil. Gower, short of runs after a splendid start to the tour, batted with the elegance and easy assurance that hallmarks the class player. Botham continued to prove that he is the most exciting allround cricketer since Sobers. Miller, absent from many amateur selector's list when the touring party was announced, visibly came of age as a Test match bowler. Follow-through problems had resulted in a slight change of action which encouraged flight and the exploitation of a cross-breeze for outswing. Australia's selectorial trio of Ridings, Loxton and Harvey – none of whom had played first-class cricket for 16 years – erred badly in choosing Cosier instead of a specialist opening batsman. A reasonable start was essential to a batting side desperately short of experience and depth.

Australia could boast a major discovery in Hogg who bowled with superb control and cut the ball back off the pitch at a pace only slightly behind that of Willis.

The wicket-keeping of Bob Taylor will remain an outstanding memory. His timing in difficult conditions was superb; they say that you cannot hear the ball meeting his gloves. He set an exceptionally high standard which inspired both bowlers and outfielders; surprisingly his five catches in the first innings constituted an England record against Australia.

AUSTRALIA 1st Innings v ENGLAND 1st Test

at Woolloongabba, Brisbane on December 1, 2, 3, 5, 6, 1978

IN	OUT	MINS	No.	BATSMAN	HOW OUT	BOWLER	RUNS
11·00	11·45	45	1	WOOD	CT TAYLOR	OLD	7
11·00	11·03	3	2	COSIER	RUN OUT (GOWER)		1
11·05	11·14	9	3	TOOHEY	BOWLED	WILLIS	1
11·16	12·15	59	4	YALLOP *	CT GOOCH	WILLIS	7
11·47	12·21	34	5	HUGHES	CT TAYLOR	BOTHAM	4
12·17	12·25	8	6	LAUGHLIN	CT SUB (J.K. LEVER)	WILLIS	2
12·23	(3·16)	135	7	MACLEAN †	NOT OUT		33
12·27	1·46	40	8	YARDLEY	CT TAYLOR	WILLIS	17
1·47	3·06	78	9	HOGG	CT TAYLOR	BOTHAM	36
3·07	3·09	2	10	HURST	CT TAYLOR	BOTHAM	0
3·11	3·16	5	11	HIGGS	BOWLED	OLD	1

* CAPTAIN   † WICKET-KEEPER

TEST DEBUTS: R.M. HOGG
             J.A. MACLEAN

| | | | | | EXTRAS | b - lb 1   w - nb 6 | 7 |

TOTAL (OFF 37·7 OVERS IN 218 MINS.) **116**

BOWLER	O	M	R	W	nb	HRS	OVERS	RUNS		RUNS	MINS	OVERS	LAST 50 (in mins)
WILLIS	14	2	44	4	-	1	11	17		50	121	21·1	121
OLD	9·7	1	24	2	4	2	10	31		100	190	32·6	69
BOTHAM	12	1	40	3	3	3	10	48					
GOOCH	1	0	1	0	-								
EDMONDS	1	1	0	0	-								
Extras / Run Outs			7	1									
	37·7	5	116	10									

WKT	TOTAL	6ˢ	4ˢ	BALLS	NOTES ON DISMISSAL
3	14	.	.	30	Offside edge to forward push.
1	2	.	.	2	Failed to beat cover-point's direct hit on 'keeper's wicket.
2	5	.	.	12	Drove outside break-back (middle and off stumps)
4	22	.	.	40	Edged half-cock push at ball leaving him - comfortable 2nd slip catch.
5	24	.	.	24	Offside driving outswinger - not at 'pitch'.
6	26	.	.	3	Hooked bouncer to long-leg — top edge.
.	.	.	2	83	–
7	53	.	2	40	Offside edge attempting drive - not at 'pitch'.
8	113	.	5	67	Edged firm-footed, offside push.
9	113	.	.	4	Beaten by lifting outswinger.
10	116	.	.	5	Yorked.

0⁶ 9⁴ 310 balls (including 7 no balls)

10 OVERS 3 BALLS/HOUR
3.06 RUNS/OVER
37 RUNS/100 BALLS

LUNCH: 48-6 MACLEAN 12* (27b, 38') YARDLEY 12* (32b, 34')
OFF 21 OVERS IN 121 MINUTES

AUSTRALIA ALL OUT AT 3.16pm 1st DAY
TEA TAKEN AT THE END OF THE INNINGS

R.W. TAYLOR (5 ct) equalled the series record of dismissals in an innings shared by W.A.S. Oldfield, G.R.A. Langley, A.T.W. Grout (twice), J.M. Parks, and R.W. Marsh (twice). TAYLOR established new record for most catches in an innings for England against Australia.

AUSTRALIA's total was their second-lowest in any Test on the Woolloongabba Ground.

WKT	PARTNERSHIP		RUNS	MINS
1ˢᵗ	Wood	Cosier	2	3
2ⁿᵈ	Wood	Toohey	3	9
3ʳᵈ	Wood	Yallop	9	29
4ᵗʰ	Yallop	Hughes	8	28
5ᵗʰ	Hughes	Laughlin	2	4
6ᵗʰ	Laughlin	Maclean	2	2
7ᵗʰ	Maclean	Yardley	27	40
8ᵗʰ	Maclean	Hogg	60	78
9ᵗʰ	Maclean	Hurst	0	2
10ᵗʰ	Maclean	Higgs	3	5

116

AUSTRALIA v ENGLAND   1st Test
at Brisbane

1st DAY	BOWLERS				BATSMEN					AUSTRALIA 1st INNINGS						
	Umpire: M.G. O'Connell		Umpire: R.A. French		SCOREBOARD LEFT				SCOREBOARD RIGHT		NOTES	END-OF-OVER TOTALS				
	VULTURE St END		STANLEY St END													
TIME	BOWLER	O.	BOWLER	O.	SCORING	BALLS	6s/4s	SCORING	BALLS	6s/4s		O.	RUNS	W.	'L' BAT	'R' BAT	EXTRAS
					WOOD cap (LHB)			COSIER No cap			Heavy cloud cover & humidity.						
11·00			WILLIS	1	¹ 3S P ··	3		· ¹ 7 9LO	2	–	WILLIS Round wkt to left-hand bat.	0⁵	2		1	1	–
03								TOOHEY cap			ATTENDANCE (1st): 14,026					0	
05			"	1				·· x	3			1					
07	OLD	1			·· ¹ 3	6		·· x x ⊙1 7	9		NB NB/1	2	5			2	1
12½			"	2				·· W	12	–		2³	5	2	2	1	1
14	"							YALLOP Helmet-cap (LHB)			Yallop wearing helmet-type cap.					0	
16			"	2				↑ L ·	5		M1	3					
19	"	2			P x ⊙ ·· L 7	14		·	6		NB NB/2	4	7		3		2
26			"	3	7	15		8 2 ······	13		Damaged ball appeal– turned down.	5	10		4	2	
31½	"	3			····· 2	21		·· x	15			6	11		5		
37			"	4	·· x 9	26		···	18		WILLIS over wkt	7	12		6		
42	"	4			·¹ 7 ·W E	30	–	·· 1	21			7⁷	14	3	7	3	
45					HUGHES cap											0	
47	"	4			· 1	1						8					
48			"	5	·· ↑ 4	4		·· x 3S	26			9	15			4	
53	"	5						·······	34		M2	10					
58			"	6	··· 8E	9		· ⊙1 EP4S	37		1 HR →	11	17		1	5	
12·03 05	DRINKS	6			L ······	16		1	38		● DROPPED 2nd SLIP (GOOCH)	12	18			6	
10	6-1-7-1(-)		"	7	x 1E ·2·1	20		3 W E	40	–	● EDGED low to 4th SLIP (OLD)	12⁶	22	4	4	7	2
15								LAUGHLIN No cap (LHB)			OLD off (injured hand) LEVER sub.					0	
17			"	7				2 2 ··	2			13	24			2	
19	BOTHAM	1			··· W E	24	–					13⁴	24	5	4	2	2
21					MACLEAN cap											0	
23	"	1			4 2···	4						14	26		2		
25			"	8				↑ W	3	–		14¹	26	6	2	2	2
27			"	8	x x ···	11		YARDLEY cap				15				0	
32	"	2						······· EP x	8		M3	16					
36			"	9	··· 1E 9 4·1	17	1	↑ ·	10		M4 ● Between 2nd & 3rd slips	17	31		7		
42	"	3			·· 3 x	22		8 ·· 1	13			18	33		8	1	
47			"	10	8 1E 8 1 ·1	26		8 · 3 1 · 1	17		● Bat handle – ducked	19	41		11	6	
53	"	4	10-2-28-3(1)		8 1	27		···· P4 7 4··1	24	1		20	47		12	11	
57	4-1-10-1(1)		GOOCH	1		27	1	x· ···· x 8 ·1	32	1	● stumping attempt 2 HR →	21	48	6	12	12	2
1·01	LUNCH		1-0-1-0(-)								M4 NB/2 OLD back*				L U N C H	
1·40	BOTHAM	5			P· ··	29		19E x ·· x 8 4···1	38	2	● DROPPED 2nd SLIP (GOOCH)	22	53			17	
45			WILLIS	11				P· W E	40	2		22²	53	7	12	17	2
46								HOGG Helmet			HOGG wearing white crash helmet.					0	
47			"	11	·	30		···· 8 1	5			23	54			1	
51½	6-1-16-1(2)	6	11-2-29-4(1)		···· x	36	1	7 ·1	7	–	M4 NB/2	24	55	7	12	2	2

AUSTRALIA v ENGLAND — 1st Test

at Brisbane

1st DAY TIME	BOWLERS (O'CONNELL) VULTURE St END BOWLER	O.	(FRENCH) STANLEY St END BOWLER	O.	BATSMEN SCOREBOARD LEFT SCORING	BALLS	6s/4s	SCOREBOARD RIGHT SCORING	BALLS	6s/4s	AUSTRALIA 1st INNINGS NOTES	O.	RUNS	W.	L BAT	R BAT	EXTRAS
					MACLEAN	36	1	HOGG	7	-	M4 NB 2	24	55	7	12	2	2
1·56			WILLIS	12	...LB..	41		.↑ 7s	10		(LB)	25	58			4	3
2·01	BOTHAM	7	"		2·3	43		4 8 L 6 / 4·1 ·003	18	1	(NB)(NB) NB/3 4	26	71		15	12	5
07½			"	13				...4...4	26	3		27	79			20	
14	"	8			6↑?8↑● 2·4·0··	52	2				(NB) NB/5 *Hit in midriff	28	86		21		6
19½	8-1-33-1(4)		"	14	.	53		2↑● ✗ ?1E 4...	33	4	*Warning (intimidation) Brearley/French summit	29	91			25	
28	OLD	7	14-2-44-4(4)		7s 1	54		2✗●2 2··1	40		JKLEVER sub for Willis (blistered feet) ●RO chance (Maclean) *Gower throw missed.	30	95		22	28	
33			BOTHAM	9	L4 ·1	57		✗··↑	45		3HR →	31	96		23		
39	"	8			✗L4● L 2O··	66					●c4 3rd slip (Botham) (NB) NB/6	32	99		25		7
44/46 DRINKS			"	10	·.L	68		P... 3 ·1	51			33	100			29	
50	"	9			8 1	69		1 3 2·4·	58	5	50 p'ship in 65 min.	34	108		26	36	
56	9-1-21-1(1)		"	11	↑ 3 L8 ✗ ·2·2··	77						35	112		30		
3·01	EDMONDS	1			F P	66					M5	36					
04	1-1-0-0(-)		"	12	1E 1	79		W	67	5		36³	113	8	31	36	7
06								HURST cap								0	
07			"	12				..W E	4	-		36⁷	113	9	31	0	7
09								HIGGS cap								0	
11			"	12				·1				37					
13	OLD 9·7-1-24-2(-)	10	12-1-40-3(4)		P 3 6 ·① 1	83	2	✗ 3 ·W ✗ ·1	5	-	NB/7	37⁷	116	10	33	1	7
3·16	AUSTRALIA ALL OUT										M5 NB/7		ALL OUT				
	BATTING TIME: 218 MINUTES							310 balls									

5 Celebrating 50 years of Test cricket in Brisbane — A commemorative medal especially struck for the toss is delivered by air male.

6 Australia are all out for 116 — Higgs is yorked by Old and Australia have been dismissed for their second-lowest total in any Test at The Gabba.

ENGLAND 1st Innings

In reply to AUSTRALIA'S 116 all out

IN	OUT	MINS	No.	BATSMAN	HOW OUT	BOWLER	RUNS
3.35	5.17	91	1	BOYCOTT	Cᵗ HUGHES	HOGG	13
3.35	3.53	18	2	GOOCH	Cᵗ LAUGHLIN	HOGG	2
3.55	2.13	223	3	RANDALL	Cᵗ LAUGHLIN	HURST	75
5.19	2.36	172	4	TAYLOR †	LBW	HURST	20
2.15	2.34	19	5	BREARLEY *	Cᵗ MACLEAN	HOGG	6
2.35	4.45	111	6	GOWER	Cᵗ MACLEAN	HURST	44
2.38	4.39	102	7	BOTHAM	Cᵗ MACLEAN	HOGG	49
4.41	11.20	93	8	MILLER	LBW	HOGG	27
4.47	5.02	15	9	EDMONDS	Cᵗ MACLEAN	HOGG	1
5.06	(12.05)	113	10	OLD	NOT OUT		29
11.21	12.05	44	11	WILLIS	Cᵗ MACLEAN	HURST	8
* CAPTAIN † WICKET-KEEPER				EXTRAS	b 7 lb 4 w - nb 1		12

TOTAL (OFF 95.4 OVERS IN 511 MINUTES) 286

J.A. Maclean equalled series record of 5 dismissals in an innings.

BOWLER	O	M	R	W	nb
HURST	27.4	6	93	4	3
HOGG	28	8	74	6	1
LAUGHLIN	22	6	54	0	-
YARDLEY	7	1	34	0	-
COSIER	5	1	10	0	-
HIGGS	6	2	9	0	-
Extras			12		
	95.4	24	286	10	

HRS	OVERS	RUNS
1	11	25
2	11	35
3	11	23
4	13	28
5	10	29
6	12	58
7	10	37
8	12	35

RUNS	MINS	OVERS	LAST 50 (in mins)
50	110	20.2	110
100	230	44	120
150	309	57.7	79
200	362	68.4	53
250	443	83.2	81

2ⁿᵈ NEW BALL taken at 4.11 pm 2nd day –
ENGLAND 180-5 after 65.2 overs.

WKT	TOTAL	6s	4s	BALLS	NOTES ON DISMISSAL
2	38	.	1	67	Edged to 3rd slip - left-handed catch.
1	2	.	.	13	Edged lifting outswinger via thighpad to gully.
3	111	1	10	196	Edged off drive low to gully - superb diving catch (left-handed)
5	•120	.	.	115	Shuffled across stumps - played back.
4	120	.	1	13	Short ball hit glove - leg-side catch.
7	219	.	5	90	Edged cut at short offside ball.
6	215	.	5	73	Edged (bat shoulder) attempted hook at bouncer.
9	266	.	1	70	Shuffled across stumps - beaten on back stroke.
8	226	.	.	9	Edged flick at short legside ball - diving left-handed catch.
.	.	.	2	102	-
10	286	.	1	20	Edged attempted offside steer wide to keeper's right.

1⁶ 26⁴ 768 balls (including 4 no balls)

11 OVERS 2 BALLS/HOUR
2.99 RUNS/OVER
37 RUNS/100 BALLS

R.M. Hogg took 6 wickets on debut.

TEA TAKEN BETWEEN INNINGS   BLSP 4.59pm - 5.10pm
11 MINUTES LOST

BAD LIGHT STOPPED PLAY at 5.45pm 26 MINS LOST ON 1ST DAY

STUMPS 1ST DAY : 60-2   RANDALL 43* (76b, 99')   TAYLOR 2* (21b, 26')
OFF 22 OVERS IN 119 MINUTES

RSP 11.54 - 12.25 31 MINUTES LOST

LUNCH : 90-2   RANDALL 62* (159b, 189')   TAYLOR 10* (75b, 116')
OFF 39 OVERS IN 209 MINUTES

TEA : 176-5   GOWER 20* (50b, 67')   BOTHAM 30* (52b, 64')
OFF 63 OVERS IN 332 MINUTES

STUMPS 2ND DAY : 257-8   BLSP at 5.55pm. 36 MINS LOST ON 2ND DAY
MILLER 19* (55b, 74')   OLD 17* (40b, 48')
OFF 83.4 OVERS IN 446 MINUTES

WKT	PARTNERSHIP		RUNS	MINS
1st	Boycott	Gooch	2	18
2nd	Boycott	Randall	36	71
3rd	Randall	Taylor	73	149
4th	Taylor	Brearley	9	21
5th	Taylor	Gower	0	1
6th	Gower	Botham	95	102
7th	Gower	Miller	4	4
8th	Miller	Edmonds	7	15
9th	Miller	Old	40	68
10th	Old	Willis	20	44

286

23

AUSTRALIA v ENGLAND　　1st Test

at Brisbane

1st DAY TIME	BOWLERS (O'CONNELL) VULTURE St END BOWLER	O.	(FRENCH) STANLEY St END BOWLER	O.	BATSMEN SCOREBOARD LEFT SCORING	BALLS	6s 4s	SCOREBOARD RIGHT SCORING	BALLS	6s 4s	ENGLAND 1st INNINGS NOTES	END-OF-OVER TOTALS O.	RUNS	W.	L BAT	R BAT	EXTRAS
					BOYCOTT cap			GOOCH Hat									
3.35			HURST	1	x · · · · · ·	8					M1	1					
40	HOGG	1						7 2 · · · E· x · x ·	8		· short of 4th slip	2	2			2	
46			·	2	· · · · · ↑ x · ·	16					M2	3					
51	·	2	}					· · · E · W	13	–	· DROPPED GULLY (LAUGHLIN)	3⁵	2	1	0	2	–
53								RANDALL cap								0	
55	·	2	}					· · · x	3		M3	4					
57½			·	3	85 ·1	18		· · · x ·	9			5	3		1		
4.03	·	3			· · · · · · · ·	26					M4	6					
09	3-2-2-1 (-)		·	4				48 4 · · · · · L L49 4	17	2		7	11			8	
15	LAUGHLIN	1			8 ·1	28		· · · · · ·	23			8	12		2		
19			·	5	7 ↑ 7 1 · 1	31		3 7· 1 2 · · ·	28		· Hit in abdomen	9	17		4	11	
24¼	·	2			· · · 6 · ·	35		8 · 4 · ·	32	3		10	22		5	15	
29			·	6	x · 8 · 7 · · 2 · 1	42		· · ·	33		1HR→	11	25		8		
34	·	3			· · · · · · · ·	50					M5	12					
38			·	7				· · · · ·2②2· ·	42		NB/1	13	29			19	
43	·	4	7-2-21-0 (2)		· · · · E · 3 4	58	1					14	33		12		
48	4-1-10-0 (2)		HOGG	4				EP · · · · E ·	50		· Appeal v. light. M6	15					
54 57	DRINKS YARDLEY	1	4-3-2-1 (-)		85 1	59	1	8F 4 ·	52	4	M6 NB/1	15³	38	1	13	23	–
4.59	BLSP										11 Mins lost		B L S P				
5.10	YARDLEY	1						· · · · ·	57			16					
12			HOGG	5	· · · · · x · E · W	67	1				M7	17	38	2	13	23	–
17					TAYLOR Helmet cap										0		
19	·	2						E 8 · P · 6 · · 4 · · 6 ·	65	1/5	· Appeal v. light.	18	48			33	
24	2-0-15-0 (2/1)		·	6	· · · · ↑2 ·1	6		· · ·	67			19	49		1		
30	LAUGHLIN	5			· · · · · · · ·	14					M8	20					
34			·	7	· · · ↑· · 19	19		x 8 7 · 4 1	70	1/6	· Hit on shoulder	21	54			38	
40	·	6	7-4-8-2 (1)		· 8 · 1	21	–	5 8 · · · · 4 1	76	1/7	· Hit on arm 2HR→	22	60	2	2	43	–
5.45	6-1-16-0 (3) BLSP										M8 NB/1		B L S P				
6.00	STUMPS		(1ST DAY)								26 Minutes lost 1st day.		S T U M P S				
2ND DAY 11.00			HURST	8	LB · · · ·	25		· · · · x	80		LB M9	23	61				1
06	HOGG	8			2 · ③ · B	28		2E · · · · 8	86		B NB/2	24	67		5	45	2
13			·	9	LB · · ·	30		2 · 9 · 4 · 1 ·	92	1/8	· Appeal at wkt (leg side) LB	25	73			50	3
19	·	9			8 ·1 · ·	34		7 1E · · 2 1	96		RANDALL's 50: 115' · DROPPED 1st slip (Yallop)	26	77		6	53	
25			·	10				· · · · · · · ·	104		M10	27					
29	·	10			7 1 · ·	37		· 7 3 · 2 1	109		ATTENDANCE (2nd) 11,157	28	81		7	56	
36			·	11				· · · ↑ ↑ 48 · 1	117			29	82			57	
41	·	11	11-4-27-0 (3)					· · · · · · · ·	125		M11	30					
47			LAUGHLIN	7	· · · · L · · ·	45					· Randall to boundary M12 spectator moved by screen.	31					
53	11-3-5-2-2 (1)	12	7-3-16-0 (3)		t. ·	47	–	9 ·1	126	1/8	t RAIN M12 NB/2 RSP at 11.54 am	31³	83	2	7	58	3

24

AUSTRALIA v ENGLAND — 1st Test
at Brisbane

2ND DAY TIME	BOWLER (O'CONNELL) VULTURE St. END	O.	BOWLER (FRENCH) STANLEY St. END	O.	SCOREBOARD LEFT SCORING	BALLS	6s/4s	SCOREBOARD RIGHT SCORING	BALLS	6s/4s	NOTES	O.	RUNS	W.	L.BAT	R.BAT	EXTRAS
11.54	R.S.P.				TAYLOR	47	–	RANDALL	126	1/8	31 MINUTES LOST M12 NB/2	31³	83	2	7	58	3
12.25	HOGG	12			. . . ↑ . .	52						32					
29			LAUGHLIN	8				L L	134		M13 3 HR →	33					
33	"	13			↑↑↑ .7 . . 1	57		. . 1E 1	137			34	85		8	59	
39			"	9				L	145		M14	35					
43	"	14			. . . E .7. .2. .	65					○ 1+1 over throw	36	87		10		
49	14·5·26·2 (1)		"	10	.	66		. . . . . 9E 1	152		50 p'ship in 107 min	37	88			60	
53	COSIER	1			. . . ↑	69		. . . . 8 1	157		↑ Round wkt	38	89			61	
58	1·0·1·0 (–)		"	11	. . . . .	75	–	.2. 1	159	1/8	M14 NB/2	39	90	2	10	62	3
1.01 LUNCH			11·5·18·0 (3)								LUNCH						
1.40	COSIER	2			. .7 . 1	77		. . . LB 1	165		(LB)	40	92		11		4
44			LAUGHLIN	12	.9 1 . . .	81		.1. L . 8 1	169			41	94		12	63	
49	"	3						. . . . . . .4 9Ex 1	177	1/9		42	98			67	
53			"	13	L . . . R↑ . .	89					○ Appeal ct sh.leg M15	43					
56½	"	4						. . . ↑ .4 6	185	1/10	↑ Round wkt	44	102			71	
2.01½			"	14	27 23	91		8 2. .EP. .7 2	191			45	111		17	75	
06	"	5	14·6·29·0 (3)		 x	99					M16 4HR →	46					
11	5·1·10·0 (2)		HURST	12	)			. . . . E W	196	1/10		46⁵	111	3	17	75	4
13					)			BREARLEY (padded cap)								0	
15			"	12	)			.x. . .	3		M17	47					
18	HOGG	15			.7 2.	107						48	113		19		
24			"	13				1E .4 .2. 9 . . P 1	11	1		49	119			6	
28	"	16			. . . . .2 1	113		.G W 1	13	1		50	120	4	20	6	4
34								GOWER (Helmet cap) (LHB)								0	
35			"	14	.L W	115	–					50²	120	5	20	0	4
36					BOTHAM (Helmet cap)											0	
38			"	14	↑ . 9E 1	4		. .	2			51	121		1		
41½ DRINKS	"	17			.x .87 . 21	9		.↑ L↑ 1	5			52	124		4		
44 / 50			"	15	. .2. 13	14		.2. 5 1	8		● DROPPED GULLY (LAUGHLIN)	53	129		7	2	
54	"	18	15·5·39·2 (4)		.4 3 .↑. .3 1	19		. .3 5	11		○ DROPPED MACLEAN – skied attempted hook	54	136		11	5	
3.01	18·5·39·3 (1)		LAUGHLIN	15	.4 1	24		. .3 4	14			55	140		12	8	
06	YARDLEY	3						. . .x .x 22	22		Round wkt to LMB M18 5 HR →	56					
11			"	16	9E 1	25		2B .2. .4 .x 29	29		(2B)	57	147		13	12	6
16	"	4			. . . . .2 4. 33	33	1					58	151		17		
20			"	17				. . . . . .4 37	37	2		59	155			16	
24	"	5			.55 .24 .73 .2 1 40	40	2		38			60	164		26		
28½	"	18			.xx .9 .2 . 48	48					○ DROPPED MACLEAN (offside – knee high)	61	166		28		
34	"	6	18·6·44·0 (5)		.6. .2. 51	51		4B 4 1 43	43		(4B) 50 p'ship: 56' DROPPED deep–	62	173		30	17	10
38	6·1·31·0 (4/1)		HIGGS	1	. 52	52	2	. . . . .2 2↑4 1 50	50	2	Mid on – HIGGS – diving forward. ↑ Round wkt	63	176	5	30	20	10
3.42½ TEA			1·0·3·0 (–)								M18 NB/2					TEA	

AUSTRALIA v ENGLAND
at Brisbane
1st Test

2ND DAY TIME	BOWLERS (O'CONNELL) VULTURE ST END BOWLER	O.	(FRENCH) STANLEY ST END BOWLER	O.	BATSMEN SCOREBOARD LEFT SCORING	BALLS	6s/4s	SCOREBOARD RIGHT SCORING	BALLS	6s/4s	NOTES	ENGLAND 1ST INNINGS END-OF-OVER TOTALS O.	RUNS	W.	L BAT	R BAT	EXTRAS
					BOTHAM	52	2	GOWER	50	2	Sun through partial cloud M18 NB/2	63	176	5	30	20	10
4.01	YARDLEY	7			.¹.	54		....³	56		Round wkt to LHB	64	179			23	
06	7-1-34-0(4)		HIGGS	2				x....x E †P	64		† Round wkt M19	65					
10	HOGG	19	2-1-3-0(-)		1⁷ 3 IE	56		.†.¹P 3 4 4.3	70	3	† NEW BALL/2 taken at 4.11 pm	66	190		34	30	
17			HURST	16	....³1	61		x..	73			67	191		35		
22	.	20			.4.1³	65	3	.↑.Y5.2	77		6HR →	68	198		40	32	
28½			.	17	x.⁷1 ↑8 4.x	71	4	↑7 .³	79			69	206		45	35	
34	.	21			↑7 †E 4W	73	5	.³ ⁹ ..4.1	84	4		69⁷	215	6	49	40	10
39					MILLER Helmet cap	1									0		
41	.	21			.¹	1						70					
42			.	18				L...2E 4W	90	5		70⁶	219	7	0	44	10
45								EDMONDS cap								0	
47			.	18	.	2		LB .	1		(LB)	71	220				11
49	.	22			.2.1³ ⁹	7		⁸.1	4			72	224		3	1	
55			.	19	...⁸.2...	15						73	226		5		
5.00	.	23	19-5-54-3(6)					.¹.⁴w	9	-		73⁵	226	8	5	1	11
02	DRINKS							OLD Helmet-cap (LHB)								0	
06			.	23				↑ x .†.—	3		M20	74					
08			LAUGHLIN	19	....¹⁸	21		.†P	5			75	227		6		
12	.	24			x.....↑	29					M21	76					
18	24-7-70-5(5)		.	20	.2⁵	30		.....²1	12			77	230		8	1	
23	HURST	20			1	34		.4.1²	16	1	7HR →	78	235			6	
28			.	21	.....⁶	40		66 21	18			79	238			9	
33	.	21	21-6-51-0(5)		↑↑⁷.②	44		....⁴3	23		NB/3	80	243		10	12	
39			HIGGS	3				....²2...	31			81	245			14	
43	.	22			.2.....³	52						82	247		12		
48			.	4				....²2...	39			83	249			16	
51	23-4-5-74-3(R)	23	4-1-7-0 (-)		↑2 2 .4 3	55	1	2† 1	40	1	† light appeal	83⁴	257	8	19	17	11
5.55	BLSP										M21 NB/3	.			BLSP		
6.00	STUMPS		(2ND DAY)								36 minutes lost 2nd day.				STUMPS		
3RD DAY 11.00	HURST	23			²3	56		x x ..Q̇..	44		(NB) NB/4	84	261		22		12
04	23-5-77-3(R)		LAUGHLIN	22	....⁵3	63		.45	45		ATTENDANCE (3RD) 12,250	85	264		25		
08	HOGG	25	22-6-54-0(5)		⁸1	64		.52	52			86	265		26		
14			HURST	24	...⁷1	68		56	56			87	266		27		
19	.	26			.W	70	1					87²	266	9	27	17	12
20					WILLIS No cap										0		
21	.	26			↑.......↑	6					M22	88					
25			.	25				..Y....4³	64			89	269			20	
30	.	27						..xP.↑.4	72		8HR →	90	270			21	
36	27-8-72-6(5)		26-6-81-3(R)	26	⁶	6	-	x........x	80	1	M23 NB/4	91	270	9	0	21	12

26

AUSTRALIA v ENGLAND

at Brisbane

1st Test

3RD DAY	BOWLERS (O'CONNELL) VULTURE St END	O.	(FRENCH) STANLEY St END	O.	BATSMEN SCOREBOARD LEFT	BALLS	6s/4s	SCOREBOARD RIGHT	BALLS	6s/4s	ENGLAND 1st INNINGS NOTES	O.	RUNS	W.	'L' BAT	'R' BAT	EXTRAS
TIME					WILLIS	6	–	OLD	80	1	M23 NB/4	91	270	9	0	21	12
11.41	HOGG	28			↑ . . ² ₁	12		. . ⁴ ₁	82			92	272		1	22	
48	28-8-74-6 (5)		HIGGS	5				. . . .	90		M24	93					
52	HURST	27			. . ⁴₁ P:	16		²4 . . ¹	94	2		94	278		2	27	
58			·	6				. . . . ²2	102			95	280			29	
12.00 03	DRINKS (10) 37-9-6-93-9	28	6-2-9-0 (-)		x ²²E :42W	20	1		102	2	M24 NB/4	95	286	10	8	29	12
12·05	ENGLAND ALL OUT								768 balls				ALL OUT				
	BATTING TIME: 511 MINUTES.				ENGLAND LEAD: 170												

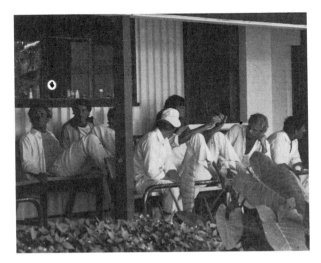

7 Brearley c Maclean b Hogg 6 *(left)* – Australia's new wicket-keeper claims his first dismissal: a sprawling legside catch off the England captain's glove.

8 and 9 The tourists dry out *(right)* – *Top:* Tropical hang-up beside the unique boundary-side Cricketers' Club. *Bottom:* Edmonds, Tolchard, Taylor, Gower and Barrington mirror the tenseness of the cricket.

AUSTRALIA 2nd Innings

170 runs behind on first Innings

IN	OUT	MINS	No.	BATSMAN	HOW OUT	BOWLER	RUNS
12.17	12.18	1	1	COSIER	BOWLED	WILLIS	0
12.17	2.24	88	2	WOOD	LBW	OLD	19
12.19	12.26	7	3	TOOHEY	LBW	BOTHAM	1
12.28	12.36	347	4	YALLOP *	Cᵗ AND BOWLED	WILLIS	102
2.26	5.05	481	5	HUGHES	Cᵗ EDMONDS	WILLIS	129
12.38	12.51	13	6	LAUGHLIN	LBW	OLD	5
12.53	2.32	63	7	MACLEAN †	LBW	MILLER	15
2.34	4.12	79	8	YARDLEY	Cᵗ BREARLEY	MILLER	16
4.14	4.55	41	9	HOGG	BOWLED	BOTHAM	16
4.57	4.58	1	10	HURST	BOWLED	BOTHAM	0
5.01	(5.05)	4	11	HIGGS	NOT OUT		0
* CAPTAIN † WICKET-KEEPER				EXTRAS	b 9 lb 5 w - nb 22		36

TOTAL   (OFF 116.6 OVERS IN 572 MINUTES)   **339**

BOWLER	O	M	R	W	nb
WILLIS	27.6	3	69	3	11
BOTHAM	26	5	95	3	6
OLD	17	1	60	2	7
MILLER	34	12	52	2	-
EDMONDS	12	1	27	0	-
Extras			36		
	116.6	22	339	10	

HRS	OVERS	RUNS
1	11	27
2	10	54
3	13	36
4	14	31
5	14	33
6	11	38
7	10	31
8	13	39
9	15	28

RUNS	MINS	OVERS	LAST 50 (in mins)
50	91	15.5	91
100	154	28.2	63
150	252	50.4	98
200	330	68	78
250	418	82.7	88
300	493	99.5	75

2nd NEW BALL taken at 11.50am. 4ᵗʰ day.
AUSTRALIA 188-3 after 65 overs.

WKT	TOTAL	6^s	4^s	BALLS	NOTES ON DISMISSAL
1	0	·	·	1	Played outside breakback which hit off stump. **FIRST BALL OF INNINGS**
3	49	·	1	50	Beaten by late movement.
2	2	·	·	9	Misjudged line - hit low on shin.
4	219	·	8	307	Mistimed straight drive - right-handed, waist-high catch.
10	339	2	8	411	Pulled short ball to deep, wide mid-on - high, left-handed catch.
5	228	·	·	8	Yorked on boot.
6	261	·	1	63	Deceived by flight - missed on-drive.
7	310	·	1	70	Edged 'arm ball' low to 1st slip's left - left-handed catch.
8	339	·	1	35	Late on yorker.
9	339	·	·	2	Missed full toss - off stump out.
·	·	·	·	2	-

2^6 20^4 958 balls (including 24 no balls)

12 OVERS 2 BALLS/HOUR
2.90 RUNS/OVER
35 RUNS/100 BALLS

LUNCH: 20-2   WOOD (26b, 44') 9*
YALLOP (30b, 33') 8*
OFF 8 OVERS IN 44 MINUTES

TEA: 102-3   YALLOP (146b, 154') 57*
HUGHES (50b, 74') 18*
OFF 31 OVERS IN 165 MINUTES

STUMPS 3RD DAY : 157-3   BLSP at 5.35pm   25 MINUTES LOST ON 3RD DAY
YALLOP (225b, 250') 74*
HUGHES (141b, 170') 51*
OFF 60 OVERS IN 261 MINUTES

LUNCH: 232-5   HUGHES (248b, 294') 78*
MACLEAN (8b, 11') 2*
OFF 77 OVERS IN 385 MINUTES

TEA: 303-6   HUGHES (354b, 416') 117*
YARDLEY (60b, 63') 11*
OFF 104 OVERS IN 507 MINUTES

WKT	PARTNERSHIP		RUNS	MINS
1st	Cosier	Wood	0	1
2nd	Wood	Toohey	2	7
3rd	Wood	Yallop	47	77
4th	Yallop	Hughes	170	267
5th	Hughes	Laughlin	9	13
6th	Hughes	Maclean	33	63
7th	Hughes	Yardley	49	79
8th	Hughes	Hogg	29	41
9th	Hughes	Hurst	0	1
10th	Hughes	Higgs	0	4

339

AUSTRALIA v ENGLAND

1st Test

at Brisbane

3RD DAY TIME	BOWLERS (FRENCH) VULTURE ST END BOWLER	O.	(O'CONNELL) STANLEY ST END BOWLER	O.	BATSMEN SCOREBOARD LEFT SCORING	BALLS	6s/4s	SCOREBOARD RIGHT SCORING	BALLS	6s/4s	NOTES	O.	RUNS	W.	'L' BAT	'R' BAT	EXTRAS
					COSIER (Bare-headed)			WOOD cap (LHB)			AUSTRALIA 2ND INNINGS END-OF-OVER TOTALS						
12.17	WILLIS	1			x W	1	–					0'	0	1	0	0	–
18					TOOHEY cap										0		
19	"	1			· · · 0 E·1 7E	6		· ·	2		NB NB/1	1	2		1		1
24			BOTHAM	1	L L W	9	–				WILLIS OFF FIELD ONE OVER (LEVER SUB)	1³	2	2	1	0	1
26					YALLOP (Helmet-cap)(LHB)										0		
28			"	1	· · · · E	5					M1	2					
30	"	2						· · · · L P	10		M2	3					
35			"	2	· 7 ·1	7		↑ · · 2 2 2T 2(2)4	17	1	NB/2	4	11		1	8	
41½	"	3	2-1-9-1 (1)		· · · · · · · E x	15					M3	5					
47			OLD	1	· 7 1	17		3S ↑ · · ·	23			6	13		2	9	
52	"	4	1-0-2-0 (-)		↑ · · 9	23		· ·	25			7	14		3		
58	4-2-2-1 (-)		MILLER	1	3 F 3 · 41 · · · L	30	1	LB ·	26	1	Round wkt. LB	8	20	2	8	9	2
1.01	LUNCH		1-0-5-0 (1)								M3 NB/2			LUNCH			
1.40	WILLIS	5			· · 9	34		9 ↑ · ↑	30		•Fended half-chance to close point (EDMONDS)	9	22		9	10	
45			OLD	2	· · · · · · x x	42					M4	10					
50	"	6			· · ! 2 ·-3	47		· 5 1 O ·	34		NB NB/3 1HR →	11	27		12	11	3
57			"	3	4 4 4 2(2)3	50		8 x · · · 7S 2 · · · 1	40		NB NB/4	12	37		19	14	
2.03	"	7			· · · · 0 E·7·	58		9 1	41		•C⁺ Brearley (1ˢᵗ slip) •Appeal ct wkt (glove)	13	39			15	4
10			"	4	· · 7 · 4	63	2	9E · 2E · 1	44			14	46		24	17	
15	"	8			x 7 ↑·	69		5 3 · ·	46			15	49		25	19	
21½			"	5				· · L W	50	1		15⁴	49	3	25	19	4
24								HUGHES cap								0	
26			"	5				9 2 · · ·	4			16	51			2	
28	"	9			2 3 · 7S · 2 2 ·	74		· · 1 7E	7		•Fended half-chance to close point (EDMONDS)	17	57		30	3	
35	9-2-18-1 (-)		"	6	9 · 7 9 1 41	77	3	8 1 · 0 · 1	13		NB NB/6	18	66		36	5	5
40 DRINKS 43	BOTHAM	3			· · · · · · · ↑ x	85					M5	19					
47			"	7	· 0 · 7 8 41	91	4	· 7 · · 1	16		NB NB/7	20	73		41	6	6
53	"	4	7-1-35-1 (3)		9 5S 1 1°	93		13E ↑↑8 1 · · · 40 1 23	23	1	•R.O. appeal (Randall) NB NB/8 2HR →	21	81		43	11	7
59			MILLER	2	· · · · x	101					Round wkt to LHB M6	22					
3.03	"	5						L 17 ↑ · · 4 · · ·	31	2		23	85			15	
08			"	3	x · 2 1 · · · ·	108		3S 1	32			24	87		44	16	
11	"	6			2 · 33 4 · · · 1	113	5	1 L Y	35			25	93		49	17	
17			"	4	· 4 · · 1	116		· · · · · · 1	40		YALLOP'S 50: 131 min	26	94		50		
20	"	7			· · · · 4 · · ·	124	6					27	98		54		
25			"	5				· · · · · · · 1	48		M7	28					
28	"	8			· 2 2 · · · · 1	131		↑ · 1	49		50 p'ship in 63 min	29	101		57		
33½	8-2-33-1 (5)		"	6	· · · · · x 1	139					M8	30					
37	EDMONDS	1	6-3-8-0 (1)		· · · · · · F	146	6	8 1	50	2		31	102	3	57	18	7
3.40	TEA 1-0-1-0 (-)										M8 NB/8			TEA			

AUSTRALIA v ENGLAND — 1st Test

at Brisbane

AUSTRALIA 2ND INNINGS

3RD DAY / TIME	BOWLER (FRENCH, Vulture St End)	O.	BOWLER (O'CONNELL, Stanley St End)	O.	SCOREBOARD LEFT — SCORING	BALLS	6s/4s	SCOREBOARD RIGHT — SCORING	BALLS	6s/4s	NOTES	O.	RUNS	W.	'L' BAT	'R' BAT	EXTRAS
TEA					YALLOP	146	6	HUGHES	50	2	M8 NB/8	31	102	3	57	18	.7
4.00			MILLER	7	.....	151		..1	53		Round wkt to LHB	32	103			19	
03	WILLIS	10						2..0 62..	62	2	(NB) NB/9	33	114			29	8
10			"	8	1 . 8	155		.1	66		3HR→	34	117		59	30	
14	"	11			.21	158		O....	72		(4NB) NB/10	35	124		62		12
20			"	9	....	166					M9	36					
23	"	12			4	168		..4	78	3		37	130		63	35	
29			"	10	1	173		P...	81			38	131		64		
33	"	13			2	181					*DROPPED 2ND SLIP (GOOCH - diving rt.)	39	133		66		
39	13-2-39-1 (1/1)		"	11	...1	186		..1	84			40	134			36	
42	BOTHAM	9			1	191		..3	87			41	137			39	
47			"	12				....	95		M10	42					
50	"	10			....	199					M11	43					
54			"	13				..4...	103	4		44	142			44	
58	"	11	13-5-19-0 (2)					......↑	111		M12	45					
6.02 / 05	DRINKS		EDMONDS	2	.1	203		2...	115		Round wkt to RHB	46	145		68	45	
09			"	12	..1	206		....	120			47	146		69		
13			"	3	...2	214					4HR→	48	148		71		
16	"	13						x ↑ †	128		†Round wkt M13	49					
20	13-5-37-1 (5)		"	4	...1	219		...	131		100 p'ship in 157min	50	149		72		
24	OLD	8			..1	223		2..	135		WILLIS off - LEVER sub †LIGHT appeal	51	152		73	47	
31	8-1-38-1 (3)		"	5	.1	225	6	..4	141	5	†over wkt HUGHES' 50: 169min	52	157	3	74	51	12
5.35	B.L.S.P.		5-0-12-0 (1)								M13 NB/10		B L S P				
6.00	STUMPS		(3RD DAY)								25 MIN LOST 3RD DAY Some cloud - humid		STUMPS				
4TH DAY 11.00	MILLER	14			..1	228		.....	146		Round wkt to LHB	53	158		75		
04			BOTHAM	14	..x..1	235		↑	147		ATTENDANCE (4TH): 4,990	54	159		76		
09	"	15			..3	238		.....	152		*via bowler's stumps to long-on. (3B)	55	165		79		15
12			"	15	..1	243		..1	155			56	168		80	53	
16	"	16						.....	163		Sides level at 11.19am	57	170			55	
20			"	16	1	249		..	165			58	171		81		
24	"	17			.1	255		..	167			59	172		82		
27			"	17	.1	257		..4.	173	6		60	178		83	60	
31½	"	18	17-5-48-1 (6)		..1	260		...1	178			61	180		84	61	
35			EDMONDS	6	1	261		.....	185		Round to RHB 5HR→	62	181		85		
38½	"	19			....	269					(LB) M14	63	182				16
42			"	7	.4...F	277	7					64	186		89		
46	"	20	7-0-17-0 (2)		.1	279		.1...L	191			65	188		90	62	
50			WILLIS	14	↑2E	280		↓3	198		†NEW BALL/2 taken at 11.50am	66	190		91	63	
56	BOTHAM	18			E...	284		4.21	202		*Appeal ct wkt (leg side)	67	197			70	
12.00 / 03	DRINKS 18-5-55-1 (7)		" 15-2-43-1 (1/1)	15	↑2E	287	7	.0..	208	7	(NB) 150 p'ship 237' NB/11 M14	68	200	3	92	71	17

31

AUSTRALIA v ENGLAND

at Brisbane

4TH DAY TIME	BOWLERS (FRENCH) VULTURE ST END BOWLER	O.	(O'CONNELL) STANLEY ST END BOWLER	O.	BATSMEN SCOREBOARD LEFT SCORING	BALLS	6s/4s	SCOREBOARD RIGHT SCORING	BALLS	6s/4s	NOTES	END-OF-OVER TOTALS O.	RUNS	W.	'L' BAT	'R' BAT	EXTRAS
					YALLOP	287	7	HUGHES	208	1/7	M14 NB/11	68	200	3	92	71	17
12.08	BOTHAM	19			···· 52 41	294	8	7 1	209			69	206		97	72	
14			WILLIS	16				4B ·O····	218		M15 (4B)(NB) NB/12	70	211				22
20	"	20	16-3-43-1 (1/1)		·9 ··8 1	300		10 2 1	220		* Hit on shoulder (ducked)	71	214		99	73	
26	20-5-64-1 (8)		OLD	9	6s 1	303		····7 1	225		YALLOP'S 100 in 337' (his 10th in F-C cricket)	72	216		100	74	
31	WILLIS	17			·8 5 ·2·W	307	8	··7 1	228			72⁷	219	4	102	75	22
36					LAUGHLIN NO cap LHB										0		
38	"	17			· 1						6HR →	73					
39			"	10	·O 3	4		····O· 1	235		(NB)(NB) NB/13,14	74	225		3	76	24
45	"	18			8 7 1	7		3 1 x	240			75	228		5	77	
51			"	11	L W	8		−				75¹	228	5	5	77	24
					MACLEAN cap										0		
53			"	11	····7	5		O··	243		(NB) NB/15	76	230		1		25
58	19-3-51-2 (1/1)	19	11-1-45-2 (3)		··7 1	8		x Lx 9 ···· 1	248	1/7		77	232	5	2	78	25
1.04	LUNCH										M15 NB/15	LUNCH					
1.40			BOTHAM	21	··!·O·-2 16	16		7 3	249		(NB) NB/16	78	238		4	81	26
46	OLD	12	21-5-69-1 (8)		P 22	22		8 ·1	251			79	239			82	
51			WILLIS	20	···2··! 29	29		1	252			80	242		6	83	
57	"	13			····Y 36	36		5 1	253			81	243			84	
2.03			"	21	7 1 37	37		2 ··O· x 1	261		(NB) NB/17	82	246		7	85	27
08	"	14			···3 1 43	43		·7 3	263		7HR →	83	250		8	88	
14			"	22	·!· 46	46		····2 1	268			84	251			89	
19	"	15			·LO···L 54	54		7 1	269		(NB) NB/18	85	253			90	28
25	15-1-52-2 (3)		BOTHAM	22	47+88 240 60	60	1	·3 x 1	272		NB/19	86	261		15	91	
30	MILLER	21			L L W 63	63	1				Lever sub for Willis	86³	261	6	15	91	28
32					YARDLEY cap										0		
34	"	21			···2 1 4	4		9 1	273			87	263		1	92	
36			"	23	2 6 ··1 6	6		2 x 8 ··1 ·1	279			88	267		3	94	
41 43½ DRINKS	"	22			2B 14	14					(2B) M16	89	269				30
47			"	24	4B 15	15		···O· x EP97 4 ·2 11	287		(NB)(LB) NB/20	90	275			98	32
52		23	24-5-85-1 (9)		····P 20	20		8 ··1	290			91	276			99	
55			OLD	16				·····EP9 Y ·2	298		HUGHES' 100: 374' (his 5th in F-C cricket)	92	278			101	
3.01			"	24	8 ·1 22	22			304		THE SLOWEST 100 FOR AUSTRALIA v ENG.	93	279		4		
04			"	17	9 2 x ·1 4 · 29	29	1	7 1	305			94	285		9	102	
09	"	25	17-1-60-2 (4)					L x 313	313		M17	95					
12			EDMONDS	8	·LB ··· 34	34		775 ·21	316		(LB) 8HR →	96	289			105	33
16	"	26						6 6····· 25 1	324	2/7		97	296			112	
19½			"	9	·8 ·1 39	39			327			98	297			113	
23	"	27						······P 335	335		M18	99					
26	27-9-41-1 (2/1)		10-0-25-0 (2)	10	··4 ·· 45	45	1	77 21	337	2/7	PROPPED close point (GOOCH). M18 NB/20	100	301	6	10	116	33

32

AUSTRALIA v ENGLAND — 1st Test

at Brisbane

4TH DAY TIME	BOWLERS (FRENCH) VULTURE St END — BOWLER	O.	(O'CONNELL) STANLEY St END — BOWLER	O.	BATSMEN — SCOREBOARD LEFT — SCORING	BALLS	6s/4s	SCOREBOARD RIGHT — SCORING	BALLS	6s/4s	AUSTRALIA 2nd INNINGS — NOTES	END-OF-OVER TOTALS O.	RUNS	W.	'L' BAT	'R' BAT	EXTRAS
					YARDLEY	45	1	HUGHES	337	2/7	M 18 NB/20	100	301	6	10	116	33
3.30	MILLER	28						....	345		M 19	101					
32½			EDMONDS	11	....	53					M 20	102					
35	"	29						....	353		M 21	103					
39	29-11-41-2(3/1)		"	12	...1...(6)	60	1	...1(8)	354	2/7	M 21 NB/20	104	303	6	11	117	33
3.42 TEA	12-1-27-0(2)										T E A						
4.00½	MILLER	30						.7.2.....	362			105	305			119	
04			WILLIS	23	12/21	62		......	368			106	308		14		
09	"	31			7/2.....W (E)	70	1					107	310	7	16	119	33
12					HOGG (cap)								0			
14			"	24	↑ 1	1	x...0...9①	377		NB NB/21/22	108	312			120	34
20	"	32			..2(2)	4		....1(8)	382			109	315		2	121	
24			"	25	LB+1	6	L..1.P(7)	388		LB • Avoided bouncer - hit on backside	110	317			122	35
30	"	33			....E P E	14					M 22 9 HR •	111					
33			"	26			....2.4(7)	396			112	319			124	
38	"	34	26-3-64-2(1/1)		.4.....P(5)	22	1					113	323		6		
42	34-12-52-2(3/1)		BOTHAM	25	.1(2)	24		1...4.(6) x9x	402	2/8		114	329		7	129	
47	WILLIS	27			.2①..3(8) E6	30		L...(7)	405		• hit on hip NB NB/23	115	335		12		36
53			"	26	.2②.W(7) 61	35	1				• Botham cautioned (intimidation) NB/24	115⁴	339	8	16	129	36
55					HURST (cap)								0			
57			"	26	.W (xF)	2	-					115⁶	339	9	0	129	36
58 DRINKS					HIGGS (cap)								0			
5.01			"	26	..	2						116					
02	27.6-3-69-3(6)	28	26-5-95-3(10)			2	-	Y...W(6)	411	2/8	M 22 NB/24	116⁶	339	10	0	129	36
5.05	AUSTRALIA ALL OUT								958 balls			ALL OUT					

BATTING TIME: 572 MINUTES   ENGLAND REQUIRE 170 RUNS IN A MINIMUM OF 405 MINUTES.

10 and 11 The heroes of Australia's great fightback – Graham Yallop (*above*) and Kim Hughes move towards their centuries and the highest partnership of the rubber.

ENGLAND 2nd Innings

Requiring 170 runs to win in a minimum of 405 minutes

IN	OUT	MINS	No.	BATSMAN	HOW OUT	BOWLER	RUNS
5.15	11.50	98	1	BOYCOTT	RUN OUT (TOOHEY)		16
5.15	11.05	53	2	GOOCH	CT. YARDLEY	HOGG	2
11.07	(3.14)	210	3	RANDALL	NOT OUT		74
11.52	12.46	54	4	BREARLEY *	CT MACLEAN	YARDLEY	13
12.48	(3.14)	109	5	GOWER	NOT OUT		48
			6	BOTHAM			
			7	MILLER			
			8	EDMONDS	DID NOT BAT		
			9	OLD			
			10	TAYLOR †			
			11	WILLIS			
				EXTRAS	b 12 lb 3 w - nb 2		17

* CAPTAIN   † WICKET-KEEPER

TOTAL (FOR 3 WICKETS)   170

(OFF 53.5 OVERS IN 265 MINS.)

BOWLER	O	M	R	W	nb	HRS	OVERS	RUNS		RUNS	MINS	OVERS	LAST 50 (in mins)
HOGG	12.5	2	35	1	1	1	11	20		50	115	20.6	115
HURST	10	4	17	0	-	2	11	35		100	187	38.7	72
YARDLEY	13	1	41	1	1	3	15	34		150	239	48.4	52
LAUGHLIN	3	0	6	0	-	4	12	67					
HIGGS	12	1	43	0	-								
COSIER	3	0	11	0	-								
Extras/Run Out			17	1									
	53.5	8	170	3									

34

WKT	TOTAL	6s	4s	BALLS	NOTES ON DISMISSAL
2	37	·	·	82	Toohey (cover) fielded Randall's off-drive and threw down striker's leg stump.
1	16	·	·	33	Edged poor defensive backstroke to 3rd slip's left (diving catch)
·	·	·	5	175	-
3	74	·	1	51	Edged cut at off break.
·	·	·	4	90	-

-⁶ 10⁴ 431 balls (Including 2 no balls)

12	OVERS	BALLS/HOUR
3·17		RUNS/OVER
39		RUNS/100 BALLS

STUMPS: 16-0 **4TH DAY**
BOYCOTT (41 b, 48') 9*
GOOCH (32 b, 48') 2*
OFF 9 OVERS IN 48 MINUTES

LUNCH: 82-3
RANDALL (99 b, 116') 37*
GOWER (16 b, 15') 4*
OFF 35 OVERS IN 171 MINUTES

ENGLAND WON BY 7 WICKETS
at 3.14 p.m. on the fifth (last) day.
ENGLAND'S FIRST WIN IN BRISBANE SINCE 1936-37.

MAN OF THE MATCH: D.W. RANDALL

TOTAL MATCH ATTENDANCE: 43,523. TIME LOST: 87 MINUTES

WKT	PARTNERSHIP		RUNS	MINS
1st	Boycott	Gooch	16	53
2nd	Boycott	Randall	21	43
3rd	Randall	Brearley	37	54
4th	Randall	Gower	96*	109
			170	

AUSTRALIA v ENGLAND — 1st Test

at Brisbane

4TH DAY	BOWLERS				BATSMEN						ENGLAND 2ND INNINGS						
	(FRENCH) VULTURE ST. END		(O'CONNELL) STANLEY ST. END		SCOREBOARD LEFT			SCOREBOARD RIGHT			NOTES	END - OF - OVER TOTALS					
TIME	BOWLER	O.	BOWLER	O.	SCORING	BALLS	6s 4s	SCORING	BALLS	6s 4s	Sparse cloud - light good	O.	RUNS	W.	'L' BAT	'R' BAT	EXTRAS
					BOYCOTT cap			GOOCH Hat			CARLSON sub for WOOD (Gastro-enteritis)						
5.15			HOGG 1		L 7 4B 1 ·2····⊙2·	9					④B (NB) NB/1	1	9		4		5
22	HURST 1							····× ·L··	8		M1	2					
27	"		"	2	·· 5 ↑	12		····	13			3	10		5		
33	"	2			7 2·↑····	20						4	12		7		
38			"	3				···† 3 ·2··	21		Round wkt ↑ over wkt	5	14			2	
43	"	3			↑ ·····L·	28					M2	6					
48			"	4				·········	29		M3	7					
54	"	4	4-1-7-0 (-)		·····1 7	35		·	30			8	15		8		
59	4-2-3-0 (-)		YARDLEY 1		P·P· 8	41	–	··L·	32	–	M3 NB/1	9	16	–	9	2	5
6.03	STUMPS		(4TH DAY) 1-0-1-0 (-)											STUMPS			
5TH DAY 11.00	HURST 5				L × Y	49					M4	10					
05			HOGG 5					E W	33	–	ATTENDANCE (5TH): 1,100 (Estimated)	10¹	16	1	9	2	5
								RANDALL cap								0	
07			"	5	4s 1	50		3 9 2·1···	6		1 HR →	11	20		10	3	
11½	"	6			···· 8 2 ·2·1	58						12	23		13		
17½			"	6	9 7s ·1 ↑	61		↑8 ·1··×	11			13	26		15	4	
23	"	7			········↑	69					M5	14					
28			"	7	····	73		···7	15			15	27			5	
33	"	8			·7	76		2 ·7 2·1· Y	20			16	31		16	8	
39			"	8	LB ·····↑	82		†LB	22		(LB) † Round wkt (LB) M6	17	33				7
45	"	9	8-2-15-1 (-)		RD	82	–	4 ·!·4 4····	30	1		18	37	2	16	12	7
50					BREARLEY Helmet cap						Batsmen crossed					0	
52			YARDLEY 2		···2 7	4		7 6 ·4·1	34	2		19	44		2	17	
56½	"	10			8 ↑	5		L YL 7 9 ··1·1	41			20	47		3	19	
12.01 05	DRINKS 10-4-17-0 (1)		"	3	·	6		2B 6·7 ····41	48	3	(2B) °4 all run/1	21	54			24	9
09	LAUGHLIN 1				··L···	12		L·↑ ·1	50		2 HR →	22	55			25	
13			"	4				········ P	58		M7	23					
17	"	2			LB	13		·····2 1	65		(LB)	24	57			26	10
21			"	5	P·P·	19		6 ·1	67			25	58			27	
24½	"	3			2 Y 9 2·1	26		4 1	68			26	62		6	28	
28½	3-0-6-0 (-)		"	6	9 8 ·4·1	33	1	1 3·1	69			27	70		11	31	
33	HIGGS 1							·······×	77		Leg breaks turning sharply. M8	28					
37			"	7	··7 2·····	41						29	72		13		
40	"	2			·····1	46		··1 4	80			30	73			32	
43			"	8	···· E ····W	51	1	·6 1	82			30⁷	74	3	13	33	10
46					·GOWER (Hat) LHB										0		
48			"	8	·	1						31					
49	"	3			·····L·	8		6F ·1	83			32	75			34	
53	3-1-2-0 (-)		9-1-26-1 (3)	9	····1	12	–	P ··1 7	87	3	Round wkt to LHB M8 NB/1	33	76	3	0	35	10

36

AUSTRALIA v ENGLAND
at Brisbane

1st Test

5TH DAY TIME	BOWLERS (FRENCH) VULTURE ST END — BOWLER	O.	(O'CONNELL) STANLEY ST END — BOWLER	O.	BATSMEN — SCOREBOARD LEFT — SCORING	BALLS	6s/4s	SCOREBOARD RIGHT — SCORING	BALLS	6s/4s	ENGLAND 2ND INNINGS — NOTES	END-OF-OVER TOTALS O.	RUNS	W.	'L' BAT	'R' BAT	EXTRAS
					GOWER	12	–	RANDALL	87	3	M8 NB/1	33	76	3	0	35	10
12.57	HIGGS	4			·4.	15	1	····1	92			34	81		4	36	
59½	4-1-7-0 (1)		YARDLEY	10	·	16	1	······1 6s	99	3	M8 NB/1	35	82	3	4	37	10
1.03	LUNCH		10-1-27-1 (3)		·							LUNCH					
1.40	HIGGS	5			·1	18		1 ·4···1	105	4		36	88		5	42	
44			YARDLEY	11	1	19		·····:.	112		•Appeal ct slip 3 HR→	37	89		6		
49	·	6			·:4/3 t··	24		Y.6	115		†Round wkt	38	93		9	43	
52½	·		·	12	··1	27		1 22·Q	121		(NB) NB/2	39	100		10	48	11
57	·	7			··1	31		····	125			40	101		11		
2.00½			·	13	1 ··1	35		·1 ·4·	129	5	RANDALL'S 50: 140'	41	108		13	53	
05		8	13-1-41-1 (4)		···· ·1	41		Y·3	131			42	112		14	56	
10			COSIER	1	41	43	2	···1 5s	137		Round wkt to LHB	43	118		19	57	
15	·	9			·24·1	48	3	···1	140		50 p'ship : 51 mins	44	125		26		
19	9-1-29-0 (3)		·	2	··1	52		489·1	144		(4B)	45	131		27	58	15
25	HOGG	9			··1 8s	55		·2·1 6·6	149		Round wkt to LHB	46	135		28	61	
31			·	3	······3	62		·	150			47	138		31		
35	·	10	3-0-11-0 (1)		1·3 8 x4·2·1	69		3·3	151			48	146		36	64	
41 45	DRINKS		HIGGS	10	74 41	71	4	·21 94 2B···	157		Gower - helmet-cap. (2B) 4 HR→	49	156		41	67	17
50	·	11			·2 1	74		·····	162			50	157		42		
56			·	11	F ·3 ·3	81		9	163		•DROPPED. COVER (WOOD) diving	51	161		45	68	
3.00	·	12			···	84		46F L98 ·22·1	168			52	166			73	
06½			·	12	2 1	85		···4·1	175			53	168		46	74	
10	12·5-2-35-1 (-)	13	12-1-43-0 (4)		1·E·2 2	90	4		175	5	M8 NB/2	53⁵	170	3	48	74	17
3.14	ENGLAND WON BY SEVEN WICKETS										431 balls						
	BATTING TIME : 265 MINUTES																

12 Clown turns acrobat – Derek Randall, soon to be voted 'Man of the Match', just fails in a spectacular attempt to run out Yallop (a brilliantly-timed picture by the *Brisbane Courier-Mail's* chief photographer, Jim Fenwick).

THE SECOND TEST AT PERTH

Australia should have kicked themselves for losing this match. Halfway through the final day they seemed to be heading safely towards a draw. That they lost by the substantial margin of 166 runs, almost two hours before the close, was due as much to inept batting and imaginative umpiring as to inspired bowling.

This match was heralded not only by the now familiar pageant and a squall of skydivers, but also by a helicopter landing on the outfield; the cricket was becoming incidental.

Western Australia's vehicle registration plates proclaim it as the 'State of Excitement', and 1979, the 150th anniversary of the founding of Swan River Colony, has been decreed the 'Year of Excitement'. When a freak storm ended play prematurely on the fourth day, someone suggested that Perth had got so excited that it wet itself. It could well have been through Randall's antics at the airport when he made a few interesting adjustments to his dress and strolled jerkily around like a marionette being operated by a drunk.

Perth is my favourite Australian city for reasons of scenery, climate, and lack of pollution, traffic and stress. The 'WACA' has a delightful and friendly country atmosphere and normally boasts the fastest pitch in the world. On this tour no pitch lived up to expectations. The one at Perth cut all sorts of capers in England's warm-up match against WA and had produced a contest which ended almost two days prematurely. Like that at Brisbane,

the Test pitch again encouraged the ball to move about throughout the match. The ball constantly hit the pads or the bat's edge, resulting in numerous appeals and the eventual retirement of umpire Brooks.

Irrespective of the final Australian capitulation wherein six wickets fell to 66 balls in 47 minutes, England's victory owed much to the extraordinary contribution of Boycott. Here was a man, patently struggling to find even a vestige of his standard form, mentally plagued by a strange diversity of torments, refusing to capitulate and battling on hour after hour. His dots were as numerous as Perth's flies. Lindsay Hassett rated Boycott's marathon as 'an exceptional innings by someone who could not find the middle of the bat'.

The ground's large retinue of gulls did not rate it at all. When Gooch forgot to score while Boycott pushed four singles in 40 minutes, they rose, angrily circled the players and then flew away.

Boycott made possible Gower's remarkable innings. With a brickwall at the other end, the left-hander was free to assault the bowling. He sped from 83 to 101 off nine balls aided by Boycott's feeding him the strike; at one stage the Yorkshireman faced only four balls in as many overs. Gower's hundred, remarkably only his fifth in 96 first-class innings but his second in 11 innings for England, took just 214 minutes. It deservedly won the Victoria Sporting Club's Award of 100 bottles of champagne, a prize which causes John Arlott much anxiety: 'A terrible responsibility for a young cricketer and one which compels me to offer some assistance'.

Well as Hogg bowled to take ten wickets in the match, he did so in very helpful conditions and Gower would most certainly have been my choice for the Benson and Hedges 'Man of the Match' award.

13 Western Australia Cricket Association (WACA) Ground, Perth

ENGLAND 1st Innings v AUSTRALIA 2nd Test

at W.A.C.A. Ground, Perth, on December 15, 16, 17, 19, 20 1978

IN	OUT	MINS	No.	BATSMAN	HOW OUT	BOWLER	RUNS
11.00	12.29	454	1	BOYCOTT	LBW	HURST	77
11.00	11.19	19	2	GOOCH	CT MACLEAN	HOGG	1
11.21	11.23	2	3	RANDALL	CT WOOD	HOGG	0
11.25	2.01	117	4	BREARLEY *	CT MACLEAN	DYMOCK	17
2.03	11.32	254	5	GOWER	BOWLED	HOGG	102
11.34	12.18	44	6	BOTHAM	LBW	HURST	11
12.20	3.22	145	7	MILLER	BOWLED	HOGG	40
12.31	2.01	52	8	TAYLOR †	CT HURST	YARDLEY	12
2.03	3.03	60	9	LEVER	CT COSIER	HURST	14
3.05	3.46	41	10	WILLIS	CT YALLOP	HOGG	2
3.24	(3.46)	22	11	HENDRICK	NOT OUT		7
* CAPTAIN	† WICKET-KEEPER			EXTRAS	b 6 lb 9	w 3 nb 8	26

TOTAL (OFF 117.5 OVERS IN 612 MINUTES) **309**

BOWLER	O	M	R	W	nb/w	HRS	OVERS	RUNS		RUNS	MINS	OVERS	LAST 50 (in mins)
HOGG	30.5	9	65	5	3/1	1	11	10		50	153	29.7	153
DYMOCK	34	4	72	1	3/-	2	13	20		100	237	47.2	84
HURST	26	7	70	3	2/1	3	12	33		150	313	63.2	76
YARDLEY	23	1	62	1	2/1	4	12	41		200	402	78.4	89
COSIER	4	2	14	0	-	5	13	39		250	500	97	98
						6	10	46		300	585	112.7	85
Extras			26			7	11	19					
	117.5	23	309	10		8	10	30					
						9	12	39					
						10	12	27					

2ND NEW BALL taken at 5.21pm on 1st DAY
- ENGLAND 157-3 after 65 overs.

WKT	TOTAL	6s	4s	BALLS	NOTES ON DISMISSAL
6	224	.	1	337	Beaten by breakback. His 49th Test fifty. 2000 runs v Aus when 47.
1	3	.	.	10	Edged forward defensive stroke at late outswinger.
2	3	.	.	3	Checked hook at sharply lifting ball. Top-edged skier to square-leg.
3	41	.	1	104	Edged backfoot force at ball leaving him.
4	199	.	9	221	Beaten by breakback – played back.
5	219	.	1	28	Played back to breakback.
9	300	.	4	104	Beaten by sharp breakback.
7	253	.	1	59	Pulled off-break to mid-wicket. Mistimed stroke.
8	295	.	.	40	Edged offside push low to 1st slip.
10	309	.	.	20	Skied straight drive – steepling catch held by mid-off behind bowler.
.	.	.	1	25	-

0⁶ 18⁴ 951 balls (including 10 no balls)

11 OVERS 4 BALLS/HOUR
2.63 RUNS/OVER
32 RUNS/100 BALLS

LUNCH: 30-2
BOYCOTT 17* (93b, 120 min)
BREARLEY 9* (87b, 95 min)
OFF 24 OVERS IN 120 MINUTES

TEA: 104-3
BOYCOTT 36* (182b, 241 min)
GOWER 46* (87b, 98 min)
OFF 48 OVERS IN 241 MINUTES

STUMPS 1ST DAY: 190-3
BOYCOTT 63* (269b, 365min)
GOWER 101* (198b, 221 min)
OFF 72 OVERS IN 365 MINUTES

LUNCH: 242-6
MILLER 8* (21b, 42 min)
TAYLOR 8* (38b, 31 min)
OFF 94 OVERS IN 487 MINUTES

TEA INTERVAL TAKEN AT END OF INNINGS

WKT	PARTNERSHIP		RUNS	MINS
1st	Boycott	Gooch	3	19
2nd	Boycott	Randall	0	2
3rd	Boycott	Brearley	38	117
4th	Boycott	Gower	158	254
5th	Boycott	Botham	20	44
6th	Boycott	Miller	5	9
7th	Miller	Taylor	29	52
8th	Miller	Lever	42	60
9th	Miller	Willis	5	17
10th	Willis	Hendrick	9	22

309

AUSTRALIA v ENGLAND   2nd Test

at Perth

1st DAY	BOWLERS Ump: T.F.BROOKS GRANDSTAND END		RIVER END Umb: R.C.BAILHACHE		BATSMEN SCOREBOARD LEFT			SCOREBOARD RIGHT			ENGLAND 1st INNINGS NOTES	END-OF-OVER TOTALS					
TIME	BOWLER	O.	BOWLER	O.	SCORING	BALLS	6s/4s	SCORING	BALLS	6s/4s	NOTES	O.	RUNS	W.	'L' BAT	'R' BAT	EXTRAS
					BOYCOTT cap			GOOCH cap Helmet			Overcast. Strong wind from River End.						
11·00			HOGG	1	Y · PP · P	8					M 1	1					
05	DYMOCK	1			L · · L · ·	15		SS 1	1		ATTENDANCE (1st):- 7,883	2	1			1	
10	"		"	2				· · · · · · · ↑	9		M 2	3					
15	"	2			8 L 2 · · · · · ·	23						4	3		2		
19			"	3	⟩			E W	10	-		4'	3	1	2	1	-
								RANDALL cap								0	
21			"	3	⟩			↑ ↑E W	3	-		4⁴	3	2	2	0	-
23					⟩			BREARLEY padded cap								0	
25			"	3	⟩			· · · ·	4		M 3	5					
28	"	3			· · 2 · 1	26		· · · · ·	9			6	4		3		
32			"	4	L · · · · · ·	34					M 4	7					
37	"	4	4-4-0-2 (-)					P L · · · · ·	17		M 5, M 6	8					
42			HURST	1	· · · · L · E° ·	42					*Short of 3rd slip *Appeal ct wkr (legside)	9					
47	"	5						P E° ·4 · · ⊙2	26		*Short of 2nd slip (NB) NB/1	10	7			2	1
52			"	2	L · 4 7 · 2 1	46		L · · · ·	30		1 HR→	11	10		6		
57 / 59	DRINKS "	6			· · · · 7 1	52		· P 2	32			12	11		7		
03			"	3	· · · 7 1	56		4 P L 2 · · 1	36			13	14		8	4	
08	"	7			· 7 1 ·	59		· · · · 7 1	41			14	16		9	5	
12			"	4				P L P 2LB · · · · · 2	49		(2LB) M 7	15	18				3
17	"	8			7 1	60		· · · · · ·	56			16	19		10		
22			"	5	· · ↑ · 7 1	66		· ·	58			17	20		11		
26	"	9			· 8 1	70		· · · ·	62			18	21		12		
31	9-1-11-0 (-)		"	6	7 2 · · · 1	75		· · 2 2	65		Sunny interludes	19	26		15	7	
36	HOGG	5	6-2-12-0 (-)		· · · · · · · ↑	83					M 8	20					
42			DYMOCK	10	·	84		· · · · · · ↑9 1	72			21	27			8	
47	"	6			·	85		· L · x · 7 1	79			22	28			9	
52	6-5-1-2 (-)		"	11	· · · · · · ·	87					M 9	23					
56	YARDLEY	1	11-2-12-0 (-)		3 2 · · · · · E	93	-		87	-	M 9 NB/1	24	30	2	17	9	3
1·00	LUNCH 7-6-1-0 (-)										2HR↗	LUNCH					
1·40			DYMOCK	12	· · · 9 1	97		· · · 4 1	91			25	32		18	10	
44	HOGG	7			9 1 ·	98		P P° 9 · · · · · 1	98		*chance to nonexistent silly mid-off	26	34		19	11	
51			"	13	· · x · · · 8 1	103		⊙4·1	102	1	(NB) NB/2	27	40			16	4
56	"	8			· · · · ° ↑	110		2 1	103		*Appeal ct wkr leg-side	28	41			17	
2·01			"	14	⟩			E W	104	1		28'	41	3	19	17	4
03					⟩			GOWER Helmet -cap (LHB)								0	
05			"	14	⟩ · · · · ·	115		12 2 1	2			29	44			3	
09	"	9						↑° 6 °11 · · · · 2 · 41	10	1	*Hit on helmet *chance to 3rd slip (Yardley)	30	51			10	
14			"	15				3 2 P · 2 · · · · ·	18			31	53			12	
19	10-5-13-2 (1)	10	15-2-24-1 (1)		· · · · 7 2 ·	123	-		18	1	M 9 NB/2	32	55	3	21	12	4

AUSTRALIA v ENGLAND

2nd Test

at Perth

1ST DAY TIME	BOWLERS (BROOKS) GRANDSTAND END BOWLER	O.	(BAILHACHE) RIVER END BOWLER	O.	BATSMEN SCOREBOARD LEFT SCORING	BALLS	6³ 4s	SCOREBOARD RIGHT SCORING	BALLS	6³ 4s	ENGLAND 1ST INNINGS NOTES	O.	RUNS	W.	'L' BAT	'R' BAT	EXTRAS
					BOYCOTT	123	-	GOWER	18	1	overcast M 9 NB /2	32	55	3	21	12	4
2.25			DYMOCK	16	···· 4 2···	26						33	57			14	
29	HURST	7	16-2-26-1 (1)		↑·¹ 3 1	126		· 2···	31			34	60		22	16	
35			COSIER	1	········	134					M 10	35					
39	"	8			· 2···· 8 P	141		9 1	32		3HR→	36	63		24	17	
43 46	DRINKS		"	2				······ L P	40		M 11	37					
50	"	9			2 1	142		7·· 4 1 1 2···2·4	47	2		38	72		25	25	
56			"	3	8E 7 4·····	149	1	·	48		· 2+2 overthrows	39	77		30		
59	·	10			E 4 ·······1	156		↑	49			40	78		31		
3.04			"	4	7 1	157		2 3 ···4··4	56	4		41	87		32	33	
08	"	11	4-2-14-0 (3)		··· 4	161		3 ···3	60		50 p'ship: 70 min	42	91		33	36	
13			YARDLEY	2	···	164		8 ····1	65			43	92			37	
18	"	12			8 7 ··2·↑·↑	170		7 ·1	67		· Appeal ct wkt ~hooking.	44	95		35	38	
23	12-2-35-0 (1)		"	3	·	171		4 ······3	74			45	98			41	
27	HOGG	11						x ········	82		M 12	46					
33			"	4	·········	179					E.W. Swanton arrived. M 13	47					
36	12-6-19-2 (1)	12	4-1-6-0 (-)		·· 7 1	182	1	9 3 2 1 1 ·2	87	4	4 HR→	48	104	3	36	46	4
3.41	TEA										M13 NB/2					T E A	
4.00			YARDLEY	5	E 7 ··1····1	188		··	89			49	105		37		
04	HOGG	13			3 L 7s ···2·1	894		··	91		Round wkt to LHB.	50	108		40		
10			"	6	3	195		P ······	98		Sunny interludes	51	109		41		
14	"	14			L Y ↑ P 8↑ ····(3)·	203		8 ·1	99		NB/3	52	113		44	47	
20			"	7	·····	207		8 4 2··3	103		GOWER'S 50: 120'	53	118			52	
24	"	15			x ···· ↑	213		Y 5 ·1	105			54	119			53	
30	15-6-27-2 (1)		"	8				9 2 ····· ····	113		· RO appeal. sent back by Boycott.	55	121			55	
34	DYMOCK	17			8 9E ·2·1·	217		x ·····	117		· Short of wkt ~diving · 2000 v AUS (8th ENG)	56	124		47		
38	"	18			8 3	218		L ······	124		BOYCOTT's 50: 280' his 49th Test fifty.	57	127		50		
43	"	18			8 ······1	225		8 ·1	125			58	129		51	56	
47	"		"	10	7 ·····2·	232		6 1	126			59	132		53	57	
50	"	19			···	235		5 2 ··23	131			60	137			62	
55			"	11				5 8 4····2·	139	5	100 p'ship: 153 5HR→	61	143			68	
58 5.01	DRINKS "	20			· ↑8	237		1E 2·····1	145		· skier behind wk	62	146		54	70	
06			"	12	·· 2 1	240		8 ·2··1	150			63	149		55	72	
10	"	21			7 ·1	242		L P1 ···4	156	6		64	154		56	76	
16	21-2-44-1 (2)		"	13	3 ···0·1	249		①··	159		NB NB NB /5 Round wkt to LHB	65	157		57		6
21	HOGG	16	13-1-31-0 (1)		7 ↑1	250		·①··xxx	168		† NEW BALL /2 · ct 1st gully NB NB	66	160		58		8
30			HURST	13	··x···	258					NB/67 M14	67					
34	"	17						4 x 2·····1	176			68	162			78	
41	"		"	14	6s 1	259		8 47 ↑···2·1	183			69	168		59	83	
46	18-6-4-2 (3)	18	14-3-41-0 (1)		7 ·2	261	1	3 37 ··4·41	189	8	M14 NB/7	70	179	3	61	92	8

43

AUSTRALIA v ENGLAND — 2nd Test
at Perth

TIME	BOWLER (Grandstand End)	O.	BOWLER (River End)	O.	SCOREBOARD LEFT – SCORING	BALLS	6s/4s	SCOREBOARD RIGHT – SCORING	BALLS	6s/4s	NOTES	O.	RUNS	W.	L BAT	R BAT	EXTRAS
					BOYCOTT	261	1	GOWER	189	8	M14 NB/7	70	179	3	61	92	8
5.53			HURST	15	7 1	262		4 3 2 2 ·· 6 ·4·↑	196	9	GOWER's 100:214' 6HR	71	189		62	101	
59	DYMOCK	22	15-3-51-0 (2)		·····7①	269	1	··	198	9	*Appeal at wkt NB/8	72	190	3	63	101	8
6.03	22-2-45-1(2) STUMPS		(1ST DAY)								M14 NB/8		STUMPS				
2ND DAY 11.00			HURST	16	+·· 2 8 2·1	273		····	202		150 p'ship:222' (W)	73	194		66		9
05	HOGG	19	16-3-54-0 (2)		·8· ↑	276		····7 1	207		strong cross wind (from legside bowling at Grandstand End)	74	196		67	102	
11			DYMOCK	23				x ·····	215		M15	75					
16	"	20			·····+↑	282		··	217		(W) M16	76	197				10
23			"	24	x ··+1	287		···	220		ATTENDANCE (2nd): 8,791	77	198		68		
27	"	21			E·↑····7 1	293		x W	221	9	†Round wkt	77⁷	199	4	69	102	10
32								BOTHAM Helmet cap								0	
34	"	21						··	1			78					
35			"	25	x ··7 2·····	301						79	201		71		
40	"	22			8· 1	302		LB ······	8		(LB) *Dropped short leg (HUGHES)	80	203		72		11
46			"	26	···↑8 2····	310						81	205		74		
50	"	23			·2·	313		····7 1	13		7HR→	82	208		76	1	
57			"	27	↑7 1	317		·4· 1 x	17			83	210		77	2	
12.02 04	DRINKS "	24			↑·↑·	325					M17	84					
10	24-8-48-3(3)		"	28	·	326		···7 4·3	24	1		85	217			9	
15	HURST	17						·4 L 2 W	28	1		85⁴	219	5	77	11	11
18								MILLER Helmet cap								0	
20	"	17						·x·	4			86					
22			"	29	·······4B	334					(4LB) M18	87	223				15
26	"	18			L W	337	1	LB	6		(LB)	87⁵	224	6	77	0	16
29					TAYLOR Helmet cap											0	
31	"	18			···	3					M19	88					
33			"	30				······1 2·	14			89	226			2	
37	"	19			·○○·4··· L	13	1				(NB) NB 8 10	90	232		4		18
44			"	31	·····x 1	20		4 3	15			91	236		5	5	
48	"	20	31-4-65-1(3)		···7 2·	28					8HR→	92	238		7		
54			YARDLEY	14	·8· 1	30		·4· 3 ····	21			93	242		8	8	
58	21-5-62-2(2) "	21	14-1-35-0(1)		Y	38	1		21	–	M20 NB/10	94	242	6	8	8	18
1·02	LUNCH												LUNCH				
1·41			YARDLEY	15	····2 3	43		3B ··	24		(3B)	95	248		11		21
45	HOGG	25			····P 1	51					M21	96					
51			"	16				E·P·5 ···4	32	1		97	252			12	
55	"	26			↑·1E·	58		·	33		Dropped wkt (in front of 1st slip)	98	253		12		
2·00	26-9-49-3(3)		"	17	W 7	59	1		33			98⁶	253	7	12	12	21
01					LEVER No cap											0	
03			17-1-46-1(2) "	17	·7 2·1 2S	4	–	··6 1	36	1	M21 NB/10	99	257	7	3	13	21

AUSTRALIA v ENGLAND
at Perth

2nd Test

2ND DAY	BOWLERS (BROOKS) GRANDSTAND END	O.	(BAILHACHE) RIVER END	O.	BATSMEN SCOREBOARD LEFT	BALLS	6s/4s	SCOREBOARD RIGHT	BALLS	6s/4s	ENGLAND 1ST INNINGS NOTES	O.	RUNS	W.	'L' BAT	'R' BAT	EXTRAS
TIME	BOWLER	O.	BOWLER	O.	SCORING	BALLS	6s/4s	SCORING	BALLS	6s/4s	NOTES	O.	RUNS	W.	'L' BAT	'R' BAT	EXTRAS
					LEVER	4	–	MILLER	36	1	M21 NB/10	99	257	7	3	13	21
2.06	HOGG	27			4 1	5		2 • 8↑ 2↑ 1 · · 4 · 4 ·	43	3	*Appeal ct wkt	100	267		4	22	
13			YARDLEY	18	· P · 6 · · ·	12		8 1	44			101	269		5	23	
17	"	28			· ·	14		↑ ↑ 5 5 5 · · · 2 1	50		† Round wkt	102	272			26	
24	28-9-62-3 (5)		"	19	5 4 1	16		P 3B · · ·	56		CARLSON sub for HOGG (3B)	103	276		6		24
29	HURST	22			2 1	17		Y · · ! · · ·	63		9 HR →	104	277		7		
35			"	20	9E · 3	19		· · 6 · 7 · x	69		Hogg back for 105th over (W)	105	283		10	28	25
39 41	DRINKS	23			· · · · E · ! ↑	27					M22	106					
46			"	21	LB	28		· · · · 1 6 1 7 1	76		(LB)	107	286			30	26
50	"	24			· · · ·	32		5 ↑8 · 2 · 1	80			108	289			33	
55			"	22	P · 5	35		· · 2 · · P	85			109	291		11	34	
3.00	"	25			8 E1 E · 2 · 1 W	40	–	↑8 1	86			109 (6)	295	8	14	35	26
03					WILLIS No cap	2									0		
05	"	25			· ·	2						110					
06			"	23				· · · 3 · 4 · · x	94	4		111	299			39	
10	"	26	23-1-62-1 (3)		x P · Y E · · · ·	10					M23	112					
16	26-7-70-3 (3)		DYMOCK	32	· ·	11		· · · · · 9	101			113	300			40	
21	HOGG	29						· Y x · W	104	4		113 (3)	300	9	0	40	26
22								HENDRICK No cap	4						0		
24	"	29			· ·	12		· · x 4 1	4			114	301			1	
28			"	33				E · · · · · x 1 2	12		•Dropped 3rd slip – low (YARDLEY)	115	302			2	
32	"	30			x 3 · 1	14		x 2 · · 1 · · ·	18		10 HR →	116	304		1	3	
38			"	34	2 1	15		L · Y · 4 · x 4 ·	25	1		117	309		2	7	
43	30-5-9-65-5 (5)	31	34-4-72-1 (4)		· · x · 5 · W	20	–		25	1		117 (5)	309	10	2	7	26
3.46	ENGLAND ALL OUT										M23 NB/10		ALL		OUT		
	TEA TAKEN				BATTING TIME: 612 MINUTES			951 balls									

14 The finest innings of the rubber – David Gower, rated by his captain as 'a minor genius', and by many others as the most exciting English batting prospect since May and Cowdrey.

AUSTRALIA 1st Innings
In reply to ENGLAND'S 309 all out

IN	OUT	MINS	No.	BATSMAN	HOW OUT	BOWLER	RUNS
4.06	4.18	12	1	WOOD	LBW	LEVER	5
4.06	5.58	112	2	DARLING	RUN OUT (BOTHAM → MILLER)		25
4.20	5.03	43	3	HUGHES	BOWLED	WILLIS	16
5.09	5.27	18	4	YALLOP *	BOWLED	WILLIS	3
5.29	(3.39)	272	5	TOOHEY	NOT OUT		81
11.00	11.33	33	6	COSIER	Cᵗ GOOCH	WILLIS	4
11.36	11.38	2	7	MACLEAN †	Cᵗ GOOCH	MILLER	0
11.40	12.23	43	8	YARDLEY	Cᵗ TAYLOR	HENDRICK	12
12.26	2.10	68	9	HOGG	Cᵗ TAYLOR	WILLIS	18
2.13	3.31	78	10	DYMOCK	BOWLED	HENDRICK	11
3.33	3.39	6	11	HURST	Cᵗ TAYLOR	WILLIS	5
* CAPTAIN † WICKET-KEEPER				EXTRAS	b - lb 7 w 1 nb 2		10

TOTAL (OFF 66.5 OVERS IN 354 MINUTES) **190**

BOWLER	O	M	R	W	nb/w	HRS	OVERS	RUNS		RUNS	MINS	OVERS	LAST 50 (in mins)
LEVER	7	0	20	1	-	1	11	34		50	101	17.5	101
BOTHAM	11	2	46	0	-/1	2	10	31		100	194	36.1	93
WILLIS	18.5	5	44	5	2/-	3	12	28		150	315	60.1	121
HENDRICK	14	1	39	2	-	4	12	28					
MILLER	16	6	31	1	-	5	12	26					
Extras/Run Out			10	1									
	66.5	14	190	10									

2ND NEW BALL taken at 3.28pm on 3rd day
- AUSTRALIA 182-8 after 65 overs.

WKT	TOTAL	6s	4s	BALLS	NOTES ON DISMISSAL
1	8	.	.	12	Beaten by late movement — pushed forward to inswinger.
4	60	.	1	63	Sent back by Toohey (striker) — beaten by mid-wicket return to bowler.
2	34	.	1	44	Played inside length ball which left him and broke off stump.
3	38	.	.	17	Late on fast break back which clipped off stump.
.	.	.	6	184	-
5	78	.	.	24	Edged firm-footed off-drive to 4th slip.
6	79	.	.	2	Top-edged sweep via leg to silly point.
7	100	.	.	44	Edged defensive push at leg-cutter.
8	128	.	2	67	Breakback took inside edge.
9	185	.	.	72	Beaten by late inswing — attempted off drive (new ball).
10	190	.	1	6	Edged attempted off-drive. Previous ball hit off stump.

0^6 11^4 535 balls (Including 2 no balls)

11 OVERS 2 BALLS/HOUR
2.85 RUNS/OVER
36 RUNS/100 BALLS

STUMPS: 60-4   TOOHEY 6* (25b, 29 min)
2ND DAY   OFF 19.7 OVERS IN 112 MIN

LUNCH: 121-7   TOOHEY 35* (116b, 152min)
HOGG 13* (32b, 37 min)
OFF 44 OVERS IN 235 MINUTES

TEA INTERVAL TAKEN AT END OF INNINGS

WKT	PARTNERSHIP		RUNS	MINS
1st	Wood	Darling	8	12
2nd	Darling	Hughes	26	43
3rd	Darling	Yallop	4	18
4th	Darling	Toohey	22	29
5th	Toohey	Cosier	18	33
6th	Toohey	Maclean	1	2
7th	Toohey	Yardley	21	43
8th	Toohey	Hogg	28	68
9th	Toohey	Dymock	57	78
10th	Toohey	Hurst	5	6

190

15 Yallop b Willis 3 – Taylor and Brearley seem to be under the illusion that Yallop has edged this fast breakback but, Willis, bowling at his fastest, has found the off stump.

16 Dymock b Hendrick 11 – Geoff Dymock's 78-minute vigil is ended immediately he faces the new ball and the highest partnership of the innings is over.

AUSTRALIA v ENGLAND — 2nd Test

Test At Perth

AUSTRALIA 1st INNINGS

TIME	BOWLER (Grandstand End)	O.	BOWLER (River End)	O.	SCOREBOARD LEFT — SCORING	BALLS	6s/4s	SCOREBOARD RIGHT — SCORING	BALLS	6s/4s	NOTES	O.	RUNS	W.	L BAT	R BAT	EXTRAS
					WOOD cap (LHB)			DARLING Helmet cap									
4.06	LEVER	1			·· xx ··· 2·×	8						1	2		2		
11			BOTHAM	1	· 2/3	10		·4 LB ·· ↑9/2	6		(LB)	2	8		5	2	1
17	"	2			·W L	12	–					2²	8	1	5	2	1
18					HUGHES cap								0				
20	"	2			8/1	1		·P·P·P	11			3	9		1		
24			"	2	·7/1 x ··· LB	7		·7/1	13		(LB)	4	12		2	3	2
29	"	3			x ·· P7/2·1	15						5	14		4		
34	3-0-5-1 (–)		"	3	4/2 ·· TE/1 1	20		6/1 +·1 3	16		(W)	6	21		8	5	3
39	WILLIS	1	3-0-13-0 (–)		··· ⊙··9	28		↑1	17		(NB) NB 1	7	23		9		4
45			HENDRICK	1	L7/·1	30			23			8	24		10		
50	"	2			···· 2 1E/4·2	38	1					9	30		16		
55			"	2	··	40		·· 4/2·1 7	29			10	33			8	
5.00	"	3			··· x W	44	1	↑8/1	30		off stump broken	10⁵	34	2	16	9	4
03	DRINKS 5.05				YALLOP Helmet cap LHB								0				
09	"	3			·· xx	3					1 HR →	11					
11			"	3	x ·····1	8		·· 7/1	33			12	35			10	
16	"	4						···· x	41		M1	13					
21			"	4	··· 8/2···1 7	16						14	38		3		
26	"	5			W x	17	–					14¹	38	3	3	10	4
27					TOOHEY cap								0				
29	"	5			·····5/·3	7						15	41		3		
34			"	5	·········	15					M2	16					
38	"	6	5-1-8-0 (–)		·	16		x ····O3 4	49		(NB) NB/2	17	45			13	5
45			BOTHAM	4	·	17		E·P 4 2 7/4 2·1	56	1	Eager just short of wk	18	52			20	
50	"	7	4-0-20-0 (1)		··6/1 E	22		7/1 ↑8	59			19	55		4	22	
55	7-1-17-2 (1)		MILLER	1	9/2··	25		3·4/2·1 RO	63	1		19⁷	60	4	6	25	5
5.58	STUMPS (2nd DAY)		0.7-0-5-0 (–)					COSIER No cap			M2 NB/2	STUMPS				0	
3RD DAY 11.00			MILLER	1	·	26					ATTENDANCE (3rd) 9,802	20					
01½	WILLIS	8			··P 9/4·1	32	1	5/·1	2		RO chance - mid wkt (Boycott) 2HR →	21	65		10	1	
07			"	2	···· 9/·1	37		·· 7/1	5		Sunny - humid	22	69		13	2	
11	"	9			8/·2···1 6	45						23	72		16		
16			"	3	·· T · P ·	53					M3	24					
19	"	10						↑·······2 8t	13			25	74			4	
24			"	4	8/2··1 6	57		····	17			26	77		19		
28	"	11			3/1	58		··· x W E	24	–		27	78	5	20	4	5
33	11-1-28-3 (2)				MACLEAN cap						Delay for Botham drink					0	
36			"	5	9/·1	59		E W	2	–		27³	79	6	21	0	5
38								YARDLEY cap Helmet								0	
40			"	5	····	63	1	6/1	1	–	M3 NB/2	28	80	6	21	1	5

AUSTRALIA v ENGLAND   2nd Test

at Perth

3RD DAY TIME	BOWLERS (BROOKS) GRANDSTAND END BOWLER	O.	(BAILHACHE) RIVER END BOWLER	O.	BATSMEN SCOREBOARD LEFT SCORING	BALLS	6s 4s	SCOREBOARD RIGHT SCORING	BALLS	6s 4s	AUSTRALIA 1ST INNINGS NOTES	O.	RUNS	W.	'L' BAT	'R' BAT	EXTRAS
					TOOHEY	63	1	YARDLEY	1	–	M3 NB 2	28	80	6	21	1	5
11.42	WILLIS	12			↑·8··1	66		···2/3 ·	6			29	84		22	4	
47½			MILLER	6	6/3	67		·······	13			30	87		25		
51	"	13			···↑···↑	75					M4	31					
57	13-2-32-3 (2)		"	7	·	76		····3 8 2·1	20			32	90			7	
12.00 03	DRINKS LEVER	4			·	77		Y·P···4/3	27		• Brilliant stop by cover (Randall) 3HR	33	93			10	
08	"		"	8				E···1 2··	35			34	95			12	
13	"	5			··8 2···3 2·	85						35	99		29		
18	5-0-12-1 (–)		"	9				·······	43		M5	36					
21	HENDRICK	6			7·1	86		E W	44	–		36²	100	7	30	12	5
23								HOGG	Helmet							0	
26	"	6						····1 P 4·	6	1		37	104			4	
30			"	10	·········	94					M6	38					
34	"	7	10-3-22-1 (–)		···6 1··	100		8 LB 1·	8		(LB)	39	107		31	5	6
39			BOTHAM	5				×·×···	16		M7	40					
44	"	8			×·P·7··	104		···b 3	20		follow on saved at 12.48pm	41	111		32	8	
49			"	6	·9 1	106		↑·9 1· 2LB 4·· 4·1	26	2	Round wkt (4 balls) (2LB)	42	119		33	13	8
54	"	9			×·····6	114						43	120		34		
58	9-1-20-1 (1)		"	7	↑9 1·	116	1	·E·····	32	2		44	121	7	35	13	8
1.03	LUNCH		7-1-27-0 (2)								M7 NB/2		LUNCH				
1.40	WILLIS	14			·····P·×·	124					M8 4HR→	45					
46			MILLER	11				·:····P·	40		• Dropped sh. leg (Botham) • st change	46					
50	"	15			·········	132					M9 M10	47					
55			"	12				····	48		M11	48					
58	"	16			8·1 8·1	134		×··· 7 2 ·1↑1	54			49	125		37	15	
2.04			"	13				···· 3 8 2·1	62			50	128			18	
07	"	17						P E W	67	2		50⁵	128	8	37	18	8
10								DYMOCK	Cap (LHB)						0	
13	"	17						···	3		M12	51					
15			"	14	·7 1 4 1	137		3s 1····	8			52	131		39	1	
19	"	18			·····1E 4··	145	2					53	135		43		
25	18-5-40-4/3		"	15				·····×	16		M13	54					
29	HENDRICK	10			9 4·7 2 2·1	148		····×	21		•4 + 1 overthrow (Boycott returned wide)	55	140		48		
35			"	16	3 2·1	151		·····	26		TOOHEY'S 50: 208'	56	143		51		
38	"	11	16-6-31-1 (–)		×·7 ·1·	155		···4 3	30		5HR→	57	147		52	4	
43 46	DRINKS		BOTHAM	8	·156			···L·7··	37			58	148			5	
50	"	12						×···9 1	45			59	149			6	
55			"	9				L E 53	53		•Ball rebounded in air and hit shoulder.	60					
59	"	13			8·1 8·1	159		·4 3 ···	58		M14	61	154		54	9	
3.05	13-1-35-1 (1)		"	10	7·1 ↑4 2·1	163	2	↑····	62	–	M14 NB/2	62	157	8	57	9	8

50

AUSTRALIA v ENGLAND
at Perth

2nd Test

3RD DAY TIME	BOWLERS (BROOKS) GRANDSTAND END BOWLER	O.	(BAILHACHE) RIVER END BOWLER	O.	BATSMEN SCOREBOARD LEFT SCORING	BALLS	6s/4s	SCOREBOARD RIGHT SCORING	BALLS	6s/4s	AUSTRALIA 1ST INNINGS NOTES	O.	RUNS	W.	'L' BAT	'R' BAT	EXTRAS
					TOOHEY	163	2	DYMOCK	62	-	M14 NB/2	62	157	8	57	9	8
3.10	LEVER	6			.x5 5.../ .3 4...	170	3	LB .		63	(LB)	63	165		64		9
16			BOTHAM	11	..442.4	177	6	4/1		64	50 p'ship in 67 min	64	180		78	10	
21	.	7	11-2-46-0 (5)		LB	178		.P..9...	71		(LB)	65	182			11	10
28	7-0-20-1 (1)		HENDRICK	14	2..1	182		x W	72	-	umps & Brearley discussions about	65	185	9	81	11	10
31								HURST cap .			bouncers to Dymock (+ NEW BALL /2)					0	
33			..	14	L..	184		4/1	1			66	186			1	
35	WILLIS	19	14-1-39-2 (1)			184	6	x2 xE /.4..W	6	1	• Appeal ct wkt - (off stump hit)	66	190	10	81	5	10
3.39	AUSTRALIA ALL OUT										M14 NB/2		ALL OUT				
	TEA TAKEN				BATTING TIME: 354 MINUTES			535 balls									

17 Toohey hooks Botham for his third boundary in five balls – For virtually the only time in the rubber Peter Toohey lived up to the high reputation he had earned against India and West Indies. He showed maturity of temperament and technique as he contributed just over half of his team's total. Incredibly his other nine innings against England's bowlers produced only 68 runs and five scores of one or nought.

ENGLAND 2nd Innings

2nd Test

119 runs ahead on 1st Innings

IN	OUT	MINS	No.	BATSMAN	HOW OUT	BOWLER	RUNS
4.00	11.06	128	1	BOYCOTT	LBW	HOGG	23
4.00	11.52	174	2	GOOCH	LBW	HOGG	43
11.08	12.38	90	3	RANDALL	C⁺ COSIER	YARDLEY	45
11.54	11.55	1	4	BREARLEY *	C⁺ MACLEAN	HOGG	0
11.57	1.45	68	5	GOWER	C⁺ MACLEAN	HOGG	12
12.41	2.13	52	6	BOTHAM	C⁺ WOOD	YARDLEY	30
1.47	3.06	79	7	MILLER	C⁺ TOOHEY	YARDLEY	25
2.15	3.00	45	8	LEVER	C⁺ MACLEAN	HURST	10
3.02	3.38	36	9	TAYLOR †	C⁺ MACLEAN	HOGG	2
3.08	(3.45)	37	10	WILLIS	NOT OUT		3
3.40	3.45	5	11	HENDRICK	BOWLED	DYMOCK	1

* CAPTAIN † WICKET-KEEPER

EXTRAS	b - 16 6	w - nb 8	14

TOTAL (OFF 66·3 OVERS IN 368 MINUTES   208

BOWLER	O	M	R	W	nb
HOGG	17	2	57	5	3
DYMOCK	16.3	2	53	1	7
HURST	17	5	43	1	-
YARDLEY	16	1	41	3	-
Extras			14		
	66.3	10	208	10	

HRS.	OVERS	RUNS
1	11	31
2	12	27
3	10	35
4	10	56
5	11	41
6	12	17

RUNS	MINS	OVERS	LAST 50 (in mins)
50	113	21.2	113
100	190	34.3	77
150	239	43.1	49
200	315	56.5	76

2ND NEW BALL taken at 3.35pm on 4th day
- ENGLAND 206-8 after 65 overs.

WKT	TOTAL	6s	4s	BALLS	NOTES ON DISMISSAL
1	58	·	·	103	Beaten by breakback on backstroke.
2	93	·	5	131	Beaten by sharp breakback.
4	135	·	3	65	Gloved sweep behind 'keeper to 1st slip.
3	93	·	·	1	Involuntary offside edge to breakback – tried to withdraw bat.
5	151	·	·	47	Top-edged cut.
6	176	·	4	39	Mistimed lofted off drive – skier to deep mid-off.
8	201	·	3	42	Mistimed pull – gentle skier to mid-wicket.
7	201	·	·	54	Edged defensive push.
9	206	·	·	33	Edged defensive push
·	·	·	·	21	–
10	208	·	·	5	Drove outside near half-volley.

0^6 15^4 541 balls (including 10 no balls)

```
10  OVERS   7  BALLS/HOUR
     3·13    RUNS/OVER
     38   RUNS/100 BALLS
```

STUMPS : 58-0   BOYCOTT 23* (100b)
3RD DAY   GOOCH   26* (88b)
LEAD: 177   OFF 23 OVERS IN 122 MINUTES

LUNCH : 150-4   GOWER   12* (45b, 63 min)
                 BOTHAM   15* (13b, 19 min)
LEAD : 269   OFF 44 OVERS IN 242 MINUTES

TEA TAKEN AT END OF INNINGS

R.M. HOGG took FIVE WICKETS IN AN INNINGS for the third time in two Tests (17 WICKETS, average 13.58, in 2 matches).

AUSTRALIA REQUIRE 328 RUNS TO WIN

WKT	PARTNERSHIP		RUNS	MINS
1st	Boycott	Gooch	58	128
2nd	Gooch	Randall	35	44
3rd	Randall	Brearley	0	1
4th	Randall	Gower	42	41
5th	Gower	Botham	16	24
6th	Botham	Miller	25	26
7th	Miller	Lever	25	45
8th	Miller	Taylor	0	4
9th	Taylor	Willis	5	30
10th	Willis	Hendrick	2	5

208

AUSTRALIA v ENGLAND
at Perth

2nd Test

3RD DAY TIME	BOWLERS (BAILHACHE) GRANDSTAND END BOWLER	O.	(BROOKS) RIVER END BOWLER	O.	BATSMEN SCOREBOARD LEFT SCORING	BALLS	6s/4s	SCOREBOARD RIGHT SCORING	BALLS	6s/4s	ENGLAND 2ND INNINGS NOTES	END-OF-OVER TOTALS O.	RUNS	W.	'L' BAT	'R' BAT	EXTRAS
					BOYCOTT cap			GOOCH Helmet cap									
4.00	HOGG	1			.7.2....1	8						1	3		3		
06			DYMOCK	1	...7.1 ..	14		.8.1	2			2	5		4	1	
10	"	2			↑.↑4LB	17		.....8.1	7		• off HEAD (4LB)	3	10			2	4
16			"	2	.:.	19		.....4.1	13		• Appeal ct wkt	4	11			3	
21	"	3						........†	21		M1	5					
26			"	3	!..4.2....	27					STREAKER (MALE) • Darling misfield	6	13		6		
31	"	4			.2.2	28		L....8.1.	28			7	15		7	4	
37			"	4	!8.⊙.2!.21	35		.3.1	30		(NB) NB/1	8	21		11	5	5
42	"	5			2.....	40		.↑L.2	33		† Round wkt (2 balls)	9	23		12	6	
49	5-1-8-0 (-)		"	5	7.1↑	42		4.LB.9 2...·1	39		(LB) off arm	10	28		13	9	6
54	HURST	1			.7.2.	45		2	44		1HR →	11	31		15	10	
59 5.02	DRINKS		"	6	.1	46		.9.2...7.1	51			12	34			13	
06	"	2						↑P↑8 .4....	59			13	38			17	
12			"	7	8↑ 2.⊙.....	55					(NB) NB/2	14	41		17		7
17	"	3						L	67		M2	15					
22			"	8	..⊙....3.1	64					(NB) NB 3	16	43		18		8
27	"	4			...9.1	68		1	71			17	44		19		
31	4-1-8-0 (1)		"	9	...7.1	72		↑x...	75			18	45		20		
36	HOGG	6	9-0-21-0 (-)		.....8.1	78		.·..	77		• Appeal ct wkt	19	46		21		
42			YARDLEY	1	....L..-.	86		—			M3	20					
47	"	7			8.2....	91		.4.·1	80			21	49		23	18	
53	7-1-12-0 (-)		"	2				.6.4.47 22..	88	2	50 p'ship in 113 min.	22	57			26	
57	DYMOCK	10	2-1-8-0 (1)		⊙......↑.	100 _			88	2	(NB) NB/4 M4	23	58	—	23	26	9
6.02	STUMPS (3RD DAY) 10-1-21-0 (-)										2HR ↗		STUMPS				
4TH DAY 11.00			HURST	5				L	96		M5	24					
05	HOGG	8	5-2-8-0 (1)		.L W	103 _					ATTENDANCE (4th): 4,698	24³	58	1	23	26	9
06					RANDALL cap										0		
08	"	8			....1.4	5						25	59		1		
12			DYMOCK	11	...7.1	9		....	100			26	60		2		
16	"	9			.3.3 4.1	14	1	...	103			27	65		7		
23			"	12	.2.3 ↑!.	19		.2. 4⊙1	107	3	(NB) NB/5	28	74		10	31	10
28½	"	10						....↑x1.x.4.:.	115	4		29	78			35	
34			"	13	..x.⊙..	27					• Appeal ct wkt M6	30					
39	"	11			.9.1	28		8.·....6 .3	122	5	• ½ chance (Randall)	31	86		11	42	
45			"	14	.7.·1 7.4.·	32	2	↑x.8 ..⊙.1	127		(NB/6) NB/6	32	93		16	43	11
50	"	12	14-2-36-0 (2)					L.L W	131	5		32⁴	93	2	16	43	11
52								BREARLEY Helmet cap								0	
54	"	12						E W	1 _			32⁵	93	3	16	0	11
55	12-2-30-3 (3)					32	2				M6 NB/6						

54

18 Occupational therapy – The Geoffrey Boycott defence in action; his boundaryless 100 runs in nine hours 42 minutes may have tested even the most enthusiastic of his devotees but his experience and sheer professionalism provided the basis of England's victory.

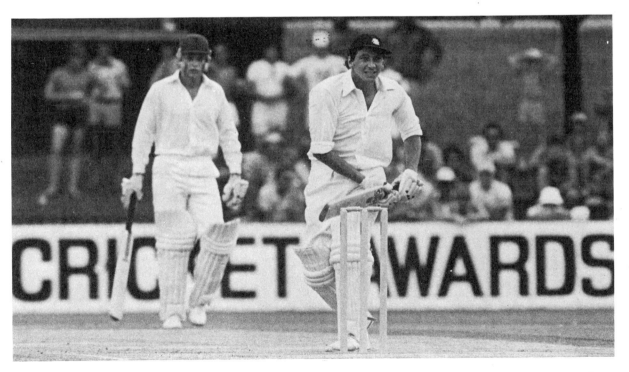

19 The Randall mishook in action – This attempted hook off a Dymock bouncer is on its way over the wicket-keeper's head for four watched by Gower and the stroke's creator. Randall was out when he skied a hook at his third ball in the first innings and the Australian bowlers were able to exploit this compulsion for that stroke on two later occasions.

AUSTRALIA v ENGLAND — 2nd Test

at Perth

4th DAY	BOWLERS (BAILHACHE) GRANDSTAND END		(BROOKS) RIVER END		BATSMEN SCOREBOARD LEFT			SCOREBOARD RIGHT			ENGLAND 2ND INNINGS NOTES	END-OF-OVER TOTALS					
TIME	BOWLER	O.	BOWLER	O.	SCORING	BALLS	6s/4s	SCORING	BALLS	6s/4s	NOTES	O.	RUNS	W.	'L' BAT	'R' BAT	EXTRAS
					RANDALL	32	2	GOWER (Helmet cap) (LHB)			M6 NB/6	32.5	93	3	16	0	11
11.57	HOGG	12						...	3		M7 3HR→	33					
59 12.01	DRINKS		DYMOCK	15	2 . E× . . 29 2 21	39		. 4	4			34	98		21		
06	"	13			. . 8 . 6 . . 2 . . 2 . .	47						35	102		25		
13	13-2-34-3(3)		"	16	. 2 6 1E . . 23 4 42	52	3	LB . 3 . 3	7		(LB)	36	115		34	3	12
18	HURST	6	16-2-53-0(3)		6 . . 1 2 . . 1 1	57		. 3 . 7 . 3 1	10			37	123		38	7	
25			YARDLEY	3	1 . . 8 1	61		9 . . . 1	14			38	126		40	8	
30	"	7			. 3 6 . 2 3	64		 3	19			39	134		45	11	
36			"	4	G W	65	3	LT 2 . . . 1	23		Round wkt to LHB	39.5	135	4	45	12	12
38					BOTHAM (Helmet cap)										0		
41			"	4	. 4 . 9	3	1					40	139		4		
43	"	8						. . . . . ×	31		M8	41					
47			"	5	. . . 44 9 . 44 . 1	10	3	.	32			42	148		13		
52	"	9			. 7 1	12		. . . . .	38		4HR→	43	149		14		
57	9-3-25-0(1)		"	6	8 1	13	3	 45	45	−		44	150	4	15	12	12
1.00	LUNCH		6-1-26-1(4)								M8 NB/6		LUNCH				
1.40	HOGG	14			 8	19		E× E . W	47	−	Round wkt to LHB • Near mid wkt	45	151	5	16	12	12
45 47			YARDLEY	7	×× . L . . ×08	27		MILLER (Helmet cap)	1		"Corner misfield	46	152		17	0	
52		15			6 . 7 1 EP5 1 . . 24 . 2	34	4	9 . 1	1			47	162		26	1	
58			"	8	.	35		 4	8			48	163			2	
2.02		16			6 . 7 . 2.2	38		O . (4) . 2 9 . . 1	16	1	(NB) Round wkt 7 balls NB/789	49	175		30	9	13
11	16-2-56-4(5)		"	9	4 W	39	4	9 . 1	17			49.2	176	6	30	10	13
13					LEVER (No cap)										0		
15			"	9	2 1	5		. 3 . 2	18		Carlson sub for DARLING	50	180		1	13	
18	HURST	10			. Y E0 . . 6 .	11		7 . . 8 . 4	20	2	• Short of 1st slip.	51	186		2	18	
24			"	10	6 . 2	19						52	188		4		
28½	"	11			.	20		. . ×. . . 7	27			53	189			19	
33			"	11	.	24		. . . 8 . 1	31		5HR→	54	190			20	
37	"	12			. . . . 7 1	29		. 3 . 1 . 4 1	34	3		55	196		5	25	
42 45	DRINKS		"	12	E 3	36		.	35			56	197		6		
48	"	13			9 × . 1E . 2 . . . 1	43		.	36			57	200		9		
54			"	13	 4	49		. L	38			58	201		10		
58	"	14			. ×× E . W	54	−					58.5	201	7	10	25	13
3.00					TAYLOR (Helmet cap)						Taylor batted with a runner (Randall)				0		
02	"	14			. . . 1	3					− strained groin. M9	59					
05			"	14				E0 . 7 . . . W	42	3	• Near wkt kpr.	59.4	201	8	0	25	13
06								WILLIS (No cap)								0	
08			"	14	. .	5		. 1 95	2		• Near wkt kpr	60	202			1	
10	"	15			P . P . . 1	11		. 1 75	4			61	203			2	
16	15-4-42-1(3)		15-1-40-3(4)	15	 1	18	−	8 . 1	5	−	M9 NB/9	62	204	8	0	3	13

AUSTRALIA v ENGLAND — 2nd Test

at Perth

4TH DAY	BOWLERS (BALHACHE GRANDSTAND) END	O.	BOWLERS (BROOKS) RIVER END	O.	BATSMEN SCOREBOARD LEFT SCORING	BALLS	6s/4s	SCOREBOARD RIGHT SCORING	BALLS	6s/4s	ENGLAND 2ND INNINGS NOTES	O.	RUNS	W.	'L' BAT	'R' BAT	EXTRAS
TIME	BOWLER	O.	BOWLER	O.	SCORING	BALLS	6s/4s	SCORING	BALLS	6s/4s	NOTES	O.	RUNS	W.	'L' BAT	'R' BAT	EXTRAS
					TAYLOR 18	-		WILLIS 5	-		M 9 NB/9	62	204	8	0	3	13
3·20	HURST	16						·····x P·	13		M 10	63					
25			YARDLEY	16	·····1²	24		··	15			64	205		1		
30	·	17	16-1-41-3(4)		···1²	28		····	19			65	206		2		
35	17-5-43-1(3)		HOGG	17	†····W E	33	-				† NEW BALL/2	65⁵	206	9	2	3	13
38					HENDRICK (NO cap)										0		
40			·	17)	··1²	1		·· P x	21		6HR→	66	207		1		
43	DYMOCK	17	17-2-57-5(5)		··⊙ W (P x)	5	-		21	-	(NB) NB/10	66³	208	10	1	3	14
3·45	ENGLAND ALL OUT 16-3-2-53-1(3)										M 10 NB/10		ALL	OUT			
	TEA TAKEN				BATTING TIME :			368 MINUTES			541 balls						
	AUSTRALIA		REQUIRE		328 RUNS		IN A	MINIMUM		OF 475	MINUTES						

20 Rodney Hogg, 10 wickets and 'Man of the Match' – Australia's amazing new star dismisses Gower for the second time in the match. Unable to gain selection for his native Victoria, Hogg moved to Adelaide in 1975 but was 27 years and eight months of age before he gained his first Test cap.

AUSTRALIA 2nd Innings

Requiring 328 runs to win in a minimum of 475 minutes

IN	OUT	MINS	No.	BATSMAN	HOW OUT	BOWLER	RUNS
4.05	4.18	13	1	DARLING	Cᵗ BOYCOTT	LEVER	5
4.05	3.11	243	2	WOOD	Cᵗ TAYLOR	LEVER	64
4.20	11.41	54	3	HUGHES	Cᵗ GOOCH	WILLIS	12
11.43	12.26	43	4	YALLOP *	Cᵗ TAYLOR	HENDRICK	3
12.28	12.29	1	5	TOOHEY	Cᵗ TAYLOR	HENDRICK	0
12.31	2.58	109	6	COSIER	LBW	MILLER	47
3.00	3.18	18	7	MACLEAN †	Cᵗ BREARLEY	MILLER	1
3.13	3.37	24	8	YARDLEY	Cᵗ BOTHAM	LEVER	7
3.21	3.29	8	9	HOGG	BOWLED	MILLER	0
3.31	(3.45)	14	10	DYMOCK	NOT OUT		6
3.39	3.45	6	11	HURST	BOWLED	LEVER	5
* CAPTAIN † WICKET-KEEPER				EXTRAS	b - lb 3 w 4 nb 4		11

TOTAL (OFF 46.1 OVERS IN 275 MINUTES) — **161**

BOWLER	O	M	R	W	nb/w	HRS	OVERS	RUNS		RUNS	MINS	OVERS	LAST 50 (in mins)
WILLIS	12	1	36	1	4/4	1	10	35		50	85	13.3	85
LEVER	8.1	2	28	4	-	2	9	25		100	185	30.2	100
BOTHAM	11	1	54	0	4/-	3	11	39		150	264	44.2	79
HENDRICK	8	3	11	2	-	4	10	44					
MILLER	7	4	21	3	-								
Extras			11										
	46.1	11	161	10									

WKT	TOTAL	6s	4s	BALLS	NOTES ON DISMISSAL
1	8	.	1	9	Fended viciously lifting ball to mid-on. (Bat knocked from grip).
6	143	.	3	168	Given out in response to appeal for offside catch. Bowler did not appeal.
2	36	.	1	45	Cut break back hard to 4th slip's left (shoulder-high, 2 handed)
3	58	.	.	23	Leg side catch from inside edge - bat hit by leg-cutter.
4	58	.	.	1	Edged firm-footed off drive at offside ball - 1st ball.
5	141	.	4	74	Missed sweep at ball which swung away.
7	143	.	.	16	Edged defensive stab at faster ball to 1st slip.
9	151	.	1	19	Edged off drive to 2nd slip - left-handed falling catch.
8	147	.	.	8	Beaten by quicker ball.
.	.	.	1	9	-
10	161	.	.	5	Drove over yorker.

0⁶ 11⁴ 377 balls (Including 8 no balls)

10	OVERS	BALLS/HOUR
3.49		RUNS/OVER
43		RUNS/100 BALLS

BAD LIGHT AND HEAVY RAIN STOPPED PLAY AT 4.33pm
87 MINUTES LOST ON 4TH DAY

STUMPS : 11 - 1 WOOD 2* (10b, 28 min)
4TH DAY HUGHES 1* (14b, 13 min)
OFF 4 OVERS IN 28 MINUTES

LUNCH: 80 - 4 WOOD 37* (97b, 151 min)
COSIER 13* (24b, 31 min)
OFF 24 OVERS IN 151 MINUTES

ENGLAND WON BY 166 RUNS
at 3.45 pm on the fifth (last) day.

ENGLAND LAST WON THE FIRST TWO TESTS OF A RUBBER
IN AUSTRALIA IN 1936-37.

MAN OF THE MATCH: R.M. HOGG

TOTAL MATCH ATTENDANCE: 35,667. TIME LOST: 87 MINUTES

WKT	PARTNERSHIP		RUNS	MINS
1st	Darling	Wood	8	13
2nd	Wood	Hughes	28	54
3rd	Wood	Yallop	22	43
4th	Wood	Toohey	0	1
5th	Wood	Cosier	83	109
6th	Wood	Maclean	2	11
7th	Maclean	Yardley	0	5
8th	Yardley	Hogg	4	8
9th	Yardley	Dymock	4	6
10th	Dymock	Hurst	10	6

161

AUSTRALIA v ENGLAND 2nd Test
at Perth

4TH DAY TIME	BOWLER (BAILHACHE) GRANDSTAND END	O.	BOWLER (BROOKS) RIVER END	O.	SCOREBOARD LEFT SCORING	BALLS	6s/4s	SCOREBOARD RIGHT SCORING	BALLS	6s/4s	NOTES	O.	RUNS	W.	'L' BAT	'R' BAT	EXTRAS
					DARLING (Helmet)			WOOD (cap)(LHB)									
4.05			WILLIS	1	2 ↑8 +·0	5	1	·× × 7s ·1	4		DROPPED 1ST SLIP (BREARLEY)(NB) NB/	1	7		5	1	1
14	LEVER	1			·· ·· W	9	1·	·· LB	6		Hit in box (hooking) Appeal-ct wkt (legside)	1⁶	8	1	5	1	2
18					HUGHES cap						(LB)				0		
20	"	1			··	2					M1	2					
22			"	2	× ·· ··· ×	8		·1 ·2	8			3	9			2	
28	2-1-1-1 (-)	2	2-0-7-0 (1)		× 4s ···· 1	14		·· LB ·1	10	-	(LB) Light appeal	4	11	1	1	2	3
4.33	BLSP				↑									B L S P			
4.41	HEAVY RAIN													R A I N			
5.10	PLAY ABANDONED										27 minutes lost on 4th day.				S T U M P S		
5TH DAY 11.00			WILLIS	3	7s ·1 ··	18		··· 3 1	14		ATTENDANCE (5th): 4,493	5	13		2	3	
05	LEVER	3			7 2 ···· ×	25		5 3	15			6	18		4	6	
11	"			4	·· ↑0 4 2	30	1	···· 7 ①	20		NB/23 (NB)	7	24		8	7	4
18	"	4			········	37		6 3	21		Edmonds sub for Willis (1 over)	8	27			10	
24			"	5				······ × ··	29		M2	9					
30	"	5			4 3 ·· 7 ·	42		7 ·3 7 1	32		1 HR →	10	35		12	14	
36	5-1-17-1 (-)			6	1 ··· W	45		··· 7 1	36	-		10⁷	36	2	12	15	4
41					YALLOP (Helmet/cap)(LHB)										0		
43			"	6	↑ 1	1						11					
44	BOTHAM	1			···· × 1	6		↑8 7 4·1	39	1	Round wkt	12	41			20	
49			"	7	1 ·· ··	9		···# 1 ↑ 8	44		(4W) * Hit on thigh	13	46			21	8
55	"	2						↑8 (4) ··1	53	2	NB/4	14	50			25	
12.00 02	DRINKS		"	8	··· E2 6· 1 2	14		·· 8 1	56		* 2 overthrows (Randall)	15	54		3	26	
08	"	3	8-1-20-1 (2)		·	15		8 2① P ··1	64		* Skier - dropped NB/ mid wkt - Boycott 5	16	57			29	
14			HENDRICK	1	·····	20		·· LB	67		(LB) M3	17	58				9
19	"	4						······ × ·	75		* Appeal ct wkt M4	18					
24			"	2	·· E W	23	-					18³	58	3	3	29	9
26					TOOHEY cap										0		
28			"	2	E W	1	-					18⁴	58	4	0	29	9
29					COSIER (No cap)										0		
31			"	2	·· 6 2·	4		·			2 HR →	19	60		2		
34	"	5			7 ↑8 1	6		66 4s ·1 ··1	81		Round wkt still	20	64		4	31	
40			"	3	········· ·	14					* Dropped ct ~ b. M5 (wide to his left)	21					
45	"	6			↑8 1	16		7· ×·9 ·2··①1	88		* Dropped m mkr (Boycott) ct Boycott. NB NB/6	22	69		5	34	10
51			"	4	L 3 ·· 3	20		···· 1	92			23	72		8		
56	7-1-28-0 (2)	7	4-2-5-2 (-)		· 7 6 × 1 4	24	1	L 2 9 ·· 20①	97	2	NB/7	24	80	4	13	37	10
1.02	LUNCH										M5 NB/7			L U N C H			
1.40			HENDRICK	5				···· × ·	105		M6	25					
46	BOTHAM	8			·· 6 3	27		··4 7 9 8 ·422	110	3	over wkt to RHB * Hit on chest	26	91		16	45	
52	8-1-39-0 (3)		6-3-7-2 (-)	6	· 7 1 ··	31	1	···· 7 1	114	3	M6 NB/7	27	93	4	17	46	10

AUSTRALIA v ENGLAND 2nd Test
at Perth

5TH DAY	BOWLERS (BALLHACHE) GRANDSTAND END	O.	(BROOKS) RIVER END	O.	BATSMEN SCOREBOARD LEFT	BALLS	6s/4s	SCOREBOARD RIGHT	BALLS	6s/4s	AUSTRALIA 2ND INNINGS NOTES	O.	RUNS	W.	L BAT	R BAT	EXTRAS
TIME	BOWLER		BOWLER		SCORING			SCORING					END-OF-OVER TOTALS				
					COSIER	31	1	WOOD	114	3	M6 NB/7 Round wkt to LHB	27	93	4	17	46	10
1.57	BOTHAM	9			x . x .	34		x . 2 3 . 2 . 1	119			28	96			49	
2.02			HENDRICK	7	. . . E E . .	41		7	120		Wood's 50: 174 min	29	97			50	
07	•	10						. . . 6 . 2 . . .	128		• Randall misfield 3 HR →	30	99			52	
12	•		•	8	. 2 . . 4 . 1 . . 1	46		3 . 1 E .	131			31	102		19	53	
17	•	11	8-3-11-2 (-)		. 6 1E5 . 42 .	51	2	. . 2 3s . 21 .	134		50 p'ship in 73 min	32	112		26	56	
24	11-1-54-0 (4)		WILLIS	9	. . 2 3 x . . .	57		9 8 1	136			33	117		29	58	
30	MILLER	1						. . . .	144		• st. appeal M7 Round wkt	34					
34			•	10	. . . 1 . 4 x . 3 . . 3	64	3	(.) .	146		(NB) NB/8	35	125		36		11
40 43	DRINKS •	2			6 3	65		. . . . x E1	153			36	129		39	59	
47			•	11	. . 3 1	68		8s 1 ↑ . . . ↑	158			37	131		40	60	
53	•	3	•		. . 7 4 8L 42 W	74	4	. 6 . 3	160		over wkt to RHB.	38	141	5	47	63	11
58					MACLEAN	cap									0		
3.00			•	12	. 7 1	2		2 1	166			39	143		1	64	
06	•	4	12-1-36-1 (3)		. . . . P	10					M8 4HR →	40					
10			LEVER	6				x W	168	3		40²	143	6	1	64	11
11								YARDLEY	Helmet cap							0	
13			•	6				. . . . x .	6		M9	41					
16	•	5			. . . . E W	16	-					41⁶	143	7	1	0	11
18					HOGG	Helmet									0		
21	•	5			. .	2					M10	42					
22			•	7				. . . . . . 2 4	14	1		43	147			4	
27			•	6	. . . . . x W	8	-					43⁶	147	8	0	4	11
29					DYMOCK	cap (LHB)									0		
31	•	6			. .	2					M11	44					
33			•	8	. 5 . 1	4		2 . 3 . E W	19	1		44⁷	151	9	1	7	11
37								HURST	cap							0	
39			•	8				4 3 1	1			45	154			3	
40	•	7			. 8 1 . 7 4 .	9	1	4 . 3 . 1	4	-		46	161		6	5	11
44	7-4-21-3 (2)		8-1-2-28-4 (1)	9		9	1	xY W	5	-	M 11 NB/8	46¹	161	10	6	5	11
3.45	AUSTRALIA ALL OUT										377 balls		ALL OUT				
	ENGLAND WON BY 166 RUNS												BATTING TIME: 275 MINUTES				

THE THIRD TEST AT MELBOURNE

Australia's emphatic victory by 103 runs, completed after only 23 minutes of play and several bugle calls of the *Last Post* on the final day, was thoroughly deserved. It also gave the series a most necessary and timely stimulant.

Australia's openers avoided running each other out for long enough to capitalise upon Brearley's extraordinary gift of predicting successfully the underside of a falling coin, their middle-order did just enough in both innings, and Hogg produced yet another exceptional bowling performance.

This defeat ended Brearley's impressive run as an unbeaten captain; his first 15 Tests since being appointed when Greig defected in 1977 had resulted in 10 wins and five draws. Only Ray Illingworth, with eight wins and 11 draws, had begun his term as England's captain with a longer unbeaten sequence. After the match Brearley announced that England did not want to make a habit of losing Tests and that morale was high. With only three clear days before the start of the next Test, he had little time in which to reconsider his own position in the side. Although he had started the rubber with a tour average of $140\frac{1}{2}$ his six innings in these Tests had produced a mere 37 runs in 214 minutes – exactly the time in which Gower had reached his hundred at Perth. Brearley had resumed his place as an opener in this match despite a wound above his right eye – sustained at an eve-of-match net practice – which had required six stitches.

The Melbourne square, with its camouflage of green and black patches, had caused its groundstaff overpowering problems. In September a glass-

21 Melbourne Cricket Ground (The MCG)

house had been erected over it to encourage a stronger growth of grass but they were still awaiting the usual second wave of couch when we arrived. Gazing at this impression of a mini coalmine, Tony Lewis felt immediately at home. 'Reminds me of Ebbw Vale', he remarked wistfully. 'When I first tapped my bat in the blockhole there I heard an answering tap from underneath.'

Australia batted very well on the first day. Wood and Darling achieved the highest opening partnership of the rubber – not that they had much to beat – and the former, atoning for another elimentary calling muddle, went on to his hundred with a display of supreme application and skill. No other player reached 50 in the game and he was an obvious choice for the Match Award.

The pitch revealed its true character on the second day. Although on the slow side and never dangerous, its extreme variations of bounce, especially at the Pavilion (Northern) End, ranged from shooters to rib-ticklers and made it impossible to combine strokeplay with any hope of survival. Miller batted 110 minutes for the slowest three runs in Test match history.

A crowd of 40,114, the best attendance for any day in the entire rubber, saw 14 wickets fall for a paltry 122 runs. Even that multitude (Lord's holds under 30,000) was lost in this vast Kremlin-like, concrete amphitheatre.

Hendrick bowled beautifully in the conditions; unlike Botham he is not a lucky bowler. His running out of Border displayed an incredibly fast reflex action. Willis, possibly still plagued by a sore undercarriage, took none for 68. It was left to the remarkable Hogg to dominate the match with the highly appropriate figures for this pitch of 10 for 66. Arthur Mailey would have enjoyed that! He and Charles (C.T.B.) Turner each took 29 wickets in their first three Tests. Hogg now had 27 which included five or more in an innings on five occasions out of six.

AUSTRALIA 1st Innings v ENGLAND 3rd Test

at Melbourne Cricket Ground on December 29, 30, 1978, January 1, 2, 3, 1979

IN	OUT	MINS	No.	BATSMAN		HOW OUT	BOWLER	RUNS
11.00	11.26	392	1	WOOD		C^T EMBUREY	MILLER	100
11.00	12.33	93	2	DARLING		RUN OUT [BOYCOTT → EMBUREY]		33
12.35	12.37	2	3	HUGHES		C^T TAYLOR	BOTHAM	0
12.39	2.40	83	4	YALLOP	*	C^T HENDRICK	BOTHAM	41
2.43	4.23	79	5	TOOHEY		C^T RANDALL	MILLER	32
4.25	11.05	105	6	BORDER		C^T BREARLEY	HENDRICK	29
11.07	12.15	68	7	MACLEAN	†	BOWLED	BOTHAM	8
11.29	11.31	2	8	HOGG		C^T RANDALL	MILLER	0
11.33	11.46	13	9	DYMOCK		BOWLED	HENDRICK	0
11.48	11.49	1	10	HURST		BOWLED	HENDRICK	0
11.51	(12.15)	24	11	HIGGS		NOT OUT		1
				EXTRAS		b - lb 8 w - nb 6		14

* CAPTAIN   † WICKET-KEEPER
Test debut: A.R. BORDER.

TOTAL (OFF 89.1 OVERS IN 441 MINUTES) 258

BOWLER	O	M	R	W	nb
WILLIS	13	2	47	0	5
BOTHAM	20.1	4	68	3	-
HENDRICK	23	3	50	3	3
EMBUREY	14	1	44	0	-
MILLER	19	6	35	3	-
Extras / Run Out			14	1	
	89.1	16	258	10	

HRS	OVERS	RUNS
1	11	47
2	12	41
3	14	38
4	13	40
5	15	46
6	10	26
7	11	15

RUNS	MINS	OVERS	LAST 50 (in mins)
50	71	12.6	71
100	145	28.5	74
150	217	44.3	72
200	284	59.5	67
250	387	80.1	103

2nd NEW BALL taken at 5.06pm on 1st DAY
- AUSTRALIA 212-4 after 65 overs.

Toss: AUSTRALIA

WKT	TOTAL	6s	4s	BALLS	NOTES ON DISMISSAL
6	250	·	6	283	Silly mid-on catch – mistimed on drive.
1	65	·	2	71	Beaten by mid-on's return to bowler – backing up – sent back.
2	65	·	·	1	Edged late outswinger – out first ball.
3	126	·	4	98	Edged outswinger – caught by 2nd slip diving to his right (one-handed)
4	189	·	1	70	On drove low to wide mid-on's left (left-handed falling catch).
5	247	·	4	115	Edged outswinger low to 1st slip – right-handed catch.
10	258	·	·	47	Drove over yorker.
7	250	·	·	5	Mistimed off-drive – comfortable extra-cover catch.
8	251	·	·	14	Pushed forward – ball took inside edge.
9	252	·	·	2	Late on defensive stab at ball which kept low.
·	·	·	·	15	

0⁶ 17⁴ 721 balls (including 8 no balls)

12 OVERS 1 BALLS/HOUR
2.89 RUNS/OVER
36 RUNS/100 BALLS

LUNCH: 88-2 WOOD 33* (87 b, 122 min) YALLOP 14* (30 b, 24 min)
OFF 23 OVERS IN 122 MINUTES

TEA: 166-3 WOOD 65* (182b, 242 min) TOOHEY 19* (53b, 56 min)
OFF 50 OVERS IN 242 MINUTES

STUMPS 1ST DAY: 243-4 WOOD 100* (267b, 366 min) BORDER 25* (107 b, 100 min)
OFF 76 OVERS IN 366 MINUTES

WKT	PARTNERSHIP		RUNS	MINS
1st	Wood	Darling	65	93
2nd	Wood	Hughes	0	2
3rd	Wood	Yallop	61	83
4th	Wood	Toohey	63	79
5th	Wood	Border	58	105
6th	Wood	Maclean	3	19
7th	Maclean	Hogg	0	2
8th	Maclean	Dymock	1	13
9th	Maclean	Hurst	1	1
10th	Maclean	Higgs	6	24

258

65

AUSTRALIA v ENGLAND — 3rd Test

at Melbourne

1ST DAY TIME	BOWLERS Southern End (Umpire: M.G. O'Connell) BOWLER	O.	Northern End (Umpire: R.A. French) BOWLER	O.	BATSMEN Scoreboard Left — WOOD (cap) SCORING	BALLS	6s/4s	Scoreboard Right — DARLING (Helmet-cap) SCORING	BALLS	6s/4s	NOTES Attendance (1*): 35,174	O.	RUNS	W.	L BAT	R BAT	EXTRAS
											Cool, some cloud. Cross wind from scoreboard side. M1						
11.00	WILLIS	1			L x x ········	8						1					
05			BOTHAM	1	2 ·4····	15	1	3 1	1		*Appeal ct 4th slip Round wkt to LHB	2	5		4	1	
10	"	2			xx P3	21		35 1	3		*Fell over	3	7		5	2	
15			"	2	··········	29					*Appeal ct wkt M2	4					
20	"	3			†5E 35 4··1	33	2	L ↑ x3S ·○·1	8		(NB) NB/1	5	14		10	3	1
26			"	3	75 ↑ L ·1	40		2E 1	9			6	16		11	4	
31		4	3-1-7-0(1)		6 1	41		2LB 2 2 ·3 2··	16		(2LB)	7	24		12	9	3
36			HENDRICK	1	9 1	42		2LB · · 6··2·	23		(2LB) *Ro chance (RANDALL)	8	29		13	11	5
42	"	5			77 6 21 1	45		7 x ·○·	29		(NB) NB/2	9	37		19	12	6
48			"	2	·· 4 ··1	49		x 4 ·3	33		*Ro chance (HENDRICK)	10	41		20	15	
53	"	6			· 35 1	52		↑8 ↑4s (4)1	39	1	Round wkt to LHB *chance to absent sh leg	11	47		21	20	
12.00 02½ DRINKS	6-1-27-0(2)		"	3	P ····	60					NB/3 M3 1HR→	12					
07	BOTHAM	4			··	62		9 7 ·2··3	45		Round wkt to LHB 50 p'ship in 71 min.	13	52			25	
13			"	4	7 1	63		LB 4 9 ··24	52	2	(LB)	14	60		22	31	7
18	"	5	4-1-14-0(1)		†9 7 21 ···	68		L 6 ·1	55			15	64		25	32	
23			EMBUREY	1				65 ···1	63			16	65			33	
26	"	6						x ········	71		*Good stop – Emburey (gully) M4	17					
31			"	2	····	73		Ro	71	2	Round wkt to LHB *Ro appeal	17⁶	65	1	25	33	7
33								HUGHES (cap)			*Appeal ct sh.leg					0	
35			"	2	·· 76	76					M5	18					
36	"	7						E W	1	–		18¹	65	2	25	0	7
37								YALLOP (Helmet-cap)(LHB)								0	
39	"	7						7 ↑ 3 2····2	7			19	69			4	
43	7-2-20-1(1)		"	3	6 ·1	78		·····	13			20	70		26		
47	WILLIS	7			8 ↑7 1 ·4	81	3	4 ··3	18		Round wkt to Wood	21	78		31	7	
53			"	4	8 ···1	85		5 5 ··1 ·4	22	1		22	84		32	12	
56	8-1-38-0(3)	8	4-1-8-0(1)		9 ·1	87	3	P 4 ·○2···	30	1	(NB) NB/5 2HR→	23	88	2	33	14	8
1.02 LUNCH											M5 NB/5				LUNCH		
1.40			MILLER	1	8 E 7 ·1 ··1	93		5 3 ·1 1	32			24	92		35	16	
44	HENDRICK	5			····	98		x 1E ·1	35			25	93			17	
49			"	2				········	43		M6	26					
52	"	6			3 1	99		L· ·	50		*LB disallowed *Dropped 1st slip (BREARLEY)	27	94		36		
57			"	3	6 1	100		5 ····4·	57	2		28	99		37	21	
2.01	"	7			···2 G··	108			59		*Damaged left hand	29	101		39		
07			"	4	5P·	114		8 ·1	59			30	102			22	
10	"	8			·	115		2 ↓2E ··4··	66	3	*Jarred hand	31	107			27	
15			"	5	·	116		6 58 ·4·21	73	4		32	114			34	
19	"	9	5-1-17-0(2)					96₀ ·2··↑·!	81		*Almost played on – Ro appeal	33	116			36	
25	9-1-25-0(2)		EMBUREY	5	8 8 ·1 1	120	3	6 58 ·21 3	85	4	*50 p'ship in 64 min. M6 NB/5	34	122	2	41	40	8

66

AUSTRALIA v ENGLAND 3rd Test

at Melbourne

1st DAY TIME	BOWLERS (O'CONNELL) SOUTHERN END BOWLER	O.	(FRENCH) NORTHERN END BOWLER	O.	BATSMEN SCOREBOARD LEFT SCORING	BALLS	6s 4s	SCOREBOARD RIGHT SCORING	BALLS	6s 4s	NOTES	AUSTRALIA 1st INNINGS END-OF-OVER TOTALS O.	RUNS	W.	'L' BAT	'R' BAT	EXTRAS
					WOOD	120	3	YALLOP	85	4	M6 NB/5	34	122	2	41	40	8
2.29	HENDRICK	10			7 1	121		· · · 2 · · ·	92			35	124		42	41	
34	10-1-27-0 (2)		EMBUREY	6	· · · · · · 2	129						36	126		44		
36	BOTHAM	8						· · · · · W	98	4	E	36⁶	126	3	44	41	8
40	DRINKS							TOOHEY	cap							0	
43	"	8						· ·	2		M7 3HR→	37					
44			"	7	3s 1	130		· · · E ·	9		Over wkt to RHB	38	127		45		
48	"	9			4 3 2 · · 1	134		· · · ·	13		• 3rd run disallowed Round wkt to LHB	39	130		48		
53			"	8	· 2 8 2 1 · P · · ·	141		4s 1	14		WOOD'S 50 in 196' •Appeal ct wkt	40	134		51	1	
56	"	10			P · · ·	145		· · · 4	18		Appeal ct sh sq leg	41	135			2	
3.00			"	9	6 2 · 1	147		· · 8 P 8 · 1	24			42	139		53	4	
04	"	11			• E 1E · · · ·	153		· · 8 2 ·	26		•Dropped ct ~ b	43	142		54	6	
09			"	10	9 · · 8 2 · 1 · ·	159		7 · 1	28		• Appeal ct wkt •Botham (sh leg) hit leg	44	146		57	7	
13	"	12			· · 3	162		E 9 · 4 · 3	33	1		45	156		60	14	
19			"	11	6 5s · · 4 1 · · ·	169	4	7 1	34			46	162		65	15	
22½	"	13	11-1-35-0 (2)		· · ·	172		· · · 2 1	39		•DROPPED (1st slip) - BREARLEY	47	163			16	
27			MILLER	6	· × · ·	174		· · · · 8	45		Hendrick (sh leg) hit on arm	48	164			17	
32	"	14						· · 7 2 ·	53			49	166			19	
36	14-3-40-2 (2)		" 7-2-18-0 (2)	7	· · · · · · · L	182	4		53	1	Round wkt to LHB M8 4HR→	50	166	3	65	19	8
3.40	TEA										NB/5				T E A		
4.00	BOTHAM	15			× 1E 3s · · 4 1	187	5	2 3 · ·	56		Round wkt to LHB	51	174		70	22	
05			MILLER	8	8 2 · · · · 2 · · 2	195					•1+1 overthrow 50 p'ship in 63 min	52	178		74		
09	"	16			· · · · × · ·	201		7 · 1	58			53	179			23	
13			"	9	· · · ·	205		· · · 8 1	62			54	180			24	
17	"	17			× Y 2 · 1	208		• · 7 2 5 · 2 3 · 3	67		•Almost played on	55	189		75	32	
22	17-3-58-2 (3)		"	10				· · 6 W	70	1		55³	189	4	75	32	8
23								BORDER	cap	(LHB)						0	
25			"	10	· ·	210		· · 3 1	3			56	190			1	
28	HENDRICK	11						· · · 2 2 · · · ·	11			57	192			3	
33			"	11	7 3	211		· E ·	18			58	195		78		
36	"	12			3s 1	212		· · ·	25			59	196		79		
41	12-1-30-0 (2)		"	12	7 1	213		· · · 7 4 · · ·	32	1		60	201		80	7	
45	EMBUREY	12			· · P 7 1	217		· · · ·	36		Round wkt	61	202		81		
49			"	13	· · · 5 1	221		· · · ·	40			62	203		82		
52	"	13			8 · 1	223		9 8 · · 4 2 · ·	46	2		63	210		83	13	
56			"	14	· · · · LB	228		· · ·	49		(LB) M9	64	211			9	
59	"	14	14-3-33-1 (3)		· 3s 1	231		· · ·	54		5HR→	65	212		84		
5.02 06	DRINKS 14-1-44-0 (3)		HENDRICK	13	† · 8 1	233		· E P P	60		† NEW BALL /2	66	213		85		
11	WILLIS	9			· · LB · · ×	239		· 9 ·	62		(LB)	67	215			14	10
16	9-1-39-0 (3)		" 14-1-34-0 (3)	14	· · ·	242	5	E · ⊙ · P 2 · 3	68	2	(NB) NB/6 M9	68	219	4	85	17	11

67

22 Hughes c Taylor b Botham 0 – England are jubilant as Hughes edges a late outswinger and is out first ball.

23 Graeme Wood, Melbourne 'Man of the Match' – Australia's opener atones for yet another run out fiasco by grafting his way to a hundred. When he was out the last four wickets could add only eight runs in 49 minutes. No other player reached 50 in the match.

AUSTRALIA v ENGLAND

3rd Test

at Melbourne

1ST DAY	BOWLERS (O'CONNELL) SOUTHERN END		(FRENCH) NORTHERN END		BATSMEN SCOREBOARD LEFT			SCOREBOARD RIGHT			AUSTRALIA 1ST INNINGS NOTES	END-OF-OVER TOTALS					
TIME	BOWLER	O.	BOWLER	O.	SCORING	BALLS	6s/4s	SCORING	BALLS	6s/4s	NOTES	O.	RUNS	W.	'L' BAT	'R' BAT	EXTRAS
					WOOD	242	5	BORDER	68	2	M9 NB/6	68	219	4	85	17	11
5.22	WILLIS	10						··········	76		M10	69					
27			HENDRICK	15	···⁴	246		····	80			70	220		86		
32	"	11			⁷1	247		·······	87		Round wkt	71	221		87		
37			"	16	⁸⁶ˣ 2·2···	255						72	225		91		
43	"	12	16-1-39-0(2)					···⁴²····	95	3	Over wkt	73	229			21	
49			BOTHAM	18	··⁶ᴱ·¹ᴱ 2···⁴	263	6				Just short of 2-slip (Hendrick)	74	235		97		
54	"	13						⁸†¹·⁹ 2····	103		† LEVER sub for HENDRICK 6HR→	75	238			24	
59	13-2-47-0(4)		19-3-68-2(4)	19	⁵3 ···	267	6	·· ᴸᴮ⁹1	107	3	LB WOOD's 100: 363' mins spectator invasion 50 p'ship in 97 mins	76	243	4	100	25	12
6.05 STUMPS	(1ST DAY)										M10 NB/6	S T U M P S					
2ND DAY 11.00	HENDRICK	17						···⁴·ᵂ	115	4	ATTENDANCE (2nd) 40,114	77	247	5	100	29	12
05								MACLEAN	cap		Warm, slight wind.					0	
07			MILLER	15	·········	275					M11	78					
10	"	18			···	278		ᴾ·····⁸	5			79	248			1	
16			"	16	ᴾ···	282		···¹	9			80	249			2	
20	"	19						⁰·······	18		NB NB/7 M12	81	250				13
26			"	17	⁶ᵂ	283	6					81¹	250	6	100	2	13
					HOGG	Helmet									0		
29			"	17	····ᵂ ·⁴	5	-					81⁶	250	7	0	2	13
31					DYMOCK	cap	(LHB)								0		
33			"	17	··	2					M13	82					
34	"	20			·····	7		··²1	21			83	251			3	
			"	18				·······ᴸ	29		M14	84					
42	"	21			·····ᴱ ·ᵂ	14	-					84⁷	251	8	0	3	13
46					HURST	cap									0		
48	"	21			⁰ˣᵂ	2	-				NB NB/8 M15	85	252	9	0	3	14
49					HIGGS	cap									0		
51			"	19	····	+		ᴾ·¹·⁴	33		7HR→	86	253			4	
55	"	22	19-6-35-3(3)		¹ᴱ1	5		ᴾ····³ ·⁴ fx	40			87	257		1	7	
12.01			BOTHAM	20	·····ᴱ ᴱ	13					M16	88					
06 09	DRINKS	23			··ᴾ	15		····²1	46			89	258			8	
14	23-3-50-3(3)		20-1-4-08-3(4)	21		15	-	ᵞᵂ	47	-		89¹	258	10	1	8	14
12.15	AUSTRALIA ALL OUT										M16 NB/8	A L L O U T					
	BATTING TIME: 441 MINUTES							721 balls									

69

ENGLAND 1st Innings
In reply to AUSTRALIA'S 258 all out

IN	OUT	MINS	No.	BATSMAN	HOW OUT	BOWLER	RUNS
12.28	12.40	12	1	BOYCOTT	BOWLED	HOGG	1
12.28	12.44	16	2	BREARLEY *	LBW	HOGG	1
12.42	2.47	88	3	RANDALL	LBW	HURST	13
12.46	3.13	110	4	GOOCH	CT BORDER	DYMOCK	25
2.50	4.09	59	5	GOWER	LBW	DYMOCK	29
3.15	4.58	83	6	BOTHAM	CT DARLING	HIGGS	22
4.12	11.15	123	7	MILLER	BOWLED	HOGG	7
5.02	5.05	3	8	TAYLOR †	BOWLED	HOGG	1
5.08	5.20	12	9	EMBUREY	BOWLED	HOGG	0
5.21	11.48	87	10	WILLIS	CT DARLING	DYMOCK	19
11.17	(11.48)	31	11	HENDRICK	NOT OUT		6
				EXTRAS	b 6 lb 4 w – nb 9		19

* CAPTAIN   † WICKET-KEEPER

TOTAL   (OFF 63.6 OVERS IN 323 MINUTES) **143**

BOWLER	O	M	R	W	nb
HOGG	17	7	30	5	6
HURST	12	2	24	1	-
DYMOCK	15.6	4	38	3	5
HIGGS	19	9	32	1	-
Extras			19		
	63.6	22	143	10	

HRS	OVERS	RUNS
1	11	21
2	10	25
3	13	35
4	12	22
5	13	24

RUNS	MINS	OVERS	LAST 50 (in mins)
50	125	22	125
100	211	41	86

WKT	TOTAL	6s	4s	BALLS	NOTES ON DISMISSAL
1	2	·	·	13	Bowled middle stump, between bat and pad by breakback.
2	3	·	·	8	Late on defensive jab at ball which kept low.
3	40	·	1	53	Played across line - hit on front pad.
4	52	·	1	91	Edged to 2nd slip a ball which left him sharply.
5	81	·	4	48	Played back - beaten by ball that kept low.
6	100	·	3	80	Drove leg-break low to cover - low, two-handed catch.
9	120	·	·	101	Drove over full toss which hit base of off stump.
7	101	·	·	4	Late on ball that cut back and kept low.
8	101	·	·	14	Late on yorker. Middle stump out.
10	143	·	·	76	Edged attempted hit to leg - skier to cover.
-	-	·	1	53	··

0⁶ 10⁴   521 balls (including 11 no balls)

11   OVERS   7   BALLS/HOUR
2·24   RUNS/OVER
27   RUNS/100 BALLS

LUNCH : 8-2   RANDALL   2* (8b, 21 min)
  GOOCH   4* (19b, 17 min)
OFF 6 OVERS IN 35 MINUTES

TEA : 75-4   GOWER   28* (44b, 50 min)
  BOTHAM   2* (21b, 25 min)
OFF 28 OVERS IN 155 MINUTES

STUMPS (2ND DAY) : 107-8   MILLER   3* (91b, 108 min)
  WILLIS   3* (39b, 39 min)
OFF 54 OVERS IN 275 MINUTES
FOURTEEN WICKETS FELL FOR 122 RUNS 2ND DAY

WKT	PARTNERSHIP		RUNS	MINS
1st	Boycott	Brearley	2	12
2nd	Brearley	Randall	1	2
3rd	Randall	Gooch	37	84
4th	Gooch	Gower	12	23
5th	Gower	Botham	29	34
6th	Botham	Miller	19	46
7th	Miller	Taylor	1	3
8th	Miller	Emburey	0	12
9th	Miller	Willis	19	54
10th	Willis	Hendrick	23	31

143

24 Randall lbw b Hurst 13 – Unlucky for some but not for the bowler or wicket-keeper who acclaim the departure of the man who scored 174 in his last Test innings on this ground.

25 Gooch in command – Watched by Gower, Graham Gooch leg glances Dymock. Although he reached 18 seven times in the rubber, not until his final innings did he score a 50.

AUSTRALIA v ENGLAND

3rd Test

at Melbourne

TIME	BOWLER (O'CONNELL) SOUTHERN END	O.	BOWLER (FRENCH) NORTHERN END	O.	SCOREBOARD LEFT SCORING	BALLS	6s/4s	SCOREBOARD RIGHT SCORING	BALLS	6s/4s	NOTES	O.	RUNS	W.	'L' BAT	'R' BAT	EXTRAS
					BOYCOTT cap			BREARLEY Helmet cap									
12·28	HOGG	1			··········	8					M1	1					
33			HURST	1	·¹³	10		4F ¹ ···· F	6			2	2		1	1	
39	"	2			·· ˣ W	13	–					2³	2	1	1	1	–
40					RANDALL cap										0		
42	"	2			⁸·¹	1		·L· W	8	–		2⁶	3	2	1	1	–
44								GOOCH Helmet cap								0	
46	"	2						PP··	2			3					
48			"	2	··⁹·1····	8		⁸·1	3		•Appeal ct wkt (leg side)	4	5		2	1	
53	"	3						⁷P···²·1	11			5	8			4	
59	3-1-4-2 (–)		"	3		8	–	↑········	19	–	M2 NB/–	6	8	2	2	4	–
1·03	LUNCH		3-1-4-0 (–)								3 wkts fell for 23 runs in pre-lunch session.		LUNCH				
1·40	HOGG	4			P·········	16					•Dropped forward short leg (HIGGS)	7					
46			HURST	4	··³4·ˣ··	22	1	⁸·1	21		²M3	8	13		6	5	
51	"	5			····	26		··↑⁹	25			9	14			6	
57			"	5				·↑·L·⁷⁷1	33			10	15			7	
2·01	"	6			··ʸ	29		L·4·01	39	1	NB NB/1 1HR→	11	21			12	1
08			"	6				········ˣ	47		M4	12					
13½	"	7			⁺⁹1	30		⑧·····2·0²⁸56	56		•Round wkt (1st two balls) NB NB/2 3	13	29		7	18	2
22	7-2-17-2 (1)		"	7	·³1	32		·····²2	62			14	32		8	20	
27	DYMOCK	1			⁸20·ˣ²·2·····	41					NB NB/4	15	37		12		3
32			"	8	⁴1	42		⁷·1 E·····	69			16	39		13	21	
37	"	2			······E·	50					•Just short of 2nd slip (border) M5	17					
41 / 44	DRINKS		"	9	·ʸL W	53	1	··³1	72			17⁶	40	3	13	22	3
47					GOWER Helmet cap (LHB)										0		
50			"	9	··	2						18					
51	"	3			P··	4		·····⁸1	78			19	41			23	
56			"	10	·↑····	9		··⁶1	81		† STREAKER (MALE)	20	42			24	
3·01	"	4			···⁴3	13		LB· ····	85		LB 2HR→	21	46		3		4
06			"	11	⁵ˢ·1 ²ᴱ·41	18	1	·L⁷·4	88			22	52		8	25	
12	"	5	11-2-23-1 (2)					··ᴱ W	91	1		22³	52	4	8	25	4
13								BOTHAM Helmet cap								0	
15	"	5						·····1	5		•Appeal ct wkt. M6	23					
18			HIGGS	1	···⁷4·³3	24	2	··	7			24	59		15		
23	"	6			·¹·⑤3	28		·····	12		Appeal ct wkt (leg side) NB/5	25	62		18		
29			"	2	⁸2·4·····	36	3					26	66		22		
32	"	7						⁹ᴱ·ᴱ 2····0↑1	21		•Nearly played on NB NB/6	27	69			2	5
37	7-2-13-1 (–)		"	3	··⁴4·⁷2···	44	4		21	–	• RO appeal	28	75	4	28	2	5
3·40	TEA		3-0-17-0 (3)								M6 NB/6		TEA				

ENGLAND 1st INNINGS

AUSTRALIA v ENGLAND 　　3rd Test
at Melbourne

2ND DAY TIME	SOUTHERN END (O'CONNELL) BOWLER	O.	NORTHERN END (FRENCH) BOWLER	O.	SCOREBOARD LEFT SCORING	BALLS	6s/4s	SCOREBOARD RIGHT SCORING	BALLS	6s/4s	NOTES	O.	RUNS	W.	'L' BAT	'R' BAT	EXTRAS
					GOWER	44	4	BOTHAM	21	–	M 6　NB/6	28	75	4	28	2	5
4.00½	DYMOCK	8						E 2 ··O·4····	30	1	NB　NB/7	29	80			6	6
05			HIGGS	4	·· 4 1	47		·····	35		Round wkt. to LHB	30	81		29		
09	"	9			L W	48	4					30¹	81	5	29	6	6
09½					MILLER	Helmet cap									0		
12			"	9	E· x ······	7					*Almost played on M7	31					
15½			"	5				L ········	43		M 8	32					
19			"	10	········	15					M 9	33					
23			"	6				x L x ·········	51		M 10　3 HR→	34					
26	"	11			x 2 ···· 1	20		x ····	54			35	82		1		
31			"	7	Y · x ·····'·	28					*DROPPED 1st SLIP (HUGHES) M 11	36					
34	"	12			···	31		9 3 6s 2··40 1	60	2	NB　NB/8	37	90			13	7
39½			"	8	····· P	37		3 ·1	62			38	91			14	
43	"	13						5 x ·····2·	70		Round wkt.	39	93			16	
47	13-4-27-2(2)		"	9	Y E ········	45					M 12	40					
50	HOGG	8			L LB ········	47		P ↑9 8↑ ··1 ·41	76	3	LB	41	100			22	8
57			"	10				3 ···W	80	3		41⁴	100	6	1	22	8
58								TAYLOR	Helmet cap							0	
59 5·02	DRINKS		"	10	··	49		3 ·1	2			42	101			1	
04	"	9						x ·W	4	–		42²	101	7	1	1	8
05								EMBUREY	No cap						0	
08	"	9			↑ ······	6					M 13	43					
11½			"	11	·········	57					M 14	44					
15	"	10						Y ······W	14	–	M 15	45	101	8	1	0	8
20								WILLIS	No cap						0	
21½			"	12	3 ······2·	65					4 HR→	46	103		3		
24	"	11			···	68		2 ··O·1	6		NB　NB/9	47	105			1	9
31			"	13	··	70		2 ·····1	12			48	106			2	
35	"	12						x E ·····	20		M 16	49					
40			"	14	········	78					M 17	50					
43	"	13						↑ L x ·······	28		Hit on shoulder M 18	51					
48½	13-6-24-4(2)		"	15	F ·······	86					M 19	52					
52	HURST	12			····	91		9 ·· 1	31			53	107			3	
57	12-2-24-1(2)		16-8-23-1(3)	16		91	–	········	39	–	M 20　NB/9	54	107	8	3	3	9
6.00	STUMPS		(2ND DAY)								ATTENDANCE (3RD): 30,038			S T U M P S			
3RD DAY 11.00	HOGG	14			L 7 ···	95		2 ··2·	43		Miller on 3 for 37'	55	110		4	5	
05			HIGGS	17	3 ···3	99		P4B P ·↑··	47		4B　Ball turning	56	117		7		13
10	"	15			B Fx W	101	–	7 ····O1	53		B NB　NB/10	56⁷	120	9	7	6	15
15					HENDRICK	No cap					Hot; no wind.				0		
17	15-6-28-5(2)	15	17-8-26-1(3)		O·	2	–		53	–	NB　NB/11 M 20	57	121	9	0	6	16

AUSTRALIA v ENGLAND

3rd Test

at Melbourne

3RD DAY	BOWLERS (O'CONNELL) SOUTHERN END	O.	(FRENCH) NORTHERN END	O.	BATSMEN SCOREBOARD LEFT	BALLS	6s/4s	SCOREBOARD RIGHT	BALLS	6s/4s	ENGLAND 1ST INNINGS NOTES	O.	RUNS	W.	'L' BAT	'R' BAT	EXTRAS
TIME	BOWLER	O.	BOWLER	O.	SCORING	BALLS	6s/4s	SCORING	BALLS	6s/4s	NOTES	O.	RUNS	W.	'L' BAT	'R' BAT	EXTRAS
					HENDRICK	2	–	WILLIS	53	–	M20 NB/11	57	121	9	0	6	16
11·18			HIGGS	18	·1	6	7 2 ·1	1E ·3 ·1	57	x 7	• Between ships	58	127		2	10	
22	HOGG	16	18-8-32-1(3)		P P↓	14					M21 5HR→	59					
27			DYMOCK	14	..E.x.	20		94 23	59			60	132			15	
32	"	17						7LB PE•7 2..	67		(2LB) • Nearly played on.	61	136			17	18
37	17-7-30-5(2)		"	15	E.x. 1E 4	28	1					62	140		6		
41	HIGGS	19			x.x.P	33		LB ..	70		(B) M22	63	141				19
45	19-9-32-1(3)		15-6-4-38-3(6)	16		33	1	1E 3 ..2..W	76	–	•DROPPED 2nd slip (BORDER)	63	143	10	6	19	19
11·48	ENGLAND ALL OUT										M22 NB/11			ALL OUT			
	AUSTRALIA LEAD :	115			BATTING TIME :	323 MIN.		521 balls									

26 Emburey b Hogg 0 – Hogg has produced the perfect ball for the tailender; a yorker which has 'done a dentist's job' on the middle stump, a splendid sight for any fast bowler.

AUSTRALIA 2nd Innings

115 runs ahead on 1st Innings

IN	OUT	MINS	No.	BATSMAN		HOW OUT	BOWLER	RUNS
12.00	2.20	100	1	DARLING		CT RANDALL	MILLER	21
12.00	2.55	136	2	WOOD		BOWLED	BOTHAM	34
2.22	5.16	153	3	HUGHES		CT GOWER	BOTHAM	48
2.57	3.38	41	4	YALLOP	*	CT TAYLOR	MILLER	16
3.59	4.32	33	5	TOOHEY		CT BOTHAM	EMBUREY	20
4.34	4.43	9	6	BORDER		RUN OUT [HENDRICK]		0
4.45	11.15	91	7	MACLEAN	†	CT HENDRICK	EMBUREY	10
5.18	5.38	20	8	HOGG		BOWLED	BOTHAM	1
5.41	11.21	41	9	DYMOCK		CT BREARLEY	HENDRICK	6
11.17	11.27	10	10	HIGGS		ST TAYLOR	EMBUREY	0
11.23	(11.27)	4	11	HURST		NOT OUT		0
* CAPTAIN † WICKET-KEEPER				EXTRAS		b 4 lb 6 w - nb 1		11

TOTAL (OFF 71.2 OVERS IN 328 MINUTES) 167

BOWLER	O	M	R	W	nb		HRS	OVERS	RUNS		RUNS	MINS	OVERS	LAST 50 (in mins)
WILLIS	7	0	21	0	-		1	12	31		50	92	19.6	92
BOTHAM	15	4	41	3	1		2	13	42		100	177	38.3	85
HENDRICK	14	4	25	1	-		3	14	28		150	254	55.7	77
MILLER	14	5	39	2	-		4	14	35					
EMBUREY	21.2	12	30	3	-		5	13	27					
Extras/Run Out			11	1										
	71.2	25	167	10										

76

WKT	TOTAL	6s	4s	BALLS	NOTES ON DISMISSAL
1	55	·	·	86	Drove low to extra-cover.
2	81	·	·	107	Bowled behind legs sweeping at slower ball.
6	152	1	4	142	Down wicket and drove waist-high to cover point
3	101	·	1	46	Changed mind; late on cut; top-edge.
4	136	·	1	30	Pulled leg-break to wide mid-on - two-handed, falling catch.
5	136	·	·	12	Backward short leg fielded sweep and threw down wicket.
8	167	·	1	77	Edged or gloved sweep to backward short leg.
7	157	·	·	21	Drove, head up, over yorker.
9	167	·	·	39	Flicked inswinger low to backward square leg.
10	167	·	·	7	Beaten by flight and turn on forward defensive stroke.
-		·	·	4	·

1⁶ 7⁴ 571 balls (including 1 no ball)

13 OVERS 0 BALLS/HOUR
2.34 RUNS/OVER
29 RUNS/100 BALLS

LUNCH : 31-0   DARLING 14* (55b, 60 min)   WOOD 15* (41b, 60 min)
OFF 12 OVERS IN 60 MINUTES

TEA : 101-3   HUGHES 22* (73b, 76 min)
OFF 39 OVERS IN 179 MINUTES

STUMPS : 163-7   MACLEAN 10* (70b, 76 min)   DYMOCK 3* (15b, 20 min)
(3RD DAY)
OFF 66 OVERS IN 301 MINUTES

WKT	PARTNERSHIP		RUNS	MINS
1st	Darling	Wood	55	100
2nd	Wood	Hughes	26	33
3rd	Hughes	Yallop	20	41
4th	Hughes	Toohey	35	33
5th	Hughes	Border	0	9
6th	Hughes	Maclean	16	31
7th	Maclean	Hogg	5	20
8th	Maclean	Dymock	10	35
9th	Dymock	Higgs	0	4
10th	Higgs	Hurst	0	4

167

AUSTRALIA v ENGLAND
at Melbourne

3rd Test

TIME	BOWLERS (FRENCH) SOUTHERN END BOWLER	O.	(O'CONNELL) NORTHERN END BOWLER	O.	BATSMEN SCOREBOARD LEFT SCORING	BALLS	6s/4s	SCOREBOARD RIGHT SCORING	BALLS	6s/4s	AUSTRALIA 2ND INNINGS NOTES	O.	RUNS	W.	'L' BAT	'R' BAT	EXTRAS
					DARLING Helmet cap			WOOD cap (LHB)									
12.00	WILLIS	1			ᴮᴱ 1 ·	2		· · · · · 9	6			1	2		1	1	
05			BOTHAM	1	· 2 · 2 ·	5		7 · Yᴸ⁴ᴮ 2 · ·	11		(LB)	2	7		3	3	1
10	"	2			· 2 · 3	7		· · 4 · 2 · 7 1 1 3	17		Round wkt to LHB	3	14		6	7	
16			"	2	· · · L Y ·	14		3 ·	18		• Ro attempt	4	15			8	
21	"	3			· · · · ·	19		· 7 9 2 1	21			5	18			11	
27			"	3				· · · · · · · · ·	29		Round wkt to LHB M1	6					
32	" ·	4			Eᵛ · · x 2 E 2 · ·	27						7	20		8		
36½	4-0-14-0 (-)		"	4	· 3 5 · 2 · · 3	32		· · 8 1	32			8	26		13	12	
42	HENDRICK	1	4-1-11-0 (-)		· · · 9 1	36		· 9 2 · ·	36		• Boycott misfield	9	29		14	14	
48			MILLER	1	· · · · · · · · ·	44					M 2	10					
51½	"	2			· · LB	47		P · · · 1E 1 ·	41		(LB)	11	31			15	2
56½	2-0-4-0 (-)		"	2	· · · · · · · · ·	55	−		41	−	M3 NB/-	12	31	−	14	15	2
1.00	LUNCH		2-2-0-0 (-)			cap					1 HR				LUNCH		
1.40	HENDRICK	3			· · 7 · x 1	59		1E 9 7 1 · 2 · 1	45		Strong crosswind from scoreboard	13	36		15	19	
44			MILLER	3				P · · · · · P4B	53		Round wkt to LHB (4B) M4	14	40				6
47	"	4			· P 4 · 1	64		· · · · · ·	56		• Appeal ct wkt (legside)	15	41		16		
52½			"	4	· · 6 · 1 ·	69		· · 3 1	59			16	43		17	20	
56	"	5			3S· 1	70		· · · 6S x 1	66		• Ro attempt (Gower)	17	45		18	21	
2.01			"	5	· · · · · · · · ·	78					M5	18					
04	"	6			· · · P ·	81		x · P 8 1	71		50 p'ship in 92 min	19	46			22	
08	6-0-13-0 (-)		"	6				· · 2 · · 2 · 1 8 1 2 8	79		LEVER sub for BREARLEY (WILLIS acting captain)	20	51			27	
13	BOTHAM	5			· · 3 1	82		L · · LB	86		[1 over] Round wkt (LB) to LHB	21	55		21		7
18			"	7	· · · W	86	−		86			21⁴	55	1	21	27	7
20					HUGHES cap										0		
22			"	7	· · 8 1	2		· ·	88			22	56		1		
24	"	6			5 9 4 · 4 · · · · ·	10	2					23	64		9		
29			"	8	7P 3 3 · · · 3	15		8 8 1 · 1	91			24	72		15	29	
34	"	7	8-4-16-1 (-)		L 6 · · · · · 1	23					2HR →	25	73		16		
39			EMBUREY	1	· · 1 1 2 1	28		· · 8 · 1	94		Round wkt to LHB	26	77		19	30	
42 45	DRINKS "	8						· · · · · · · · ·	102		M6	27					
50			"	2	· · · · · · ·	36					M7	28					
53	"	9						2 · · 6 x 2 W	107	−		28⁵	81	2	19	34	7
55								YALLOP Helmet cap (LHB)								0	
57	"	9						· · ·	3			29					
59			"	3	8 · · · · · · ·	37		· · · · · ·	10			30	82		20		
3.03	"	10			4 · 1	39		· 7 · 7 9E 2 · · 2 2	16			31	89		21	6	
08	10-2-34-1 (2)		"	4	x · · · · · · ·	47					M8	32					
10½	WILLIS	5			· · · · ·	52		· · 9 1	19			33	90			7	
16	5-0-15-0 (-)		5-3-5-0 (-)	5̃		52	2	· · · · · x	27	−	M9 NB/-	34	90	2	21	7	7

27 Behind the scenes *(left)* – Graham Yallop in the familiar surroundings of his Victoria and Australia dressing room. His only victories over England – the Third Test and two one-day internationals – were achieved on his home ground.

28 'Well bowled!' *(right)* – Ian Botham, clearly exhausted by the heat and humidity, is congratulated by Brearley, Hendrick, and Taylor after bowling Wood.

29 Hughes at his best – Perfectly balanced, with head still and a good follow-through, Hughes clips Emburey to leg watched by Taylor and Gooch.

at Melbourne

3RD DAY TIME	BOWLERS (FRENCH) SOUTHERN END — BOWLER	O.	(O'CONNELL) NORTHERN END — BOWLER	O.	BATSMEN — SCOREBOARD LEFT — SCORING	BALLS	6s 4s	SCOREBOARD RIGHT — SCORING	BALLS	6s 4s	NOTES	O.	RUNS	W.	'L' BAT	'R' BAT	EXTRAS
					HUGHES	52	2	YALLOP	27	—	M9 NB/-	34	90	2	21	7	7
3.19	WILLIS	6			.. LB	54		....1E.4.	33	1	(LB)	35	95			11	8
23			EMBUREY	6	....	62					M10	36					
26	"	7			..8.1	65		.9.1 ...	38			37	97		22	12	
31	7-0-21-0 (1)		"	7	.......P	73					M11	38					
34	MILLER	9	7-5-5-0 (-)			73	2	.1E.9..22....W46 E	46	1	Round wkt to LHB 3HR→	39	101	3	22	16	8
3.38	TEA 9-4-20-2 (-)							TOOHEY cap			M11 NB/-		TEA			0	
3.59			EMBUREY	8	6.1	74		....	7		Overcast; cool;	40	102		23		
4.02	MILLER	10			P...1.6.6	81	1/2	.7.1	8		strong wind from scoreboard side.	41	110		30	1	
06			"	9	P.......	88		8.1	9			42	111			2	
09	"	11			...35.1	93		6.3 .P.1E3	12			43	118		31	8	
13			"	10	..8.1..	98		8.1 8.1	15			44	121		32	10	
17	"	12			...1	101		E E .3.3	20			45	124			13	
20	12-4-38-2 (-)		"	11	6.F6 4.1	104	3/4	8.1 .7.1	25		Botham (sh sq leg) hit on right arm.	46	131		37	15	
25	HENDRICK	7			....	108		.4.7s.41	29	1		47	136			20	
31			"	12				6 W	30	1		47'	136	4	37	20	8
32								BORDER cap (LHB)								0	
34			"	12				P.↓.P.....	7		Round wkt to LHB M12	48					
37	"	8			L L	116					M13	49					
42			"	13				L RO	12	—		49⁵	136	5	37	0	8
43								MACLEAN cap								0	
45			"	13				...1	3		M14	50					
46	"	9			1	124					M15	51					
51½			"	14				.......P	11		M16	52					
54	"	10			P. EP	132					M17 4HR→	53					
59 5.02	DRINKS		"	15				P.......	19		M18	54					
05	"	11			..2.1	135		..4..1	24		HUGHES on 37/for 45'	55	141		38	4	
11	11-3-23-0 (2)		"	16	4.3 4.4.21 1E6	141	1/4	8.1	26		LEVER sub for HENDRICK ● Top-edged sweep	56	152		48	5	
15	BOTHAM	11			3 W	142	1/4					56'	152	6	48	5	8
16					HOGG no cap										0		
18	"	11			↑.Px E 0........	8					NB) NB/1 M19	57	153				9
23			"	17				........P	34		Hendrick back. M20	58					
26	"	12			........●	16					● Appeal at wkt M21	59					
31			"	18	P...1	19		....F6.1	39			60	154			6	
34	"	13			8.1 Y W	21	—	..5.1 F5	44			60⁷	157	7	1	8	9
38					DYMOCK cap (LHB)										0		
41	"	13			.1						Round wkt to LHB	61					
42			"	19				E	52		M22	62					
44	"	14	19-11-29-1 (2)		2.1 .L8.2	6		P. LB	55		(LB)	63	161		3	10	
49	14-4-40-3 (2)		MILLER	13	..1	8	—	....1 1E	61	1	M22 NB/1	64	162	7	3	9	10

AUSTRALIA v ENGLAND 3rd Test
at Melbourne

3RD DAY TIME	BOWLERS (French) SOUTHERN END	O.	(O'Connell) NORTHERN END	O.	Scoreboard Left SCORING	BALLS	6s/4s	Scoreboard Right SCORING	BALLS	6s/4s	NOTES	O.	RUNS	W.	L BAT	R BAT	EXTRAS
					DYMOCK	8	–	MACLEAN	61	1	M22 NB 1	64	162	7	3	9	10
5.53	BOTHAM	15			....P.?.	15		8/1	62			65	163			10	
58	15-4-41-3 (6)		MILLER	14		15	–	........P P	70	1	M23 NB/1	66	163	7	3	10	10
6.01	STUMPS		14-5-39-2 (-4) (3RD DAY)								5HR STUMPS						
4TH DAY 11.00	HENDRICK	12			P P 1 2	23					ATTENDANCE (4TH) 23,432	67	164		4		
05			EMBUREY	20	.. P 1 ° 7	26		..... P	75		• Gower misfielded round wkt to LHB.	68	165		5		
08	•	13			x 9 1	33		P	76			69	166		6		
14			•	21	LB —	35		E W	77	1	(LB)	69³	167	8	6	10	11
15					⌐			HIGGS cap								0	
17			•	22				.....	5		M24	70					
19	•	14			.... 8 ...W	39	–					70⁴	167	9	6	0	11
21					HURST cap										0		
23	•	14			.... +						M25	71					
26	14-4-25-1 (2)		21-2-12 30-3 (5)	22	+	–		P x • W	7	–	M25 NB 1	71²	167	10	0	0	11
11.27	AUSTRALIA ALL OUT				BATTING TIME: 328 MINS. 571 balls								ALL OUT				
	ENGLAND REQUIRE 283 TO WIN IN 681 MINUTES																

30 Border run out 0 – Hendrick *(left)* has just achieved the most remarkable dismissal of the rubber; fielding a firmly-hit sweep at backward short-leg, he has continued the movement, shovelled the ball into the stumps, and just beaten the left-hander's attempt to regain his crease.

ENGLAND 2nd Innings

Requiring 283 runs to win in a minimum of 681 minutes

IN	OUT	MINS	No.	BATSMAN	HOW OUT	BOWLER	RUNS
11.39	3.37	197	1	BOYCOTT	LBW	HURST	38
11.39	11.46	7	2	BREARLEY *	CT MACLEAN	DYMOCK	0
11.48	11.53	5	3	RANDALL	LBW	HOGG	2
11.55	2.11	95	4	GOOCH	LBW	HOGG	40
2.14	5.21	167	5	GOWER	LBW	DYMOCK	49
3.39	5.15	76	6	BOTHAM	CT MACLEAN	HIGGS	10
5.18	5.35	17	7	MILLER	CT HUGHES	HIGGS	1
5.24	5.58	34	8	TAYLOR †	CT MACLEAN	HOGG	5
5.37	(11.23)	44	9	EMBUREY	NOT OUT		7
11.00	11.20	20	10	WILLIS	CT YALLOP	HOGG	3
11.22	11.23	1	11	HENDRICK	BOWLED	HOGG	0
* CAPTAIN	† WICKET-KEEPER			EXTRAS	b 10 lb 7	w 1 nb 6	24

TOTAL (OFF 67 OVERS IN 341 MINUTES) **179**

BOWLER	O	M	R	W	nb/w	HRS	OVERS	RUNS		RUNS	MINS	OVERS	LAST 50 (in mins)
HOGG	17	5	36	5	1/-	1	11	41		50	77	14.2	77
DYMOCK	18	4	37	2	5/1	2	11	31		100	170	33.3	93
HURST	11	1	39	1	-	3	14	38		150	244	47.6	74
HIGGS	16	2	29	2	-	4	11	35					
BORDER	5	0	14	0	-	5	12	23					
Extras			24										
	67	12	179	10									

82

WKT	TOTAL	6s	4s	BALLS	NOTES ON DISMISSAL
4	122	·	1	155	Missed on-drive.
1	1	·	·	3	Edged firm-footed off-drive at ball leaving him.
2	6	·	·	8	Played across line of ball which kept low. (Played back)
3	71	·	5	87	Beaten on forward defensive stroke.
6	163	·	3	128	Beaten by angled ball (left-arm over) that kept low.
5	163	·	·	62	Edged offside push at leg-break.
7	167	·	·	12	Glanced quicker ball to backward short leg.
8	171	·	·	40	Followed offside ball delivered off short run.
-	-	·	·	33	-
9	179	·	·	12	Ball 'popped' to hit bat handle – backward short leg catch.
10	179	·	·	2	Breakback beat forward defensive stroke.

0⁶ 9⁴ 542 balls (Including 6 no balls)

11 OVERS 6 BALLS/HOUR
2·67 RUNS/OVER
33 RUNS/100 BALLS

LUNCH: 50-2 BOYCOTT 15* (65b, 81 min) GOOCH 26* (46b, 65 min)
OFF 15 OVERS IN 81 MINUTES

TEA: 123-4 GOWER 23* (70b, 86 min) BOTHAM 0* (2b, 1 min)
OFF 40 OVERS IN 200 MINUTES

STUMPS: 171-8 EMBUREY 2* (13b, 21 min)
(4TH DAY) OFF 62·6 OVERS IN 318 MINUTES

AUSTRALIA WON BY 103 RUNS
at 11·23 am. on the fifth (last) day
ENGLAND'S FIRST DEFEAT UNDER BREARLEY
in 16 matches. TOTAL MATCH ATTENDANCE: 139,258.

MAN OF THE MATCH: G.M. WOOD

WKT	PARTNERSHIP		RUNS	MINS
1st	Boycott	Brearley	1	7
2nd	Boycott	Randall	5	5
3rd	Boycott	Gooch	65	95
4th	Boycott	Gower	51	83
5th	Gower	Botham	41	76
6th	Gower	Miller	0	3
7th	Miller	Taylor	4	11
8th	Taylor	Emburey	4	21
9th	Emburey	Willis	8	20
10th	Emburey	Hendrick	0	1

179

31 Boycott on the attack – Geoffrey Boycott off-drives Border during his 38. The pitches and the batsman's own form allowed few glimpses of this glorious stroke.

32 Well placed! – Graham Gooch (40) bisects Border and Hughes with this edge off Dymock; his partnership with Boycott fed hopes of a dramatic victory.

AUSTRALIA v ENGLAND
at Melbourne

3rd Test

4TH DAY	BOWLERS (FRENCH) SOUTHERN END		(O'CONNELL) NORTHERN END		BATSMEN SCOREBOARD LEFT			SCOREBOARD RIGHT			ENGLAND 2ND INNINGS NOTES	END-OF-OVER TOTALS					
TIME	BOWLER	O.	BOWLER	O.	SCORING	BALLS	6s/4s	SCORING	BALLS	6s/4s	NOTES	O.	RUNS	W.	'L' BAT	'R' BAT	EXTRAS
					BOYCOTT cap			BREARLEY Helmet-cap									
11.39	HOGG	1			. . . . . . ↑	8					M1	1					
44			DYMOCK	1	)			·⊙W E	3	–	NB NB/1	1² / 1	1	1	0	0	1
46					}			RANDALL cap								0	
48			·	1	}			· . . . . ² 7	6		* Appeal ct wkt gide	2	3				2
52	·	2	)		⁸ 3	9		P L ·W	8	–		2³	6	2	3	2	1
53			}					GOOCH Helmet cap								0	
55	·	2	}		E .	11		· . LB	3		LB	3	7				2
59			·	2	. . . .	15		² ⁸ · · 4 1	7	1		4	12			5	
12.04	·	3			↑ ¹ . · 2	18		. . . . ³ 1	12		Sunny but cool cross wind from scorebox	5	15		5	6	
10			·	3	. . . .	22		² · ⁷ 4 . .	16	2		6	20			11	
14	·	4			· · · ⁹ 4	26	1	P 7 · . 3	20			7	27		9	14	
21	4-1-13-1(i)		·	4	· 2 . . ⁴	30		. . . ⁸ 1	24			8	30		11	15	
26	HURST	1			P L L · · .	36		· · ² 3	26			9	33			18	
32			·	5	· · ⊙ ⁶ 1	41		⁷ 1 · · ·	30		Round wkt (LH) NB NB/2	10	36		12	19	3
36	·	2			L ⁸ · · 3	44		· · · 7 2 ·	35		1HR →	11	41		15	21	
41			·	6	· · · · · · ⁺ (B)	50		· ·	37		W M2	12	42				4
46			3	6-1-17-1(2)	L PL · . . . ·	58					M3	13					
51			HIGGS	1	·	59		· · · ³ 4 · · ·³B	44	3	3B Ball turning	14	49			25	7
56	4-1-9-0(-)	4	1-0-4-0(i)		L · · · · · ·	65	1	⁹ ·1	46	3		15	50	2	15	26	7
1.00	LUNCH										YARDLEY sub for DARLING M3 NB/2 ?				LUNCH		
1.41			DYMOCK	7				· · ⊙ · 2 · · · ⁴	55		NB Round wkt NB/3	16	53			28	8
46	HOGG	5			³ˢ · 1	67		· · · · · LB	61		LB 50 p'ship in 76'	17	55		16		9
51			·	8				· · ⊙ 4 · · · ⁴	70	4	NB ⁺ over wkt NB/4	18	61			33	10
56½	·	6			· · B	70		⁵ ⁹E · 2 1	75		B	19	65			36	11
2.02			·	9	³ˢ · 1	72		· · · 1E LB 4	81	5	LB	20	71		17	40	12
07	·	7	)					· · L L W	87	5		20⁶	71	3	17	40	12
11			}					GOWER Helmet-cap (LHB)								0	
14	·	7	}					· ·	2		M4	21					
16			·	10	· ⁶ 1	74		· · ↓ · L	8		2HR →	22	72		18		
20	·	8			P P LB · ·	79		⁹ ⁸ 2 · 3	11		LB	23	78			5	13
26½	8-2-22-2(i)		·	11	· · · · E	84		· · ³ 1	14			24	79			6	
31	HIGGS	2	·		x x · · ·	91		⁸ ³	15		Ball turning & lifting	25	82			9	
35			· L	12	· · · · · ⁴ˢ 1	98		⁹ 1	16			26	84		19	10	
40	·	3			· · · ⁷ 1	102		· · · P E	20		Darling back.	27	85		20		
43 46	DRINKS		·	13	· · · · ⊙ · ·	111					NB NB/5 M5	28	86				14
50	·	4	13-2-33-1(4)		· · · · ⁷ 1	115		⁹E 1 · · ·	24		Round wkt to LHB	29	88		21	11	
54			BORDER	1	· · · · ³ 3	120		· · ·	27		slow left arm (round wkt. to RHB)	30	91		24		
58½	·	5			· ⁷ 1	123		1E 4 · · · ·	32	1		31	96		25	15	
3.02	5-0-15-0(2)		2-0-4-0(-)	2	· · · · · ⁶ 1	129	1	· · 1	34	1	M5 NB/5	32	97	3	26	15	14

85

AUSTRALIA v ENGLAND — 3rd Test

at Melbourne

TIME	BOWLERS (FRENCH) SOUTHERN END — BOWLER	O.	(O'CONNELL) NORTHERN END — BOWLER	O.	BATSMEN SCOREBOARD LEFT — SCORING	BALLS	6s/4s	SCOREBOARD RIGHT — SCORING	BALLS	6s/4s	NOTES	O.	RUNS	W.	'L' BAT	'R' BAT	EXTRAS
					BOYCOTT	129	1	GOWER	34	1	M5 NB/5	32	97	3	26	15	14
3.05	HIGGS	6			...... ³⁵1	136		.	35			33	98		27		
09			BORDER	3	..⁶3	139		L	40			34	101		30		
13	"	7			..⁶1 ....|	146		1	41			35	103		31	16	
16			"	4	..	148		P 4⁸ ..⁸3	47		(4B) 3HR→	36	110			19	18
20		8						....	55		M6	37					
24			"	5	⁴3 .	150		....⁶1	61		• RO chance (YALLOP) backward point	38	114		34	20	
28	"	9	5-0-14-0 (→)		¹3	152		L P B	67		(B)	39	118		37		19
33	9-1-21-0 (2)		HURST	5	⁶1 L W	155	1	⁴3	69		50 p'ship in 82'	39⁵	122	4	38	23	19
37					BOTHAM	Helmet cap									0		
39			5-1-13-1 (→)	5	LB ..	2	-		70	1	(LB)	40	123	4	0	23	20
3.40	TEA										M6 NB/5				TEA		
4.00	HOGG	9			...L L LB	8		↑x.	72		(LB) Round wkt to LHB M7	41	124		1	27	21
07			HURST	6	x. ...L 9E 1°	14		x² .⁴.	74	2	• Almost played on	42	129		1	27	
12	"	10			⁷2..¹..⁸..	20		x² 1	76			43	133		4	28	
18			"	7	L ....LB	26		1 ²3	78		(LB)	44	138			32	22
23	"	11			P	32		1E .1°	80		• DROPPED MACLEAN (offside – low)	45	139			33	
29			"	8	.⁸1	34		1x. L ..1	86		Round wkt to LHB	46	141		5	34	
35	"	12			P ..⁹1	39		x ³3 ..	89		4HR→	47	145		6	37	
41			"	9	⁶S 1	40		.1² ..⁴4.² ²x4	96	3	• Wood misfielded.	48	153		7	44	
46²	"	13	9-1-32-1 (2)		.↑L. .⁰9 1	48		7 1	97		† Round wkt (4 balls) (NB) NB/6 Hogg fell	49	156		8	45	23
52²	13-3-33-2 (1)		HIGGS	10				PL↑F FL⁶..1	105		† Round wkt	50	157			46	
58	DYMOCK	14			1 1	49		P ...L .1	112			51	159		9	47	
5.02 05	DRINKS		"	11	...F .F⁷1	56		.	113		Round wkt to LHB	52	160		10		
08²	"	15			B ...	60		.².⁷1	117		(B)	53	162			48	24
13			"	12	E W	62	-	P ...⁶1	122			53⁷	163	5	10	49	24
15					MILLER	Helmet cap									0		
18			"	12	.1	1						54					
19	"	16						....L L W	128	3		54⁶	163	6	0	49	24
21			)					TAYLOR	cap							0	
24	"	16						..	2		M8	55					
25			•	13	⁷.1	3		....P.	8			56	164		1		
28	"	17	•		P L E 1	11					Round wkt M9	57					
32			"	14	⁸W	12	-	F⁹ .2....⁸1	15			58	167	7	1	3	24
35					EMBUREY	No cap									0		
37	"	18			.L	2		....²1	21		4HR→	59	168			4	
42	18-4-37-2 (4)		"	15				L E	29		M10	60					
45	HOGG	14	•		LL P⁸ 2	10						61	170		2		
51			"	16	...	13		.⁰²1	34		• Chance to Fwd Mid off (TOOHEY)	62	171			5	
54	15-4-35-3 (1)	15	16-2-29-2 (2)		13		-	L . E W	40	-	• Appeal ct wkt (legside) out at 5.58	62⁶	171	8	2	5	24
5.58	STUMPS	(4TH DAY)									M10 NB/6				STUMPS		

AUSTRALIA v ENGLAND

at Melbourne

5TH DAY TIME	BOWLERS (FRENCH) SOUTHERN END BOWLER	O.	(O'CONNELL) NORTHERN END BOWLER	O.	BATSMEN SCOREBOARD LEFT SCORING	BALLS	6s/4s	SCOREBOARD RIGHT SCORING	BALLS	6s/4s	ENGLAND 2ND INNINGS NOTES	O.	RUNS	W.	'L' BAT	'R' BAT	EXTRAS
					EMBUREY	13	-	WILLIS	No cap		M 10 NB/6	62⁶	171	8	2	0	24
11.00	HOGG	15						··	2		M 11	63					
02			HURST	10	··· x 9 7 2·1	20		Po ·	3		* Appeal ct via pad Sh. 2H. leg	64	174		5		
07	.	16			P R L F L	28					* Appeal ct 1st slip M 12	65					
12			,	11	9 ·1	30		··· L 2 ·3	9			66	178		6	3	
18	"	17	11-1-39-1(2)		L·7 ·· 1	33		8 ·W	12	-	short run 1st 2 balls	66⁶	179	9	7	3	24
20								HENDRICK	No cap							0	
22	17-5-36-5(1)	17				33	-	x W	2	-	short run	67	179	10	7	0	24
11.23	ENGLAND ALL OUT										M 12 NB/6		ALL OUT				
	AUSTRALIA WON BY 103 RUNS										542 balls						
	BATTING TIME: 341 MINUTES										ATTENDANCE (5TH) 10,500 (Estimated)						

33 The vital breakthrough – Geoff Dymock is congratulated after trapping Gower lbw for 49. Afterwards, England's last four wickets added only 16 runs.

THE FOURTH TEST AT SYDNEY

At 5.05 pm on Thursday, 11 January, Hurst was deceived by Emburey's flight, the Ashes were retained, and England had accomplished the main objective of their tour.

Brearley hailed the result as 'the greatest comeback-from-nowhere match I've played in for England'. He had every reason to feel satisfied, not only had he been the architect of an amazing victory, but he had also recovered his form as an opener and made vital contributions with the bat. Only the second England captain after Hutton to regain and then successfully defend the Ashes, Brearley proved himself worthy of assessment as a batsman/captain allrounder, not one to be pilloried every time he prospers in only one department.

The Sydney Cricket Ground, newly dwarfed by six monstrous erections decorated in that delicate grey of battleships, and looking to Michael Melford 'like the Mona Lisa smoking a pipe', had seen rather too much activity for the good of its own square. Brearley, at last correctly guessing the topside of the coin, was able to commit the opposition to batting fourth on a pitch certain to take sufficient turn for Miller and Emburey to put a target of 200 beyond their capabilities. Yallop, not yet a giant among tacticians, failed to realise that this was a five-day match and made some naïve criticisms of England's scoring rate in the second innings.

Australia really lost the match on the fourth day when, in a temperature of

34 Sydney
Cricket Ground

over 100°F and with the humidity compelling two drinks intervals per session, they dropped five catches – mostly off the accurate leg-spin of Higgs – and seemed rather short of direction and inspiration. England had to complete their sleight of hand without the bowling of Willis or Botham and the fielding of Gower. Hendrick, finding yet another pitch with English characteristics, bowled superbly, taking two vital wickets and putting Australia behind the clock before the spinners applied the *coup de grâce*.

The Hillites were ordered to remove a banner which read: 'First convicts – then rabbits – now Botham!' because apparently it was considered denigratory to rabbits. Botham, arguably the best allrounder since Sobers, dominated England's first innings, bowled 28 overs in fierce heat and held three catches in Australia's reply, and stayed with Randall for 90 minutes in the second innings despite a virus infection and severe headache. On the final afternoon he narrowly escaped serious injury when, fielding at short-leg, he was hit on the temple of his helmet by a full-bloodied pull from Darling. He unwisely refused to leave the field and had to chase the next ball almost to the boundary. 'I felt as though I was running on air', he confided. Brian Close would have approved.

After Boycott had shown no great pleasure at being adjudged 'lbw' for his only first-ball dismissal for England and his first duck in a Test in some 68 innings, Randall took over the Yorkshireman's mantle and so disciplined himself that only once during the slowest recorded hundred in all 234 Tests between these two countries did he indulge in a full followthrough of his favourite off-drive. Without challenging the bowlers' authority he ground England back into the match and on to a position from which to snatch a famous victory.

ENGLAND 1st Innings v AUSTRALIA 4th Test

at Sydney Cricket Ground on January 6, 7, 8, 10, 11, 1979

IN	OUT	MINS	No.	BATSMAN	HOW OUT	BOWLER	RUNS
11.00	11.54	54	1	BOYCOTT	CT BORDER	HURST	8
11.00	12.36	96	2	BREARLEY *	BOWLED	HOGG	17
11.56	11.57	1	3	RANDALL	CT WOOD	HURST	0
12.01	2.24	102	4	GOOCH	CT TOOHEY	HIGGS	18
12.38	1.02	24	5	GOWER	CT MACLEAN	HURST	7
1.43	4.20	138	6	BOTHAM	CT YALLOP	HOGG	59
2.28	2.32	4	7	MILLER	CT MACLEAN	HURST	4
2.34	3.07	33	8	TAYLOR †	CT BORDER	HIGGS	10
3.09	3.18	9	9	EMBUREY	CT WOOD	HIGGS	0
3.20	(4.41)	62	10	WILLIS	NOT OUT		7
4.22	4.41	19	11	HENDRICK	BOWLED	HURST	10
* CAPTAIN † WICKET-KEEPER				EXTRAS	b 1 lb 1 w 2 nb 8		12

TOTAL (OFF 52.6 OVERS IN 281 MINUTES) **152**

BOWLER	O	M	R	W	nb/w	HRS	OVERS	RUNS		RUNS	MINS	OVERS	LAST 50 (in mins)
HOGG	11	3	36	2	5/2	1	11	18		50	120	20.6	120
DYMOCK	13	1	34	0	4/-	2	10	33		100	223	40.3	103
HURST	10.6	2	28	5	1/-	3	11	22		150	271	50.2	48
HIGGS	18	4	42	3	-	4	13	46					
Extras			12										
	52.6	10	152	10									

Toss: ENGLAND

WKT	TOTAL	6ˢ	4ˢ	BALLS	NOTES ON DISMISSAL
1	18	.	.	40	Edged forward defensive stroke to 2nd slip (dived in front of 1st slip)
3	35	.	.	80	Missed walking defensive onside push at ball which took off stump.
2	18	.	.	2	Hooked short ball hard to backward short square leg (brilliant catch).
5	66	.	1	81	Pulled short ball to deep mid-wicket (magnificent falling catch).
4	51	.	.	10	Failed to avoid ball which lifted sharply and hit gloves.
9	141	.	7	108	Edged attempted hook at bouncer to substitute 'keeper.
6	70	.	1	5	Edged firm-footed push at ball leaving him.
7	94	.	1	28	Followed leg-break — edged to gully.
8	98	.	.	11	Pushed to forward short leg - two-handed catch to his left.
.	-	.	.	43	—
10	152	.	.	24	Yorked (middle and leg stumps hit).

0⁶ 10⁴ 432 balls (Including 10 no balls)

11 OVERS 2 BALLS/HOUR
2.88 RUNS/OVER
35 RUNS/100 BALLS

LUNCH: 51-4 GOOCH 12* (41b, 61 min)
OFF 21 OVERS IN 122 MINUTES

TEA: 119-8 BOTHAM 40* (89b, 120 min)
WILLIS 4* (23b, 23 min)
OFF 45 OVERS IN 242 MINUTES

YALLOP deputised as wicket-keeper for last 93 minutes (18.6 overs) of innings and caught BOTHAM in that position. MACLEAN left field at 3.49 pm suffering from heat exhaustion and effects of blow to left eye (6 stitches) received in nets on Jan. 4.

ENGLAND'S TOTAL OF 152 WAS THEIR LOWEST IN A FIRST INNINGS AT SYDNEY SINCE 1894-95.

WKT	PARTNERSHIP		RUNS	MINS
1st	Boycott	Brearley	18	54
2nd	Brearley	Randall	0	1
3rd	Brearley	Gooch	17	35
4th	Gooch	Gower	16	24
5th	Gooch	Botham	15	41
6th	Botham	Miller	4	4
7th	Botham	Taylor	24	33
8th	Botham	Emburey	4	9
9th	Botham	Willis	43	41
10th	Willis	Hendrick	11	19

152

91

AUSTRALIA v ENGLAND — 4th Test

at Sydney

ENGLAND 1st INNINGS

Umpire: BAILHACHE PADDINGTON END — Umpire: FRENCH RANDWICK END

TIME	BOWLER (Paddington)	O.	BOWLER (Randwick)	O.	SCORING (Left)	BALLS	6s/4s	SCORING (Right)	BALLS	6s/4s	NOTES	O.	RUNS	W.	L BAT	R BAT	EXTRAS
					BOYCOTT (cap)			BREARLEY (Helmet cap)			HOT (33°C) no wind, very humid.						
11.00	HOGG	1			+ + .⋮.ˣ.˙.	8					Ⓦ Ⓦ M1	1	2				2
07			DYMOCK	1	.	9		ᴸ..ᴸ3..₁	7		ATTENDANCE (1st) 20,824	2	3			1	
12	"	2						↑₀↑ˣ......	15		*Hit on chest M2	3					
18			"	2	8E 2.ˣ......	17						4	5		2		
22	"	3						...ⓞ...² ₁	24		ⓃⒷ NB/1	5	7			2	3
28	3-2-1-0 (–)		"	3				EP	32		YARDLEY sub for HOGG (5 overs) (23 min) M3	6					
32	HURST	1			...3×2 2.1	23		8 2.	34			7	12		5	4	
37			"	4	↑...ˣ7 P 2...	31						8	14		7		
41½	"	2						E2 P .²......	42			9	16			6	
46			"	5	...9	35		.ⓞ˙...	47		*Appeal ct wkt ⓃⒷ NB/2	10	18		8	4	
51	"	3			↑..E .W	40	–					10⁵	18	1	8	6	4
54					RANDALL (cap)										0		
56	"	3			↑8 .W	2	–					10⁷	18	2	0	6	4
57	DRINKS				GOOCH (Helmet cap)										0		
12.01	"	3			⋮	1					M4 1 HR →	11					
03			"	6				..P2₉....	55			12	20			8	
08	"	4			.ᴸᴮ.ⓞ.	8		.8 .1	57		ⓁⒷ ⓃⒷ NB/3	13	23			9	6
13	4-1-8-2 (–)		"	7	.P ..	10		....P4 .1	63		Round wkt	14	24			10	
18	HOGG	4			....3 3	15		4 4 2.1 ₁9	67		NB/4	15	31		3	14	
26			"	8	......	18		.P 4 .3	72		over wkt	16	34			17	
30	"	5	8-1-12-0 (–)					.ⓞ....W ˣ	80	–	ⓃⒷ NB/5	16⁷	35	3	3	17	7
36					GOWER (Helmet cap)(LHB)											0	
38	"	5						ᴸ ⋮	1		M5	17					
39	5-3-8-1 (–)		HIGGS	1	ᴸ.P7 P ...3	24		.7 .1	3		Ball turning	18	39		6	1	
45	HURST	5			....×7 .1	30		44 21	5			19	43		7	4	
51			"	2	...8 .4...	38	1					20	47		11		
55	6-1-16-3 (–)	6	2-0-8-0 (1)		..7 .1	41	1	.2 1 7×G 2W	10	–	Round wkt to LHB 2 HR →	21	51	4	12	7	7
1.02	LUNCH							BOTHAM (Helmet cap)	7		M5 NB/5						
1.43			HIGGS	3	7 1	42		.......P	7			22	52		13	0	
46½	HOGG	6			Y.P. ..2.ⓞ	51					ⓃⒷ NB/6	23	55		15		8
53			"	4	...9	54		...1 3₀	12		*Yallop misfielded	24	56			1	
57	"	7			.6 .1	56		↑.9E .2...↑8E	18		nearly played on	25	60		16	4	
2.02			"	5	⌷.⋮....⌷	64					M6	26					
06	"	8			..9 6 .1	68		B. 7 1 7 .1	22		Ⓑ Round wkt	27	65		18	6	9
13	8-3-18-1 (–)		"	6				...ˣ......	30		M7	28					
17	HURST	7			....	76					M8	29					
22			"	7	....W	81	1	6 .1	31			29⁶	66	5	18	7	9
24	DRINKS				MILLER (Helmet cap)						Batsmen crossed				0		
28	7-2-16-3 (–)	7	7-2-11-1 (1)	7	– –			..7	33	–	M8 NB/6	30	66	5	0	7	9

92

AUSTRALIA v ENGLAND — 4th Test

at Sydney

1st DAY TIME	BOWLERS (BAILHACHE) PADDINGTON END — BOWLER	O.	(FRENCH) RANDWICK END — BOWLER	O.	BATSMEN SCOREBOARD LEFT — SCORING	BALLS	6s/4s	SCOREBOARD RIGHT — SCORING	BALLS	6s/4s	NOTES	END-OF-OVER TOTALS — O.	RUNS	W.	L BAT	R BAT	EXTRAS
					MILLER	–	–	BOTHAM	33	–	M8 NB/6	30	66	5	0	7	9
2.29	HURST	8			1E E 4·W	5	1					30⁵	70	6	4	7	9
32					TAYLOR (Helmet cap)										0		
34	"	8			3 9 1 1 2	2		8 1	34			31	73		2	8	
37			HIGGS	8	· · · · · · · · · ·	10					M9 3HR→	32					
41	"	9			x0 · ·	12		· 2 · · · 1	40		• Appeal ct wkt	33	76			11	
45½			"	9				x P5	48		• Appeal ct gully M10	34					
49 51	Maclean off	10			· · · · 8 · · ·	20					YARDLEY sub for MACLEAN — YALLOP w/k	35	78		4		
56	10-2-28-4(1)		"	10	· ·	22		3 Y 8 4 · · · · 1	54	1	Heat exhaustion	36	83			16	
3.00	DYMOCK	9						2E 5 ⊙· 2 · 2 ·	63		NB NB/7	37	88			20	10
04			"	11	6 4 E 4 · 2 · W	28	1				• 1 + 1 overthrow	37⁶	94	7	10	20	10
07					EMBUREY (Helmet cap)										0		
09			"	11	· ·	2					• Dropped fwd sh leg (HIGGS)	38					
10½	"	10			x · · · · ·	9		9	64		Sub moved from specialist position	39	95			21	
16			"	12	· 7 W	11	–	1 3	65		(Gully) – Botham protest.	39³	98	8	0	24	10
18					WILLIS (No cap)										0		
20			"	12	L ·	5						40					
22		11						1E · · · · P 4	74	2	NB/8	41	102			28	
27			"	13	F · · · · · · 9 1	13						42	103		1		
30	"	12			x 9E 1	15		3 4 7 · 442 · ·	80	4		43	114		2	38	
35			"	14	1 P P x · · · 2 · ·	23					x almost bowled.	44	116		4		
39	" 13-1-34-0(3)	13	14-4-28-3(3)			23	–	P · ⊙ · · · 8 2 · ·	89	4	NB 4HR→ M10 NB 9	45	119	8	4	40	11
3.43	TEA										YARDLEY sub for MACLEAN wk: YALLOP			T E A		
4.02			HIGGS	15	F 2E · · 1	27		6 2 2 · 3	93			46	125		5	45	
06	HOGG	9						84 · · · · · 44	101	6	BOTHAM'S 50: 30'	47	133			53	
13			"	16	8 7 P · 1 · 1 ·	32		4 3 · 1 · 1	104			48	137		7	55	
17	"	10						9 E Y E 4 · W	108	7		48⁴	141	9	7	59	11
20								HENDRICK (No cap)								0	
22	"	10			· ·	34		⊙· 3 7 3	3		NB NB/10	49	145			3	12
25			"	17	· · · ·	38		x 4 3	7			50	148			6	
29	"	11			† · ·	40		1E x 3 · 2 · · · 1	13		† short run	51	151			9	
34	11-3-36-2 (3)		"	18	· · P	43		Y · · · 1 8	18			52	152			10	
38	HURST 10·6-2-28-5(1)	11	18-4-42-3(3)			43	–	· · · L W YX	24	–		52⁶	152	10	7	10	12
4.41	ENGLAND ALL OUT										M 10 NB 10		ALL OUT				
	BATTING TIME: 281 MINUTES										432 balls						

93

AUSTRALIA 1st Innings
In reply to ENGLAND'S 152 all out

IN	OUT	MINS	No.	BATSMAN	HOW OUT	BOWLER	RUNS
4.53	4.56	3	1	WOOD	BOWLED	WILLIS	0
4.53	3.08	276	2	DARLING	CT BOTHAM	MILLER	91
4.58	1.42	184	3	HUGHES	CT EMBUREY	WILLIS	48
1.44	4.23	141	4	YALLOP *	CT BOTHAM	HENDRICK	44
3.10	3.15	5	5	TOOHEY	CT GOOCH	BOTHAM	1
3.17	(12.40)	245	6	BORDER	NOT OUT		60
4.25	5.28	63	7	MACLEAN †	LBW	EMBUREY	12
5.30	5.43	13	8	HOGG	RUN OUT [MILLER→TAYLOR]		6
5.45	11.51	66	9	DYMOCK	BOWLED	BOTHAM	5
11.53	12.33	40	10	HIGGS	CT BOTHAM	HENDRICK	11
12.35	12.40	5	11	HURST	RUN OUT [MILLER]		0
* CAPTAIN	† WICKET-KEEPER			EXTRAS	b 2　lb 3　w -　nb 11		16

TOTAL (OFF 108 OVERS IN 530 MINUTES) **294**

BOWLER	O	M	R	W	nb
WILLIS	9	2	33	2	10
BOTHAM	28	3	87	2	4
HENDRICK	24	4	50	2	-
MILLER	13	2	37	1	-
EMBUREY	29	10	57	1	-
GOOCH	5	1	14	0	-
Extras/Run Outs			16	2	
	108	22	294	10	

HRS	OVERS	RUNS
1	10	49
2	13	34
3	13	40
4	12	27
5	11	40
6	14	26
7	12	29
8	14	31

RUNS	MINS	OVERS	LAST 50 (in mins)
50	60	10.2	60
100	151	29.1	91
150	234	46.5	83
200	311	63.4	77
250	433	88.3	122

2nd NEW BALL TAKEN AT 4.07pm on 2nd DAY
- AUSTRALIA 200-4 AFTER 65 OVERS.

WKT	TOTAL	6s	4s	BALLS	NOTES ON DISMISSAL
1	1	·	·	5	Edged back defensive stroke into off stump.
3	178	·	9	200	Edged on-drive at off-break to leg slip.
2	126	·	6	167	Drove shortish offside ball comfortably to mid-off. [1st ball after lunch 2nd day]
5	210	·	5	136	Steered offside ball low to 2nd slip's left (diving catch).
4	179	·	·	4	Top-edged cut to 3rd slip.
·	·	·	4	203	
6	235	·	1	58	Played back – missed defensive prod.
7	245	·	1	17	Calling muddle following Border's hit to mid-wicket (Gower returned to bowler's end)
8	276	·	·	54	Missed drive at faster ball which removed off stump.
9	290	·	·	32	Edged defensive stroke to shorter ball low to 2nd slip.
10	294	·	·	2	Called for impossible run to bowler (Miller) by Border.

0⁶ 26⁴ 878 balls (Including 14 no balls)

12 OVERS 2 BALLS/HOUR
2·72 RUNS/OVER
33 RUNS/100 BALLS

STUMPS: 56-1 (1ST DAY)
DARLING 35* (55b, 67min)
HUGHES 15* (43b, 62min)
OFF 12 OVERS IN 67 MINUTES

LUNCH: 126-1
DARLING 69* (140b, 189min)
HUGHES 48* (166b, 184min)
OFF 38 OVERS IN 189 MINUTES

TEA: 199-4
YALLOP 40* (111b, 118min)
BORDER 4* (30b, 25min)
OFF 63 OVERS IN 310 MINUTES

STUMPS: 248-7 (2ND DAY)
BORDER 31* (110b, 145min)
DYMOCK 0* (20b, 15min)
OFF 88 OVERS IN 430 MINUTES

WKT	PARTNERSHIP		RUNS	MINS
1st	Wood	Darling	1	3
2nd	Darling	Hughes	125	184
3rd	Darling	Yallop	52	84
4th	Yallop	Toohey	1	5
5th	Yallop	Border	31	48
6th	Border	Maclean	25	63
7th	Border	Hogg	10	13
8th	Border	Dymock	31	66
9th	Border	Higgs	14	40
10th	Border	Hurst	4	5

294

AUSTRALIA v ENGLAND

4th Test

at Sydney

1st DAY TIME	BOWLERS (BAILHACHE) PADDINGTON END — BOWLER	O.	(FRENCH) RANDWICK END — BOWLER	O.	BATSMEN SCOREBOARD LEFT — SCORING	BALLS	6s/4s	SCOREBOARD RIGHT — SCORING	BALLS	6s/4s	NOTES	O.	RUNS	W.	L BAT	R BAT	EXTRAS
					WOOD (Cap) (LHB)			DARLING (Helmet Cap)									
4.53	WILLIS	1			...⊙.W	5	–				(NB) NB/1	0^5	1	1	0	0	1
56					HUGHES (cap)											0	
58	"	1			↑7 .1	2		.⊙⊙ ↑AE	4		(NB)(NB) NB/3	1	4		1		3
5.01			BOTHAM	1	...3.7 4.1	7	1	...	7			2	9		6		
06	"	2			..⊙.↑6.3 4.1	14	2	⊙.↑7.7 4	10	1	(NB)(NB) NB/4 5	3	20		11	4	5
13			"	2	7s 1	15		......	17			4	21		12		
18	"	3			..⊙.L.	24					(NB) NB 6 M1	5	22				6
24			"	3	...1	27		↑8 6 2 2..21	22			6	27			9	
30	"	4						...②4.4 31 ↑8 ↑8 x↑8		3	Last ball of short run NB/7 (3ii)	7	37			19	
37	4-1-20-1 (4)		"	4	7s 1	29		↑8 4.4..	37	5	LEVER sub for WILLIS *Hit on thigh	8	46		13	27	
43	HENDRICK	1	4-0-20-0 (3)		7 1	30		......	44			9	47		14		
49			MILLER	1	.. 8 .1...	37		8 1	45		1 HR→	10	49		15	28	
52	"	2			..P	43		.2 3	47		*Hit on thigh 50 p'ship in 55 min	11	52			31	
58	2-0-4-0		2-0-6-0 (1)	2		43	2	...4...	55	6	M1 NB/7	12	56	1	15	35	6
6.00	STUMPS		(1ST DAY)										STUMPS				
2nd DAY 11.00	HENDRICK	3			P...2	49		.x	57		ATTENDANCE 2nd 20,485	13	57		16		
05			BOTHAM	5	...9 1	53		1	61		ot, humid, no wind.	14	58		17		
10			"	4	R P E2 2	61					*4LB disallowed	15	60		19		
15			"	6	.2 1	63		....7 1	67			16	62		20	36	
20	"	5			x 7 7s 9 .1 .1 1	68		4 2 .1 1	70			17	67		23	38	
25			"	7	P. 4 LB ...4.	75	3	. 1	71		(LB)	18	72		27		7
30	"	6			1E 2 ..4.2	81	4	P. ..	73			19	77		32		
35	6-0-17-0 (1)		"	8	x x ..	89					M2	20					
40	WILLIS	5	8-1-27-0 (4)		L. P ...	93		9E E 9 2 .221	77			21	82			43	
45			EMBUREY	1				....	85		M3	22					
49	"	6			L E. 2 ...1	97		...x	89		*Almost played on. 2HR→	23	83		33		
55			"	2	.....EP.	105					M4	24					
58	"	7			LB .	107		1E E 6 3 2...1 1	95		(LB)	25	88			47	8
12.04 DRINKS 07	7-1-30-1 (4)		"	3				.	103		*Randall (mid-wkt) hit Botham (sh leg) on leg	26					
10	BOTHAM	9			x .. ↑7L .2	115					/M5	27	90		35		
15			"	4	1	119		...5 1	107			28	91			48	
18½	"	10			E LIE ...4	126	5	7 3	108		DARLING'S 50: 146' over 3rd slip (GOOCH)	29	98		39	51	
24			"	5				7 7 8 4.4..2.	116	8	100 p'ship in 146 min	30	108			61	
27	"	11			...:.1 2	131		...1	119			31	109		40		
32	11-1-37-0 (5)		"	6	......	139					M6	32					
35	HENDRICK	7						.2..2xx 7.	127		*Randall misfielded	33	113			65	
41			"	7	....9E 2...	147						34	115		42		
44½	"	8	7-4-13-0 (2)		2 ...1	152		30 LB	130		*DARLING'S HS in Tests (LB)	35	118		43	66	9
50	8-0-23-0 (1)		MILLER 3-0-11-0 (2)	3	7 ..4.	158	6	6 .1	132	8	M6 NB/7 3HR→	36	123	1	47	67	9

AUSTRALIA v ENGLAND — 4th Test
at Sydney

2ND DAY TIME	BOWLERS (BAILHACHE) PADDINGTON END — BOWLER	O.	(FRENCH) RANDWICK END — BOWLER	O.	BATSMEN SCOREBOARD LEFT — SCORING	BALLS	6s/4s	SCOREBOARD RIGHT — SCORING	BALLS	6s/4s	NOTES	AUSTRALIA 1st INNINGS — END-OF-OVER TOTALS — O.	RUNS	W.	L BAT	R BAT	EXTRAS
					HUGHES	158	6	DARLING	132	8	M6 NB/7	36	123	1	47	67	9
12.54	HENDRICK	9						·····8 2··	140			37	125			69	
58½	9-0-25-0(1)		MILLER	4	······2 1	166	6		140	8	M6 NB/7	38	126	1	48	69	9
1·02	LUNCH		4-0-12-0(2)										LUNCH				
1·42	WILLIS	8			4 W	167	6					38'	126	2	48	69	9
					YALLOP Helmet Cap LHB										0		
44	"	8			····⊙··	8					NB NB/8 M7	39	127				10
49			EMBUREY	8		9		····2 8 21	147		Round wkt to LHB	40	130			72	
53	"	9			⊙··2 8	13		····2 ①	153		NB NB/8/10	41	134		2	73	11
2·02	9-2-33-2(4)		"	9				2B	161		LEVER sub for WILLIS 2B M·8	42	136				13
05	HENDRICK	10			·····P	21					M9 (ill-returned to hotel)	43					
10	"		"	10	····†8 1	27		·1	163		† over wkt	44	138		3	74	
14	"	11			····4 2·	35	1					45	142		7		
19	11-1-29-0(2)		"	11	·····	40		··3 3E	166		Round wkt to LHB	46	145			77	
23	BOTHAM	12			⊙21 ↑72	43		8E ····	172		NB NB/11	47	150		10	78	14
28			"	12	·······	51					M10 4HR→	48					
32	"	13			··1 7	54		2 ·4···	177	9	EDMONDS sub for HENDRICK 152 in 24½ heat exhaustion	49	156		11	83	
37			"	13	····1	59		··x ··	180			50	157		12		
40 43	DRINKS "	14			↑9 ··	61		·20⊙ x x	187		DARLING changed headgear to CAP.	51	161		13	85	15
49			"	14	·1·· ·4 8 6	67	2	··6	189		NB NB/12	52	167		18	86	
52½	"	15	14-6-28-0(3)		↑↑7s ··	72		2 461 ·1 ⊙21	193		NB/13	53	172		19	90	
59	15-1-55-0(6)		MILLER	5	·1 7	74		6	199			54	174		20	91	
3·03	GOOCH	1			·x· ·4·· 7 F	82	3				50 p'ship in 82 min	55	178		24		
07	1-0-4-0(1)		"	6				W E	200	9		55'	178	3	24	91	15
08								TOOHEY Cap								0	
10			"	6	·····	87		·9 ·1	2			56	179			1	
14	BOTHAM	16						:W E	4	–	HENDRICK back (off 42 min)	56²	179	4	24	1	15
15								BORDER Cap LHB								0	
17	"	16						···P ↑	6		M11	57					
21	16-2-55-1(6)		"	7	····1	92		7 4··	9	1		58	184		25	4	
26	EMBUREY	15			2···· ·· 2 3 4	100	4				5HR→	59	190		31		
30			"	8				········	17		M12	60					
32	"	16			···· P 3 1	105		·E ··	20			61	191		32		
35			"	9	··1 6 43	109	5	···	24			62	198		39		
38	17-6-36-0(4)	17	9-1-27-1(4)		·1 2S	111	5	·····	30	1	M12 NB/13	63	199	4	40	4	15
3·42	TEA										overcast, slight breeze, storm near, cool				TEA		
4·00			MILLER	10	···1 6	115		····	34			64	200		41		
03	EMBUREY	18	10-1-28-1(4)		······	123					M13	65					
07	18-7-36-0(4)		BOTHAM	17				†·2······ 6	42		NEW BALL/2	66	202			6	
12	HENDRICK	12	17-2-57-1(6)		··2·····	131	5		42	1	M13 NB/13	67	204	4	43	6	15

97

AUSTRALIA v ENGLAND   4th Test

at Sydney

2ND DAY TIME	BOWLERS (BAILHACHE) PADDINGTON END BOWLER	O.	(FRENCH) RANDWICK END BOWLER	O.	BATSMEN SCOREBOARD LEFT SCORING	BALLS	6s/4s	SCOREBOARD RIGHT SCORING	BALLS	6s/4s	AUSTRALIA 1ST INNINGS NOTES	END-OF-OVER TOTALS O.	RUNS	W.	L BAT	R BAT	EXTRAS
						131	5	...DFR	42	1	M 13 NB 13	67	204	4	43	6	15
4·17				18	·· 1E ·1	134		2 3 ·21 2·2	47			68	210		44	11	
22	HENDRICK	13			·W	136	5					68²	210	5	44	11	15
23					MACLEAN	Helmet									0		
25	"	13	18-2-63-1 (6)		P 2 ··1	4		··	49			69	211		1		
29			GOOCH	2	·········	12					M 14	70					
33		14			P2 ··1	15		···· 1	54			71	213		2	12	
39	14-1-34-1 (2)		"	3	2 1	16		··· 4 2 ···	61			72	216		3	14	
43	BOTHAM	19			··· ↑ L	24					M 15 6HR→	73					
48			·	4	···· P1E° 4	29	1	·· 2 ·1	67		* Just wide of slip 6 19	74	221		7	15	
52	"	20			··· 1 ··	35		2 9 1 ···	66			75	224		8	17	
57			·	5				··· 2	74			76	226			19	
5·00 04	DRINKS "		"	21	5-1-14-0 (2) ·!··· 2 ·1	40		··· ·	77			77	227		9		
09			EMBUREY	19	·········	48					M 16	78					
13	"	22			8 1 ··	51		2 ↑ 2 1 ··1	82		Round wkt	79	230		10	21	
18	22-3-70-1 (6)		"	20				···2··· 7	90		Round wkt	80	232			23	
21	HENDRICK	15			···· 3S ↑8 1 1	57		4 ·	92			81	235		12	24	
27			·	21	L W	58	1					81¹	235	6	12	24	15
28					HOGG	Helmet									0		
30			"	21	···· P 4 ·	7	1					82	239		4		
33	"	16			··1 2	10		x ···· 2 1	97			83	241		5	25	
38			"	22	· 6 1 ·····	17		9 3	98			84	245		6	28	
42	"	17			RO	17	1	:	99			84¹	245	7	6	28	15
43					DYMOCK	Cap (LHB)									0		
45	"	17			··· L ·	7					M 17 7HR→	85					
49			"	23	···· P	12		3 7 ·21	102			86	248			31	
53	"	18	23-8-49-1 (5)					········	110		M 18	87					
58	18-3-39-1 (2)		MILLER	11	·········	20	–		110	1	M 19 NB/13	88	248	7	0	31	15
6·00	STUMPS (2ND DAY)		11-2-28-1 (4)								ATTENDANCE (3RD) 13,659				STUMPS		
3RD DAY 11·00	HENDRICK	19			···	23		5 2 ··2·1	115		LEVER sub for WILLIS (weak from stomach his brother).	89	251			34	
06			BOTHAM	23				↑ · 9	123		Hot, humid, no wind	90	252			35	
10	" "	20						P 6P ···· ↑	131		M 20	91					
15			·	24	x 1E ·· ·	27		5 2 4 ··1	135	2	DYMOCK on 'o' for 32'	92	258		1	40	
20	·	21	24-3-77-1 (7)		·· 8 1	30		1E6 ··· 1	140		* DROPPED 3rd SLIP (GOOCH) low to his left	93	260		2	41	
26			EMBUREY	24	1E 1	32		···· P	146			94	261		3		
30	·	22			·T· 1	36		7 ·· x 2··1	150			95	264		4	43	
36	22-4-47-1 (2)		"	25	P P	44					slight cross breeze M 21 from snow gd.	96					
39	BOTHAM	25						↑8↑ 6 ··402····	159	3	NB NB/14	97	271			49	16
44			"	26	P···· 3 1	51		3 1	160		BORDER's 50 in 191'	98	275		5	52	
47	25-5-3-84-2 (8)	26	26-9-54-1 (5)		↑x· x W	54	–	4 ·1	162	3	Round wkt * Discussion (Bailhache/Bradley) re bouncers to Dymock	98⁵	276	8	5	53	16
11·51											M 21 NB 14						

98

AUSTRALIA v ENGLAND
at Sydney
4th Test

3RD DAY TIME	BOWLERS (BAILHACHE) PADDINGTON END — BOWLER	O.	(FRENCH) RANDWICK END — BOWLER	O.	BATSMEN SCOREBOARD LEFT — SCORING	BALLS 6s/4s	SCOREBOARD RIGHT — SCORING	BALLS 6s/4s	AUSTRALIA 1st INNINGS — NOTES	O.	RUNS	W.	'L' BAT	'R' BAT	EXTRAS
					HIGGS cap	–	BORDER	162 / 3	11 21 NB/14	98⁵	276	8	0	53	10
11.55	BOTHAM	26			.?...	3			8 HR→	99					
55½"			EMBUREY	27	³.1	4	..².1 ...1	169	Round wkt to LHB stumping chance	100	278		1	54	
12.00 03	DRINKS "	27			E 7 5 .1 ...	9	↑.5 ..1	172		101	280		2	55	
08			"	28	....			180	M 22	102					
11	"	28			L 7 .1	11	.↑...↑	186	3rd & 4th balls of sn. run	103	281		3		
15	28-3-87-2 (8)		"	29	...PP.³1	18	.	187		104	282		4		
19	HENDRICK	23	29-10-57-1(5)		...⁵1	22	....	191		105	283		5		
25			MILLER	12	..⁴1 ³3	26	.⁶1..	195	Round wkt to LHB	106	288		9	56	
30	"	24			P E I E .2W	32	–			106⁶	290	9	11	56	16
33					HURST cap								0		
35	"	24			..	2				107					
37	24-4-50-2 (2)		13-2-37-1(6)	13	RO 2	–	.....4.4	203 / 4	M 22 NB/14	108	294	10	0	60	16
12.40	AUSTRALIA ALL OUT						878 balls		ALL OUT						
	AUSTRALIA LEAD: 142						BATTING TIME: 530 MINUTES								

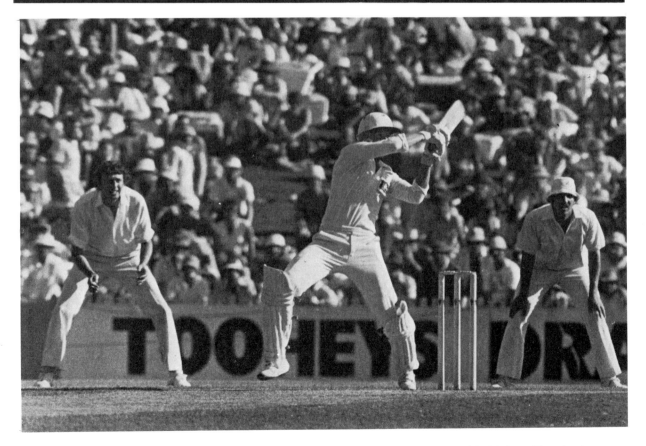

35 The bouncer hit – Rick Darling hooks Willis for yet another boundary in his highest Test innings.

ENGLAND 2nd Innings

142 runs behind on first innings

IN	OUT	MINS	No.	BATSMAN	HOW OUT	BOWLER	RUNS
12.52	12.53	1	1	BOYCOTT	LBW	HOGG	0
12.52	5.22	216	2	BREARLEY *	BOWLED	BORDER	53
12.55	5.32	582	3	RANDALL	LBW	HOGG	150
5.24	12.33	128	4	GOOCH	C˙ WOOD	HIGGS	22
12.35	3.53	98	5	GOWER	C˙ MACLEAN	HOGG	34
3.55	4.44	90	6	BOTHAM	C˙ WOOD	HIGGS	6
4.46	11.20	96	7	MILLER	LBW	HOGG	17
5.34	(12.22)	110	8	TAYLOR †	NOT OUT		21
11.22	12.11	49	9	EMBUREY	C˙ DARLING	HIGGS	14
12.12	12.13	1	10	WILLIS	C˙ TOOHEY	HIGGS	0
12.14	12.22	8	11	HENDRICK	C˙ TOOHEY	HIGGS	7

* CAPTAIN   † WICKET-KEEPER

| | | | | | EXTRAS | b 5   lb 3   w –   nb 14 | 22 |

TOTAL (OFF 146.6 OVERS IN 697 MINUTES) **346**

RANDALL'S 100, REACHED IN 406 MINUTES,
WAS THE SLOWEST FOR EITHER COUNTRY IN TESTS BETWEEN ENGLAND AND AUSTRALIA.

BOWLER	O	M	R	W	nb
HOGG	28	10	67	4	11
DYMOCK	17	4	35	0	7
HURST	19	3	43	0	–
HIGGS	59.6	15	148	5	–
BORDER	23	11	31	1	–
Extras			22		
	146.6	43	346	10	

HRS	OVERS	RUNS
1	11	42
2	12	27
3	13	27
4	14	26
5	12	24
6	13	42
7	12	39
8	10	18
9	14	22
10	13	30
11	15	22

RUNS	MINS	OVERS	LAST 50 (in mins)
50	87	15.5	87
100	192	39.6	105
150	311	64	119
200	388	82	77
250	501	102.1	113
300	599	124.2	98

2ND NEW BALL taken at 2.06 pm on 4th DAY
– ENGLAND 204-3 after 84 overs.

WKT	TOTAL	6s	4s	BALLS	NOTES ON DISMISSAL
1	0	·	·	1	Played too early at slower breakback. OUT FIRST BALL FOR 1ST TIME IN TESTS
2	111	·	2	195	Pushed forward - played inside legbreak which hit off stump.
6	292	·	13	498	Misjudged line of ball which kept low.
3	169	·	1	98	Edged via boot to silly mid-off.
4	237	·	3	68	Edged off-drive low to 'keeper.
5	267	·	·	88	Inside edge (via pad) to silly mid-off.
7	307	·	1	80	Played across line of ball that kept low - front foot.
·	·	·	1	113	-
8	334	·	1	39	Mistimed cover drive at leg-break - falling cover-point catch.
9	334	·	·	1	Edged leg-break to short gully - out 1st ball.
10	346	·	1	11	Edged drive at leg-break to short gully's right.

0⁶ 23⁴ 1,192 balls (including 18 no balls)

12 OVERS 5 BALLS/HOUR
2.36 RUNS/OVER
29 RUNS/100 BALLS

LUNCH: 11-1	BREARLEY 4* (5b, 12 min) RANDALL 7* (10b, 9 min) OFF 2 OVERS IN 12 MINUTES		
TEA: 74-1	BREARLEY 33* (110b, 134 min) RANDALL 37* (103b, 131 min) OFF 26 OVERS IN 134 MINUTES		
STUMPS (3RD DAY) 133-2	RANDALL 65* (205b, 251 min) GOOCH 6* (31b, 37 min) OFF 53 OVERS IN 254 MINUTES		
LUNCH: 191-3	RANDALL 87* (314b, 370 min) GOWER 18* (25b, 26 min) OFF 78 OVERS IN 373 MINUTES		
TEA: 247-4	RANDALL 119* (420b, 490 min) BOTHAM 2* (33b, 46 min) OFF 100 OVERS IN 493 MINUTES		
STUMPS (4TH DAY) 304-6	MILLER 16* (61b, 76 min) TAYLOR 3* (33b, 28 min) OFF 128 OVERS IN 615 MINUTES		

WKT	PARTNERSHIP		RUNS	MINS
1st	Boycott	Brearley	0	1
2nd	Brearley	Randall	111	213
3rd	Randall	Gooch	58	128
4th	Randall	Gower	68	98
5th	Randall	Botham	30	90
6th	Randall	Miller	25	46
7th	Miller	Taylor	15	48
8th	Taylor	Embury	27	49
9th	Taylor	Willis	0	1
10th	Taylor	Hendrick	12	8

346

AUSTRALIA v ENGLAND — 4th Test
at Sydney

ENGLAND 2ND INNINGS

3RD DAY TIME	BOWLER (Paddington End)	O.	BOWLER (Randwick End)	O.	SCOREBOARD LEFT SCORING	BALLS	6s/4s	SCOREBOARD RIGHT SCORING	BALLS	6s/4s	NOTES	O.	RUNS	W.	L BAT	R BAT	EXTRAS
					BOYCOTT cap			BREARLEY Helmet cap									
12.52			HOGG	1	W	1	–					0¹	0	1	0	0	–
53					RANDALL cap										0		
55			"	1	·1 ²· 4	4		·21	3			1	6		3	3	
59½	DYMOCK	1	1-0-6-1 (–)		·4 ··× 10	10	1	·1	5		M – NB/–	2	11	1	7	4	–
1.04	LUNCH																
1.40½			HOGG	2	4 0· 15	15	2	··02·1	12		NB NB NB/×/4	3	20		11	7	2
49	DYMOCK	2			···· 19	19		···1	16			4	21			8	
54			"	3	2 3 20	20		9 1·×·9 2 23	23			5	27		14	11	
59	"	3	3-0-19-1 (1)		2···4··· 28	28	3					6	33		20		
2.04	3-0-12-0 (2)		HURST	1	···· 32	32		···1	27			7	34			12	
09	HOGG	4	1-0-1-0 (–)					····2·· 35	35		LB	8	37		14	3	
15			DYMOCK	4	·1 33	33		···1	42			9	39		21	15	
21	"	5			21 35	35		·····1	48			10	42		24		
26			"	5	×········P 43	43					M1 1HR →	11					
31	"	6			··7 46	46		······Y 53	53			12	44		25	16	
36	6-0-26-1 (1)		"	6	······1 02· 55	55		8s 1 54	54		NB NB/×6	13	49		28	17	4
42	DRINKS																
45	HIGGS	1						········ 62	62		M2	14					
49			"	7	········ 63	63					M3	15					
54	"	2	7-2-18-0 (2)		··· 66	66		····4 67	67		50 p'ship in 84 min.	16	50			18	
58			HURST	2	23 1 69	69		··1 21 72	72			17	60		34	22	
3.03½	"	3			········ 77	77					M4	18					
07	3-2-1-0 (–)		"	3				······1 80	80			19	61			23	
12	BORDER	1	3-0-12-0 (–)					········ 88	88		Left-arm round wkt. M5	20					
15	1-1-0-0 (–)		HIGGS	4	× ···1 82	82		··· 91	91			21	62		35		
20	HURST	4			·1 84	84		2·4··· 97	97	1		22	69		36	29	
26			"	5	········ 92	92					M6 2HR →	23					
29	"	5			···· 96	96		···3 101	101			24	72			32	
35			"	6				········ 109	109		*Almost played on to 'flipper' - kept low. M7	25					
38	6-0-24-0 (1)	6	6-4-2-0 (–)		······1 103	103	3	·1 110	110	1	M7 NB/6	26	74	1	37	33	4
3.43	TEA																
4.01			HIGGS	7				·····4· 118	118	2		27	78			37	
03	HOGG	7			× ········ 111	111					M8	28					
10			"	8				·······1 126	126			29	79			38	
13	"	8			···· 115	115		·2·1· 130	130		*Almost played on	30	82			41	
19	"		"	9	41 117	117	4	····2·1 136	136		*one short run (ran 3)	31	90		42	44	
24	"	9			2······· 144	144						32	92			46	
30			"	10	··2····· 125	125					2B	33	96		44		6
33	"	10	10-4-17-0 (2)		········ 152	152					M9	34					
40	10-2-31-1 (1)		BORDER	2	········ 133	133	4	152		2	Left-arm round wkt. M10 NB/6	35	96	1	44	46	6

AUSTRALIA v ENGLAND — 4th Test
at Sydney

ENGLAND 2ND INNINGS

TIME	BOWLER (French) Paddington END	O.	BOWLER (Bailhache) Randwick END	O.	SCORING (Scoreboard Left)	BALLS	6s/4s	SCORING (Scoreboard Right)	BALLS	6s/4s	NOTES	O.	RUNS	W.	L BAT	R BAT	EXTRAS
					RANDALL	133	4	BREARLEY	152	2	M10 NB 6	35	96	1	44	46	6
4.44	HIGGS	11						··········	160		M11 3HR→	36					
47			BORDER	3	·· 7 6 / · 1 1	137		· 2 · / · 1 ··	164			37	99		46	47	
51	"	12			L / ·········	145					M 12	38					
54			"	4				·········	172		M 13	39					
57	"	13			····· 7 ·	151		··	174		100 p'ship in 189min	40	100		47		
5.00 03½ DRINKS			"	5	···· 8 ·	158		· 2 · 1	175			41	102		48	48	
07	"	14			·· x ···	161		·· B ····	180		B M14	42	103				7
11			"	6				··· 7 · 7 · 2 ·· 2 ·	188		BREARLEY'S 50: 205'	43	107			52	
15	"	15			7 ··· 8 / 2 ··· · 1	167		··· 1	190		Round wkt RANDALL'S 50: 207'	44	111		51	53	
20			"	7	{			····· W	195	2		44⁵	111	2	51	53	7
22								GOOCH (sun hat)								0	
24			"	7				···· E ·	3		· DROPPED MACLEAN M 15	45					
26	"	16			· 2E · 1	169		····· x	9			46	112		52		
31			"	8	········ 8	177						47	113		53		
35	"	17			7 x 3 / 2 ··· · 1	183		· 7 · 1	11		over wkt.	48	117		56	1	
38½			"	9	·····	188		·· 7 · 1	14			49	118			2	
42	"	18			8F · 1	190		· 6 · 3 ···	20		* Head-high full-toss 4HR→	50	122		57	5	
46 18-7-31-0 (2)			"	10	········· P	198					M16	51					
50	HOGG	11			·· ⊙ · 3 7	203		· 9E 1 ·· ⊙	25		NB NB NB/7 8	52	128		60	6	9
58 11-2-35-1 (1)			" 11-5-10-1 (1)	11	6 6 / 4 1	205	5	······	31	–	M16 NB/8	53	133	2	65	6	9
6.01	STUMPS		(3RD DAY)		··											STUMPS	
4TH DAY 11.02	HOGG	12			· P 2 ··· 1 ·	212		· 9 1	32		Very hot (37°C and rising) and humid.	54	135		66	7	
07			HIGGS	19	· E ····	217		·· 4 · 1	35		Leg breaks turning and bouncing high.	55	136			8	
11	"	13			L ··· 1 ↑ · ⊙	44					NB NB/9 M17	56	137				10
18			"	20	·········	225					M18	57					
21	"	14						↑ ·····	52		M19	58					
27½ 14-4-37-1 (1)			"	21	····· 2 · 1	231		· P ·	54		ATTENDANCE (4th) 9,090	59	138		67		
31	HURST	7			·· 3 · 3 ··	237		· 3D · 1	56		• Teams level (11.35)	60	142		70	9	
37			"	22	· 1E · 3	239		x ·· 8 · 1 FX	62		M20 5HR	61	146		73	10	
40 43½ DRINKS	"	8			········· L	247					Temp 38°C – two drinks intervals per session authorised.	62					
49			"	23				········ •	70		• Dropped s. mid off (Hurst)	63					
52	"	9			· x · v P 7 ···· 4	255	6				M21 TV cameraman fell 20ft from perch – (Bradman Stand).	64	150		77		
59			"	24	· 8 ········	256		LB 1E · 2 · 4 ·· 2 ··	77	1	LB • Dropped, HUGHES (sub)	65	158		78	16	11
12.03	"	10			··· 9 · 1	260		···· 1	81			66	159		79		
07 10-1-33-0 (2)			"	25	·· 8 · 1 · 7	266		· 4 · 1 · 2 · 3	83		50 p'ship in 105'	67	165		81	20	
13	DYMOCK	8			···· x x	270		··· 2 ·	87			68	166			21	
17			"	26	·· 9 · 1	273		· 4 ·· 1	92			69	168		82	22	
20 23 DRINKS	"	9	26-9-52-0 (3)		··· 2 · 1	277		···· 1	96		Left arm round wkt	70	169		83		
28 9-2-20-0 (2)			BORDER	12	········	285	6		96	1	YARDLEY sub for HURST M22 NB/9	71	169	2	83	22	11

36 Derek Randall, 'Man of the Match' – Randall drives Dymock's fourth delivery with the second new ball for the only front-of-the-wicket offside boundary of his entire innings. Patrick Eagar's superb camerawork has captured a textbook example of the off-drive.

AUSTRALIA v ENGLAND

4th Test

at Sydney

4TH DAY TIME	BOWLERS (FRENCH) PADDINGTON END BOWLER	O.	(BAILHACHE) RANDWICK END BOWLER	O.	BATSMEN SCOREBOARD LEFT SCORING	BALLS	6s/4s	SCOREBOARD RIGHT SCORING	BALLS	6s/4s	ENGLAND 2ND INNINGS NOTES	O.	RUNS	W.	L BAT	R BAT	EXTRAS
					RANDALL	285	6	GOOCH	96	1	M22 NB/9	71	169	2	83	22	11
12.32	HIGGS	27						xEW	98	1		71²	169	3	83	22	11
33								GOWER Helmet cap (LHB)			Gower batted with high temperature & throat infection / over wkt					0	
35	"	27			8/1	286		4f 4t 3.4..	5	1		72	177		84	7	
39			BORDER	13	x.......	294					M23	73					
42	"	28			3/1	295		PP9 6 ..4..3.	12	2		74	185		85	14	
46	"		"	14	1E ..	298		5 .2...	17		over wkt to LHB 6HR→	75	188		86	16	
51	"	29			P 4 1	306						76	189		87		
54	"		"	15	L	314					M24	77					
57	30-9-71-1(5)	30	15-8-19-1(1)			314	6	L5 P° .2...	25	2	*Appeal c s.mid-on M24 NB 9	78	191	3	87	18	11
1.01	LUNCH										LUNCH						
1.41			DYMOCK	10	....	322					Hurst back. M25	79					
45	HIGGS	31						....	33		M26	80					
48	"		"	11	...O..	329		2 .1	35		NB/10	81	193		88	19	
53	"	32						74 P8 ...24..1	43	3	Round wkt (8th ball)	82	200			26	
57	"		"	12	..O....	336		x3S .1	45		NB NB'11	83	202			27	12
2.02	"	33			1	342		2 .1	47		Round wkt.	84	204		89	28	
06	33-10-80-1(6)		"	13	...42-0-	351	7				NEW BALL/2 NB NB/2	85	211		95		13
12	HOGG	15			44.4..	357	10	84 21	49		Round wkt to LHB RANDALL's (2'+06')	86	226		107	31	
20 23½	DRINKS		"	14		362		x2 ..1	52		So p'ship in 161 min. 7HR→	87	227			32	
29	"	16						L P°L	60		*Appeal c wkt M27	88					
34½	"		"	15	..O.O.22..	372					Temp 36°C NB NB NB/x14	89	233		111		15
40	"	17			9/1	375		LB 3S 1	65		LB	90	236		112	33	16
48	"		"	16	1	381		3 .1	67			91	237			34	
52	"	18						EW	68	3		91'	237	4	112	34	16
53								BOTHAM Helmet cap								0	
55	"	18			9 .1	383		F.9 ...1.	5		Round wkt t over wkt	92	239		113	1	
3.00 03	DRINKS		"	17	x	391					M28	93					
08	"	19	17-4-35-0(3)					...O..	14		NB NB/15 M29	94	240				17
15	19-6-56-2(4)		HIGGS	34	E° 3 .1	394		EF .1	19		*dropped slip (HUGHES)	95	241		114		
20	HURST	11			8E	400		..	21		YARDLEY sub for HOGG (back strain)	96	242		115		
25	"		"	35	L 84 ..2.1	407			22		8HR→	97	245		118		
28	"	12			°9E	412		2 .1	25		*dropped - inside edge to wkt	98	247		119	2	
33	"		"	36				PP L ...1	33		M30	99					
36	13-2-36-0(2)	13	36-11-84-1(6)		....	420	10		33	-	*Appeal c wkt M31	100	247	4	119	2	17
3.41	TEA										M31 NB/15 / TEA						
4.00			HIGGS	37				....	41		Hogg back. M32	101					
03	HURST	14			6 .1	422		↑ ↑x	47			102	248		120		
08	"		"	38	7 1E 4.1.	427	11	2 .1	50		*Dropped slip (YALLOP)	103	254		125	3	
12	15-2-39-0(2)	15	38-12-90-1(7)		8/1	428	11	7S 1	57	-	M32 NB'15	104	256	4	126	4	17

AUSTRALIA v ENGLAND

at Sydney

4th Test

ENGLAND 2ND INNINGS

4TH DAY TIME	BOWLERS (FRENCH) PADDINGTON END BOWLER	O.	(BAILHACHE) RANDWICK END BOWLER	O.	BATSMEN SCOREBOARD LEFT SCORING	BALLS	6s/4s	SCOREBOARD RIGHT SCORING	BALLS	6s/4s	NOTES	O.	RUNS	W.	'L' BAT	'R' BAT	EXTRAS
					RANDALL	428	11	BOTHAM	57	–	M32 NB/15	104	256	4	126	4	17
4.17			HIGGS	39	·¹ ···⁸	433		··¹⁹	60			105	258		127	5	
20	HURST	16						↑1x· ↑	68		M33	106					
25	16-3-39-0 (2)		"	40	····¹⁴	438		··P⁸¹	71			107	260		128	6	
29	BORDER	16						·········	79		M34	108					
32			"	41	··⁴²⁰·¹⁸ˢ	444	12	··	81		*Darling misfielded – 4 otrun	109	265		133		
36		"	17		·¹²	446		·····	87			110	266		134		
39 42	DRINKS		"	42	¹P⁷	449		EP W	88	–		110	267	5	135	6	17
44								MILLER	sun hat							0	
46	"		"	42				····	4		9HR→	111					
47	"	18			···²⁷····	457						112	269		137		
51			"	43				······×··	12		M35	113					
54	"	19			····⁶·	464		·	13			114	270		138		
57			"	44	⁴F⁶····↑⁴⁶	470	13	·P·	15		†Round wkt (1 ball)	115	275		143		
5.02	"	20			·······P	478					M36	116					
05	20-10-23-1(1)		"	45	¹⁸	479		¹⁹E··⁶··⁴·	22	1	*Appeal ct s. mid-off	117	281		144	5	
09	HOGG	20			·····²⊙·⁸·	488					(NB) Short run (Tooday balls) NB/16	118	284		146		18
15			"	46	··¹²	491		·P¹⁸···	27		Miller changed head-gear to helmet cap	119	286		147	6	
18	"	21			·²⁴ˢ··¹²	496		··⁸	30		RANDALL's 150: 571	120	290		150	7	
24 28	DRINKS		"	47				·····⁷²··	38			121	292			9	
31	"	22			ᴸW	498	13					121	292	6	150	9	18
32					TAYLOR	cap										0	
34	"	22			ᴸY····	6					M37	122					
38			"	48				E·····⁶²··	46			123	294			11	
41	"	23			²···⊙·†·⁸	15					†short run·up 10HR (NB) NB/17→	124	297		2		19
45			"	49	·¹⁸	16		·³³·····	53			125	301		3	14	
49	"	24			···⊙†	25					(NB) †short·up (3 balls) NB/18 M38	126	302				20
54	24-8-64-3(4)		"	50				·P·†⁴P²·	61		Round wkt †over wkt	127	304		16		
59	BORDER 21-11-23-1(1)	21	50-13-123-2(10)		·P·ᴸP·	33	–		61	1	M39 NB/18	128	304	6	3	16	20
6.02	STUMPS		(4TH DAY)												S T U M P S
5TH DAY 11.00			HIGGS	51				²ᴮ····	69		(2B) M40	129	306				22
03	HOGG	25			·······P	41					M41	130					
08			"	52				·P····P	77		M42	131					
11	"	26			λλ·····↑	49					λ = short run·up M43	132					
16			"	53	×·×·×·	55		ᴸ·¹⁶¹	79		*Toohey misfielded	133	307			17	
19	"	27						ᴸW	80	1	ATTENDANCE (5TH) 8,755	133	307	7	3	17	22
20								EMBUREY	No cap							0	
22	"	27						EP†·²λ·λ	7		*Hit on shoulder	134	309			2	
26			"	54	·²⁷·····	63						135	311		5		
29	28-10-"07-4(4)	28	54-15-126-2(10)		··ᴸλ····	67	–	···ᴸ⁷¹	11	–	M43 NB/18	136	312	7	5	3	22

106

AUSTRALIA v ENGLAND
at Sydney

4th Test

5TH DAY TIME	BOWLERS (FRENCH) PADDINGTON END BOWLER	O.	(BAILHACHE) RANDWICK END BOWLER	O.	BATSMEN SCOREBOARD LEFT SCORING	BALLS	6s/4s	SCOREBOARD RIGHT SCORING	BALLS	6s/4s	ENGLAND 2ND INNINGS NOTES	O.	RUNS	W.	'L' BAT	'R' BAT	EXTRAS
					TAYLOR	67	–	EMBUREY	11	–	LEAD: 170 M43 NB/18	136	312	7	5	3	22
11.34			HIGGS	55	··¹⁷	70		····¹⁸	16			137	314		6	4	
37	HURST	17			··²·····	78					YARDLEY sub for HOGG	138	316		8		
42			"	56	ˣᴸ·····	82		ˣ⁸⁶·2·1	20		11 HR →	139	319			7	
46	·	18			····	86		···⁷1	24		• Hard chance to backw'd sqleg (DYMOCK)	140	320			8	
51			"	57	··ᴱ³1	89		⁹·⁷4·1	29	1		141	326		9	13	
55	"	19			···⁷	93		·····	33			142	327		10		
59 12.02	DRINKS 19-3-43-0(2)		"	58	⁴⁶21··¹⁸	98		⁹ᴱ·1	36			143	332		14	14	
05	BORDER	22			·³2·····	106					Round wkt	144	334		16		
10			"	59	}			··ᴡ²ᴱ	39	1		144³	334	8	16	14	22
11					}			WILLIS sun hat								0	
12			"	59	}			ᴱᴡ	1	–		144⁴	334	9	16	0	22
13					}			HENDRICK No cap								0	
14			"	59	}			ʸ¹ᴱˣ·2·	4			145	336			2	
16	·	23			···⁶·³4··1	113	1	⁹·1	5			146	342		21	3	
20	23-11-31-1 (2)		" (92) 59⁶-15-148-5	60		113		ˣˣˣ³·⁴·ᴱᴡ	11	1		146⁶	346	10	21	7	22
12.22	ENGLAND ALL OUT										M43 NB/18		ALL	OUT			
	AUSTRALIA REQUIRE 205 To WIN IN 266 MINUTES										1,192 balls		BATTING TIME: 697 MIN.				

37 The Ashes retained – John Emburey penetrates Hurst's defence, England have won a most improbable victory, and the celebrations begin.

AUSTRALIA 2nd Innings

Requiring 205 runs to win in a minimum of 266 minutes

IN	OUT	MINS	No.	BATSMAN	HOW OUT	BOWLER	RUNS
12.34	2.05	51	1	DARLING	Cᵗ GOOCH	HENDRICK	13
12.34	2.29	75	2	WOOD	RUN OUT [BOTHAM→TAYLOR]		27
2.07	3.02	55	3	HUGHES	Cᵗ EMBUREY	MILLER	15
2.31	2.39	8	4	YALLOP *	Cᵗ AND BOWLED	HENDRICK	1
2.41	3.31	50	5	TOOHEY	BOWLED	MILLER	5
3.04	(5.05)	101	6	BORDER	NOT OUT		45
3.33	3.40	7	7	MACLEAN †	Cᵗ BOTHAM	MILLER	0
4.00	4.09	9	8	DYMOCK	BOWLED	EMBUREY	0
4.12	4.17	5	9	HOGG	Cᵗ BOTHAM	EMBUREY	0
4.19	4.43	24	10	HIGGS	LBW	EMBUREY	3
4.45	5.05	20	11	HURST	BOWLED	EMBUREY	0
* CAPTAIN † WICKET-KEEPER				EXTRAS	b - lb1	w - nb1	2

TOTAL (OFF 49.2 OVERS IN 211 MINUTES) **111**

BOWLER	O	M	R	W	nb		HRS	OVERS	RUNS		RUNS	MINS	OVERS	LAST 50 (in mins)
WILLIS	2	0	8	0	1		1	11	40		50	97	18.1	97
HENDRICK	10	3	17	2	-		2	12	23		100	179	40	82
EMBUREY	17.2	7	46	4	-		3	17	37					
MILLER	20	7	38	3	-									
Extras/Run Out			2	1										
	49.2	17	111	10										

WKT	TOTAL	6s	4s	BALLS	NOTES ON DISMISSAL
1	38	.	1	37	Edged defensive push at offside ball low to 2nd slip.
2	44	.	2	64	Attempted quick single to cover's right. Hughes remained in crease
4	59	.	1	40	Edged off-break via pad to forward short leg. Ball 'lifted'.
3	45	.	.	12	Simple return catch. Checked drive - slower ball.
5	74	.	.	50	Went down wicket and missed off-drive.
.	.	.	9	115	-
6	76	.	.	11	Off-break hit glove and rebounded to silly point.
7	85	.	.	12	Edged attempted back-foot drive into stumps.
8	85	.	.	4	Edged off-break via pad to short-leg.
9	105	.	.	29	Played back — beaten by off-spin.
10	111	.	.	21	Missed drive - beaten by flight.

0⁶ 13⁴ 395 balls (including 1 no ball)

14 OVERS 0 BALLS/HOUR
2.25 RUNS/OVER
28 RUNS/100 BALLS

LUNCH: 15-0 DARLING 5* (21b, 26 min)
WOOD 9* (20b, 26 min)
OFF 5 OVERS IN 26 MINUTES

TEA: 76-6 BORDER 13* (33b, 36 min)
OFF 30.6 OVERS IN 146 MINUTES

ENGLAND WON BY 93 RUNS
at 5.05 p.m. on the fifth (last) day.
and RETAINED THE ASHES for the
first time in Australia since 1954-55.

MAN OF THE MATCH: D.W. RANDALL

TOTAL MATCH ATTENDANCE: 72,813

WKT	PARTNERSHIP		RUNS	MINS
1st	Darling	Wood	38	51
2nd	Wood	Hughes	6	22
3rd	Hughes	Yallop	1	8
4th	Hughes	Toohey	14	21
5th	Toohey	Border	15	27
6th	Border	Maclean	2	7
7th	Border	Dymock	9	9
8th	Border	Hogg	0	4
9th	Border	Higgs	20	24
10th	Border	Hurst	6	20

111

AUSTRALIA v ENGLAND 4th Test
at Sydney

5TH DAY TIME	BOWLERS (FRENCH) PADDINGTON END — BOWLER	O.	(BAILHACHE) RANDWICK END — BOWLER	O.	BATSMEN SCOREBOARD LEFT — SCORING	BALLS	6s/4s	SCOREBOARD RIGHT — SCORING	BALLS	6s/4s	NOTES	AUSTRALIA 2ND INNINGS END-OF-OVER TOTALS — O.	RUNS	W.	L BAT	R BAT	EXTRAS
					DARLING Helmet cap			WOOD cap (LHB)			LEVER sub for GOWER (throat infection).						
12.34			WILLIS	1	1 . 2	2		. . . . . 1 9	6			1	2		1	1	
38	HENDRICK	1			. . . . . .	8		. 1 2	8			2	3			2	
44			"	2				. . . . . 2·04 6 48	17	1	NB NB/1	3	10			8	1
50	"	2	EMBUREY 2-0-8-0(1)	1	. · L · 7	14		P x	19		EDMONDS sub for WILLIS (stomach virus)	4	11		2		
56	2-0-2-0(-)		EMBUREY 1-0-4-0(-)	1	F4 P9E 1 · · · · 2	21	–	8	20	1	M – NB/1	5	15	–	5	9	1
1.00	LUNCH										GOWER and WILLIS will take no further part.	LUNCH					
1.40	HENDRICK	3			. 1 7	26		3s 7s · 1	23			6	18		6	11	
46			EMBUREY	2				7 2 7 3s · · 24·21	31	2	6/3 field	7	27			20	
49	"	4						LL L · · · · ·	39		M1	8					
55			"	3	7 6 4 1 · · · ·?	32	1	· 1 2	41		hit Botham (sh sq leg) with full pull on helmet – 4 mins lost.	9	33		11	21	
2.02	"	5			6 E · 2 · · W	37	1	4 3	42			9·6	38	1	13	24	1
05			{		HUGHES cap											0	
07	"	5	3-0-19-0(2)		· ·	2					Round wkt to LHB · Skier over cover 1HR →	10					
10			MILLER	1				3E P P 2·· · · · ·	50			11	40			26	
13	"	6			P7 · 1	5		· · · · ·	55			12	41		1		
19			"	2	7 2·· · · · P	13						13	43		3		
23	"	7						· · · P · · · 1	63			14	44			27	
28			"	3				8·0	64	2		14·1	44	2	3	27	1
29			{					YALLOP Helmet cap (LHB)								0	
31			"	3	EP · · · 1	16		4 · · · 1	4			15	45			1	
34	"	8						EP · · · · · · · W	12	–	M2	16	45	3	3	1	1
39	DRINKS							TOOHEY cap								0	
41			"	4	E 9E · · · · · 3	23		8 1	1			17	49		6	1	
45	"	9						x L · · · · · · ·	9		M3	18					
50			"	5	5 P3 4·· · · 1	28	1	· · ·	12			19	54		11		
54	"	10			x 6 2 ·1· · · 3	33		7 1 · · ·	15			20	59		15	2	
59	10-3-17-2(-)		"	6	P xx EP ·· · · · W	40						20·7	59	4	15	2	1
3.02			{		BORDER cap (LHB)											0	
04			"	6	·1	1					M4	21					
06	EMBUREY	4						· · · · · · · 1	23		7/2 field · Half chance (Botham) (sh. leg). M5	22					
09			"	7	7 EP E · 4·· · · ·	9	1				2HR →	23	63		4		
12	"	5			· · 1 1	11		· · · · · 1 4	29		Round wkt to LHB	24	64			3	
16			"	8				· · · · · · · ·	37		M6	25					
19	"	6			x P P · · · · · ·	19					M7	26					
22			"	9				9 · · · · · · 2 ·	45			27	66			5	
25	"	7			7 P 4 4·· · · · 4·	27	3					28	74		12		
29	7-2-28-0(4)		"	10	{			· · · · W	50	–		28·5	74	5	12	5	1
31			{					MACLEAN cap								0	
33			" 10-3-20-2(2)	10	·	28	3	LB ·?	2	–	LB M8 NB/1	29	75	5	12	0	2

AUSTRALIA v ENGLAND — 4th Test

at Sydney

AUSTRALIA 2ND INNINGS

5TH DAY TIME	BOWLERS (FRENCH) PADDINGTON END — BOWLER	O.	(BAILHACHE) RANDWICK END — BOWLER	O.	BATSMEN — SCOREBOARD LEFT — SCORING	BALLS	6s/4s	SCOREBOARD RIGHT — SCORING	BALLS	6s/4s	NOTES	O.	RUNS	W.	'L' BAT	'R' BAT	EXTRAS
					BORDER	28	3	MACLEAN	2	–	M8 NB/1	29	75	5	12	0	2
3.35	1	8						P P P	10		M9	30					
37½	8·3·28·0 (4)		MILLER	11	.·P·7·1	33	3	G W	11	–	M9 NB/1	30⁶	76	6	13	0	2
40	TEA		10·6·3·21·3 (2)					DYMOCK cap (LHB)			TEA						
4.00			MILLER	11				·L	2			31				0	
01	EMBUREY	9			···3·2···F	41						32	78		15		
04			"	12				P P ....·	10		M10	33					
07	"	10			·272·241	45	4	E ·W	12	–		33⁶	85	7	22	0	2
09								HOGG no cap								0	
12	"	10						··	2			34					
13			"	13	....	53					M11	35					
16	"	11						EP ·W	4	–		35²	85	8	22	0	2
17								HIGGS cap								0	
19	"	11						PP L ...··	6		M12	36					
20			"	14	·4·7·4···	61	6					37	93		30		
23	"	12						..........·	14		Round wkt. Higgs objected to Lever at sh.leg	38					
27			"	15	····8E·1	66		·2·	17		M13	39	96		31	2	
31	"	13			·····F7·4	74	7				3 HR →	40	100		35		
34			"	16				P P ....·	25		M14	41					
37	"	14			·4·L·····	82	8					42	104		39		
39			"	17	····L	87		··+4	28		† over wkt to both	43	105			3	
43	"	15						L W	29	–		43¹	105	9	39	3	2
43								HURST cap								0	
45	"	15						P P·P·PP	7		* Appeal ct wkt M15	44					
48			"	18	····3	92		·E7 ··	10		* Appeal ct sh.leg.	45	106		40		
51	"	16			··P·x·4·1	99		·	11		* DROPPED deep mid off (SUB-LEVER)	46	107		41		
54			"	19	E·····E··	107					M16	47					
57	"	17						P P ....·	19		M17	48					
5·00 01	DRINKS		"	20	·E·····6·4	115	9					49	111		45		
04	17²·7·46·4 (7)	18	20·7·38·3 (5)			115	9	·W	21	–	M17 NB/1	49²	111	10	45	0	2

5·05 **AUSTRALIA ALL OUT**   395 balls   **ALL OUT**

ENGLAND WON BY 93 RUNS AND RETAINED THE ASHES

BATTING TIME: 211 MINUTES

THE FIFTH TEST AT ADELAIDE

Although they twice had England at their mercy, Australia were unable to press home their advantage and eventually indulged in a freak capitulation on a benign pitch, shedding their last eight wickets for 45 runs. Still, it was another absorbing match, with drama, humour and records in fair supply, and played on Australia's most attractive Test ground with its splendid backdrop featuring Mount Lofty. Its highlight for some was a highly testing and tasting day in the Barossa Valley which fortunately affected the journalists more than it did the players; a fractured shin, a gravel-grazed face, and an array of tormented heads paid tribute to the boundless generosity of our host, Wyndham Hill-Wood, a nephew of Clem Hill.

Australia made their most significant team change of the rubber when they replaced their vice-captain, Maclean, with their first left-handed wicket-keeper. Kevin Wright immediately established himself as a cricketer of considerable class and even the warmest admirers of his very likeable predecessor must have wondered why he had not been chosen throughout the rubber.

Yallop's gamble in bowling first on a greenish wicket which promised little help to bowlers in the later stages of the match seemed well justified when England were 27 for 5. Even their final total, which owed most to a

38 Adelaide Oval

ferocious innings by Botham, seemed inadequate for a first innings lead. Its most surprising feature was a spectacular lunging scoop by Willis which dropped the ball into the crowd behind cover-point. An attempted encore resulted in Hogg's 37th wicket and a tremendous ovation from the bowler's adopted home crowd for eclipsing Mailey's famous record.

The frightening injury to Darling in the first over unsettled Australia's vulnerable batting and a splendid bowling performance, supported by the now expected level of brilliance in the field, enabled England to snatch a narrow lead. After Boycott, aiming for a hundred, had just missed his fiftieth Test 50, Taylor, Miller and Emburey took England to the highest total of the rubber and safety. Their sheer professionalism underlined the main differences between the two teams: experience and motivation. Taylor, whose splendid 97 equalled his highest first-class score and represented a record contribution by an England No. 8 against Australia, discovered the application and concentration to play a major innings at international level. Together with fellow Maltamaniac, Alan Lee, I marked my debut as an

adjudicator by attempting to acclaim Taylor as the first wicket-keeper to win a Benson and Hedges gold medallion in 20 Tests sponsored by those worthy benefactors. We were sad to be out-voted 3–2 but few could quarrel with the choice of Ian Botham – except perhaps the Hillites at Sydney.

39 Ian Botham, 'Man of the Match' is congratulated by runner-up Bob Taylor.

ENGLAND 1st Innings v AUSTRALIA 5th Test

at Adelaide Oval on January 27, 28, 29, 31, February 1, 1979

IN	OUT	MINS	No.	BATSMAN	HOW OUT	BOWLER	RUNS
11.00	11.22	22	1	BOYCOTT	Cᵗ WRIGHT	HURST	6
11.00	11.28	28	2	BREARLEY *	Cᵗ WRIGHT	HOGG	2
11.24	11.49	25	3	RANDALL	Cᵗ CARLSON	HURST	4
11.30	11.40	10	4	GOOCH	Cᵗ HUGHES	HOGG	1
11.42	12.00	18	5	GOWER	LBW	HURST	9
11.51	3.08	158	6	BOTHAM	Cᵗ WRIGHT	HIGGS	74
12.02	2.01	80	7	MILLER	LBW	HOGG	31
2.03	2.31	28	8	TAYLOR †	RUN OUT [WRIGHT→YARDLEY]		4
2.32	2.57	25	9	EMBUREY	BOWLED	HIGGS	4
2.58	3.23	25	10	WILLIS	Cᵗ DARLING	HOGG	24
3.10	(3.23)	13	11	HENDRICK	NOT OUT		0

* CAPTAIN † WICKET-KEEPER

EXTRAS	b 1	lb 4	w 3	nb 2	10

TEST DEBUTS: P.H. CARLSON
K.J. WRIGHT

TOTAL (OFF 40.4 OVERS IN 225 MINUTES) 169

BOWLER	O	M	R	W	nb/w	HRS	OVERS	RUNS		RUNS	MINS	OVERS	LAST 50 (in mins)
HOGG	10.4	1	26	4	3/1	1	9.3	27		50	99	16.4	99
HURST	14	1	65	3	-/2	2	12.5	44		100	162	29.5	63
CARLSON	9	1	34	0	-	3	11	48		150	213	38.1	51
YARDLEY	4	0	25	0	1/-								
HIGGS	3	1	9	2	-								
Extras/Run Out			10	1									
	40.4	4	169	10									

Toss: AUSTRALIA

WKT	TOTAL	6ˢ	4ˢ	BALLS	NOTES ON DISMISSAL
1	10	·	·	21	Defensive edge to late outswinger.
2	12	·	·	14	Involuntary edge to lifting ball leaving him.
4	18	·	·	13	Edged drive low to 4ᵗʰ slip's right - superb diving right-handed catch.
3	16	·	·	10	Bouncer hit gloves - simple skier to 1ˢᵗ slip running back.
5	27	·	1	13	Beaten by break back which kept low. Played back.
9	147	2	6	97	Edged 'walking' off side push at leg-break. (Was also stumped.)
6	80	·	3	89	Played back to quicker ball.
7	113	·	·	21	Calling mix-up over 4ᵗʰ run to long-leg (HOGG) from BOTHAM sweep.
8	136	·	·	21	Played across leg-break - aimed mid-wicket push.
10	169	1	3	20	Skied big off-side hit to cover.
-	-	·	·	9	-

3⁶ 13⁴   328 balls (including 4 no balls)

10	OVERS 6	BALLS/HOUR
4·17		RUNS/OVER
52		RUNS/100 BALLS

LUNCH: 71-5	BOTHAM 14* (40b, 71 min) MILLER 25* (68b, 60 min)

OFF 22 OVERS IN 122 MINUTES

R.M. HOGG took his 37th wicket of the rubber when he dismissed WILLIS and so passed Australia's record in any rubber against England set by A.A. MAILEY in 1920-21.

TEA INTERVAL TAKEN AT END OF INNINGS

WKT	PARTNERSHIP		RUNS	MINS
1ˢᵗ	Boycott	Brearley	10	22
2ⁿᵈ	Brearley	Randall	2	4
3ʳᵈ	Randall	Gooch	4	10
4ᵗʰ	Randall	Gower	2	7
5ᵗʰ	Gower	Botham	9	9
6ᵗʰ	Botham	Miller	53	80
7ᵗʰ	Botham	Taylor	33	28
8ᵗʰ	Botham	Emburey	23	25
9ᵗʰ	Botham	Willis	11	10
10ᵗʰ	Willis	Hendrick	22	13

169

115

AUSTRALIA v ENGLAND · 5th Test

at Adelaide

1ST DAY	BOWLERS				BATSMEN					ENGLAND 1ST INNINGS					
	Umpire: R.C.BAILHACHE CATHEDRAL END		Umpire: M.G.O'CONNELL RIVER TORRENS END		SCOREBOARD LEFT			SCOREBOARD RIGHT		NOTES Hot; slight breeze	END-OF-OVER TOTALS					
TIME	BOWLER	O.	BOWLER	O.	SCORING	BALLS	6s/4s	SCORING	BALLS	6s/4s		O.	RUNS	W.	'L'BAT	'R'BAT	EXTRAS
					BOYCOTT cap			BREARLEY Helmet-cap			ATTENDANCE (1ST) 25,004						
11.00			HOGG	1	+·¹ ↑²	3		···ː·	5		(W)	1	2		1		1
07	HURST	1			+2···+··	11					(W)(W) LB	2	7		3		4
12			"	2	P·¹·3°	15		×··	9		Wood damaged hand (gully)-TOOHEY sub.	3	10		6		
19	"	2			P×_E_···W	21	–					3⁶	10	1	6	0	4
22			}		RANDALL cap										0		
24	"	2			··×	2					M1	4					
25			"	3				·2··W	14	–		4⁵	12	2	0	2	4
28								GOOCH Helmet-cap								0	
30			"	3				↑↑·	3			5					
32½	"	3			²¹²·L×	7		·↑·¹	6		(LB)	6	16		2	1	5
37½			"	4	·			↑G_W	10	–		6⁴	16	3	2	1	5
40								GOWER Helmet-cap (LHB)								0	
42			"	4				↑·↓·	4		M2	7					
45	"	4	}		⁴·²·E·PE·W	13	–					7⁶	18	4	4	0	5
49			}		BOTHAM Helmet cap											0	
51	"	4			··ː	2						8					
52			"	5	↑↑·	4		···²·3	10			9	23			5	
58	"	5	}					²·4W	13	1	1HR →	9³	27	5	0	9	5
12.00	DRINKS		}					MILLER Helmet cap								0	
02	"	5	}					·×·····	5		·Appeal ct wkt.	10					
06	5-1-11-3 (1)		"	6	·OO·↑·4···	14	1				(NB)(NB) NB/×2	11	33		4		7
14	CARLSON	1	6-1-15-2(1)					×······	13		M3 WOOD back.	12					
18			HURST	6	⁸·¹	15		×·×E··B	20		(B)	13	35		5		8
24	"	2			··PP6·3	19		·2··	24		·Dropped long leg (HURST) (LB)	14	41		8	2	9
28			"	7	⁴·3↑↑·	22		L···¹	29			15	45		11	3	
33	"	3			·	23		····↑¹	36		·Appeal ct wkt.	16	46			4	
36			"	8	·LB	25		4··3··²	42		(LB)	17	52			9	10
41	"	4			····⁸·2···	33						18	54		13		
45			"	9	···	35		1E×···↑8·1	48	1		19	59			14	
50	"	5	9-1-26-3(2)					⁸4····L·3	56	2		20	66			21	
54			YARDLEY	1				PPP·6·2··	64			21	68			23	
58	6-1-18-0(1)	6	1-0-2-0(–)		····⁸·1	40	1	⁹·2··	67	2	2HR →	22	71	5	14	25	10
1.02	LUNCH										M3 NB/2					LUNCH	
1.41			HOGG	7	···↑·↑·4	48						23	72		15		
46	CARLSON	7			⁸·1·	50		····↑9·1	73			24	74		16	26	
50			"	8	··	52		×·×⁸·①	80		NB/3	25	75			27	
57	"	8						·····⁷4··	88	3	50 p'ship · 78 min	26	79			31	
2.00	8-1-24-0(2)		"	9	⁸·1	53	1	L_W	89	3	HOGG equalled A·E series record (36 wkts)	26	80	6	17	31	10
2.01			9-1-18-3(1)								M3 NB/3						

116

AUSTRALIA v ENGLAND

5th Test

at Adelaide

1ST DAY TIME	BOWLERS (BAILHACHE) CATHEDRAL END BOWLER	O.	(O'CONNELL) RIVER TORRENS END BOWLER	O.	BATSMEN SCOREBOARD LEFT SCORING	BALLS	6S 4S	SCOREBOARD RIGHT SCORING	BALLS	6S 4S	ENGLAND 1ST INNINGS NOTES	O.	RUNS	W.	'L' BAT	'R' BAT	EXTRAS
					BOTHAM 53	1		TAYLOR Helmet-cap	6		M3 NB/3	26²	80	6	17	0	10
2.03			HOGG	9				..... P	6			27					
08	CARLSON	9			... 1E3⁸ 244 ..	61	3					28	90		27		
12	9-1-34-0 (4)		"	10				..↑. 7.2 .6 2..2	14		• Dropped 2nd slip (BORDER)	29	94			4	
18	YARDLEY	2	10-1-22-3(1)		.P.. F76.1 643	68	1/4	P	15		•4 all-run	30	107		40		
24			HURST	10	3 3	70		.↑...•	21		•Appeal ct wkt (legside)	31	110		43		
30	"	3			8 3	71		Ro	21	–	Run out going for 4th	31¹	113	7	46	4	10
31								EMBUREY Helmet cap								0	
32	"	3			.6 .1	73		P. P 5	5			32	114		47		
35			"	11	L 34 .21	76		2E ..2..	10		BOTHAM'S 50: 127 min 3 HR →	33	119		50	2	
41 44	DRINKS "	4			747 ②2.1	81		...7 ...1	14		• "dropped" Hogg (m→b) NB/4	34	125		55	3	
48	4-0-25-0(1/1)		"	12	9131 L7 44.1	85	1/6	.7 .1 ...	18			35	135		64	4	
54	HIGGS	1			.6 .1	87		x ..W	21	–		35⁵	136	8	65	4	10
57								WILLIS No cap								0	
58	"	1						...	3			36					
3.00			"	13	... 9 7 1 1	92		2 1 ..	6			37	139		67	1	
05	"	2			x 74 E .. 61 W	97	2/6	8 .1	8			37⁷	147	9	74	2	10
08			"		HENDRICK No cap										0		
10	"	2			x .:	1						38					
11			"	14				363x2x4 622.4.4.	16	1/2	[18 off the over]	39	165			20	
17	"	3	14-1-65-3(6/1)		....:.... x	9					M4	40					
20	3-1-9-2(-/1)		HOGG 10-4-1-26-4(2)	11	9		–	3 x 3 .4.:W	20	1/3		40⁴	169	10	0	24	10
3.23	ENGLAND ALL OUT										M4 NB/4		ALL OUT				
	BATTING TIME:		225 MINUTES								328 balls						

40 The worst moment of the series – Rick Darling is struck over the heart by a short ball from Willis and only the prompt reactions of Emburey and umpire O'Connell saved his life.

AUSTRALIA 1st Innings

In reply to ENGLAND'S 169 all out

IN	OUT	MINS	No.	BATSMAN	HOW OUT	BOWLER	RUNS
3.46 (3.50) / 11.06 11.37		35	1	DARLING	C† WILLIS	BOTHAM	15
3.46	12.16	210	2	WOOD	C† RANDALL	EMBUREY	35
3.54	4.01	7	3	HUGHES	C† EMBUREY	HENDRICK	4
4.03	4.12	9	4	YALLOP *	BOWLED	HENDRICK	0
4.14	4.34	20	5	BORDER	C† TAYLOR	BOTHAM	11
4.35	4.43	8	6	CARLSON	C† TAYLOR	BOTHAM	0
4.45	11.04	79	7	YARDLEY	BOWLED	BOTHAM	28
11.37	12.53	76	8	WRIGHT †	LBW	EMBUREY	29
12.18	12.20	2	9	HOGG	BOWLED	WILLIS	0
12.23	2.20	79	10	HIGGS	RUN OUT (GOWER)		16
12.55	(2.20)	47	11	HURST	NOT OUT		17

* CAPTAIN   † WICKET-KEEPER

EXTRAS	b 1 lb 3 w - nb 5	9
TOTAL (OFF 53.4 OVERS IN 296 MINUTES)		164

BOWLER	O	M	R	W	nb	HRS	OVERS	RUNS		RUNS	MINS	OVERS	LAST 50 (in mins)
WILLIS	11	1	55	1	3	1	9	27		50	103	16.4	103
HENDRICK	19	1	45	2	3	2	11	39		100	183	31.4	80
BOTHAM	11.4	0	42	4	-	3	11	31		150	274	49.2	91
EMBUREY	12	7	13	2	-	4	11	35					
Extras/Run Out			9	1									
	53.4	9	164	10									

118

WKT	TOTAL	6ˢ	4ˢ	BALLS	NOTES ON DISMISSAL
(0)	0	1	1	33	Retired hurt when 0* (5 balls, 4 min) - hit under heart by ball from WILLIS.
6	94				Hooked bouncer to long-leg.
7	114	·	1	117	Swept to deep square-leg (falling catch)
1	5	·	1	10	Pushed forward. Edged outswinger low to 4th slip.
2	10	·	·	4	Beaten by late movement - played back.
3	22	·	1	18	Edged off-drive at outswinger.
4	24	·	·	5	Edged firm-footed push at outswinger.
5	72	·	4	75	Played on via left arm - ball cut back.
9	133	·	2	69	Attempted push to mid-wicket off back foot.
8	116	·	·	1	Late on stroke. Out first ball.
10	164	·	·	63	Attempted quick single to cover.
-	·	·	1	39	-

1⁶ 11⁴ 434 balls (Including 6 no balls)

10	OVERS 7	BALLS/HOUR
3.07		RUNS/OVER
38		RUNS/100 BALLS

STUMPS : 69-4 WOOD 19* (79b, 134')
(1ST DAY) YARDLEY 28* (69b, 75')
OFF 23 OVERS IN 134 MIN.

LUNCH : 134-9 HIGGS 4* (27b, 39')
HURST 0* (7b, 7')
OFF 45 OVERS IN 256 MIN.

WKT	PARTNERSHIP		RUNS	MINS
1ˢᵗ	Darling	Wood	0*	4
	Wood	Hughes	5	7
2ⁿᵈ	Wood	Yallop	5	9
3ʳᵈ	Wood	Border	12	20
4ᵗʰ	Wood	Carlson	2	8
5ᵗʰ	Wood	Yardley	48	79
6ᵗʰ	Wood	Darling	22	31
7ᵗʰ	Wood	Wright	20	39
8ᵗʰ	Wright	Hogg	2	2
9ᵗʰ	Wright	Higgs	17	30
10ᵗʰ	Higgs	Hurst	31	47

164

AUSTRALIA v ENGLAND — 5th Test

at Adelaide

TIME	BOWLER (Cathedral End)	O.	BOWLER (R. Torrens End)	O.	SCORING (Scoreboard Left)	BALLS	6s/4s	SCORING (Scoreboard Right)	BALLS	6s/4s	NOTES	O.	RUNS	W.	'L' BAT	'R' BAT	EXTRAS
					DARLING (Helmet-cap)			WOOD (cap) (LHB)									
3.46			WILLIS	1	. . . . .	5					*Hit under heart. 'Swallowed' tongue. Carried unconscious from field on stretcher after detention by two physiotherapists. (B) Taken to hospital.	0⁵	0		0	0	–
50					HUGHES (cap)											0	
54			"	1	P 3 B . 4 .	3	1					1	5		4		1
56	HENDRICK	1			P P E W	10	1					1⁷	5	1	4	0	1
4.01					YALLOP (Helmet-cap) (LHB)											0	
03	"	1			:	1					M1	2					
04			"	2				. . (2) . . 2(6) . .	10		(NB) NB/1/2	3	10			4	2
11	"	2			. . W	4	–					3³	10	2	0	4	2
12					BORDER (cap) (LHB)											0	
14	"	2			. . 1	3		. .	12			4	11		1		
18			"	3	2 3	4		. . . . . . ↑	19			5	14		4		
24	"	3	3-0-11-0 (1)		. . . (0) . 4	10		. . .	22		(NB) NB/3	6	16		5		3
29			BOTHAM	1	7 2 1 E . 2 . 4 . . . W	18	1					7	22	3	11	4	3
34					CARLSON (Helmet-cap)											0	
35	"							P X 4 . . 2 .	30			8	24			6	
40			"	2	↑ . . E W	5	–					8⁵	24	4	0	6	3
43					YARDLEY (Helmet-cap)											0	
45			"	2	1 E↑ 3	1		. ↑	32		1HR →	9	27		3		
47	"	5			. . . . P 7	7		. ↑	34			10	28		4		
52 55	DRINKS		"	3	↑ 2 . ! . 1	11		Y P . ↑	38			11	29		5		
5.00	"	6			. 7 1 . 0 . . .	18		. 9 1	40		(NB) NB/4	12	32		6	7	4
06			"	4	8 . 1	19		E ↑ x 2 . . 3 .	47			13	36		7	10	
11	"	7	4-0-14-2 (1)		8 1	20		2 P . . 4 (0) . .	55	1	(NB) NB/5	14	42		8	14	5
17	7-1-12-2 (1)		WILLIS	4	2 1	21		. . . .	62			15	43		9		
23	EMBUREY	1			. . . .	29					M2	16					
26			"	5	2 1 8 7 . 4 . 4 1	33	2	7 . LB 2 . . 0 . ↑	67		▷DROPPED 2ND SLIP (BOTHAM) (LB) (NB) NB/6	17	56		18	16	7
33	"	2			. . . .	41					M3	18					
35			"	6	4 1 E 2 . . 4 4 1	46	4	x 6 . 1	70			19	66		27	17	
42			"	3	6-0-33-0 (5)	. . . .	54					M4 2HR →	20					
45			HENDRICK	8	. ! 1	56		L . . . . !	76		▷Dropped 2nd slip (BOTHAM)	21	68		28	18	
52	"	4			. . . .	64					M5	22					
54	4-4-0-0 (–)		9-1-15-2 (1)	9	. . . . ↑	69	4	. . 7 1	79	1		23	69	4	28	19	7
6.00	STUMPS		(1ST DAY)								M5 NB/6		STUMPS				
2ND DAY 11.00	BOTHAM	5			. ↑ . . . W	75	4	4 . 3	80		ATTENDANCE (2ND) 17,357	23⁷	72	5	28	22	7
04					DARLING	5	–				Hot: slight breeze					0	
06	"	5			1 1	6						24	73		1		
07			HENDRICK	10	x 4 7	14	1					25	77		5		
13	"	6			x 1 1	21		9 1	81			26	79		6	23	
11.18	6-0-20-3 (1)		11-1-21-2 (2)	11	. . . 6	25	1	. . . 9	85	1	M5 NB/6	27	81	5	7	24	7

AUSTRALIA v ENGLAND — 5th Test

at Adelaide

2ND DAY	BOWLERS (BAILHACHE) CATHEDRAL END	O.	(O'CONNELL) R. TORRENS END	O.	BATSMEN SCOREBOARD LEFT	BALLS	6s/4s	SCOREBOARD RIGHT	BALLS	6s/4s	AUSTRALIA 1ST INNINGS NOTES	O.	RUNS	W.	'L' BAT	'R' BAT	EXTRAS
TIME	BOWLER		BOWLER		DARLING	25	1	WOOD	85	1	MS NB/6	27	81	5	7	24	7
11.24	BOTHAM	7						···· 2⁴ ····	93		• Hit on shoulder	28	83			26	
29			HENDRICK	12	··· 2 2	30		9 · ¹LB	96		(LB)	29	87		9	27	8
34	"	8			↑7 ↑8 6· W	33	1/1	↑ 35 ·1	98			29⁵	94	6	15	28	8
37					WRIGHT	cap									0		
39	"	8			Y···	3						30					
41			"	13	8 ·2······	10		8 ·1	99		3 HR →	31	97		2	29	
47		9	13-1-27-2 (2)		• ¹E ↑6 ·· 3 ··3	16		2 ·1 7·1	101		• Appeal ct wkt	32	105		8	31	
53	9-0-37-4 (1/1)		EMBUREY	5	·······³·2	24						33	107		10		
57	WILLIS	7			·1⁸	26		6·1 ·2···⁵	107			34	111		11	34	
12.02 06	DRINKS		"	6	··1³	29		L Y L Y	112			35	112		12		
10	"	8			·1⁴ ····	34		·· 1⁴	115			36	114		13	35	
16			"	7				·W⁷	117	1		36²	114	7	13	35	8
16²								HOGG	Helmet -cap		(Batsmen crossed)					0	
18			"	7	·2·····	40						37	116		15		
20	"	9						W˟	1	–		37¹	116	8	15	0	8
20²								HIGGS	cap		LEVER sub for BOTHAM					0	
23	"	9			7 7⁴ ·24····	46	1	7s ·3	1		• 1+2 overthrows (Gower)	38	125		21	3	
28			"	8				··········	9		M 6	39					
31	"	10			··········	54					M 7	40					
36			"	9				F Y ····	17		Botham back M 8	41					
39	"	11	9-6-5-1 (–)		2 3 ˟6 ·2·4··1	62	2	•			• Ro chance (GOOCH) 4 HR →	42	132		28		
46	11-1-55-1 (7)		HENDRICK	14	2 ·1	64		˟ E ····	23			43	133		29		
52	EMBUREY	10			···· W	69	2					43⁵	133	9	29	3	8
53					HURST	cap									0		
55	"	10			···P	3					M 9	44					
57	10-7-5-2 (–)		15-1-29-2 (2)	15	˟ Y ··	7	–	˟ ·· 8·1	27	–	M 9 NB/6	45	134	9	0	4	8
1.02	LUNCH										LUNCH						
1.40	EMBUREY	11						P E 9E ···· ··3	35			46	137			7	
43			HENDRICK	16	˟·· 4·1	10		˟ ·· 6 ·1 LB	40		(LB)	47	140		1	8	9
48²'	"	12			P 4 ·4··	17	1	7·1	41			48	145		5	9	
51	12-7-13-2 (1)		"	17	··· 2 6 ·1 ·1	22		2 ·1 ˟2 ·1	44			49	149		7	11	
57	BOTHAM	10			6s ·1 ·	25		···· 2·1	49			50	151		8	12	
2.01	"			18	3 4 ·2·1	30		3s ·1 ˟··	52			51	155		11	13	
07	"	11			4 ·1	32		···· ˟ 1Ex ·2·1	58			52	158		12	15	
12			"	19	4 E ˟4 ··2··3	39		9 ·1	59			53	164		17	16	
18	11-4-0-42-4 (1)12		19-1-45-2 (2)			39	1	˟ Ro ····	63	–	M 9 NB/6	53⁴	164	10	17	16	9
2.20	AUSTRALIA ALL OUT										434 balls		ALL	OUT			
	ENGLAND LEAD : 5										BATTING TIME: 296 MINUTES						

ENGLAND 2nd Innings
5 runs ahead on 1st Innings

IN	OUT	MINS	No.	BATSMAN	HOW OUT	BOWLER	RUNS
2.32	12.16	265	1	BOYCOTT	Cᵀ HUGHES	HURST	49
2.32	4.13	82	2	BREARLEY *	LBW	CARLSON	9
4.15	5.12	57	3	RANDALL	Cᵀ YARDLEY	HURST	15
5.14	11.39	85	4	GOOCH	BOWLED	CARLSON	18
11.43	12.56	72	5	GOWER	LBW	HIGGS	21
12.20	12.50	30	6	BOTHAM	Cᵀ YARDLEY	HURST	7
12.52	5.47	235	7	MILLER	Cᵀ WRIGHT	HURST	64
12.58	12.58	361	8	TAYLOR †	Cᵀ WRIGHT	HOGG	97
5.49	1.57	147	9	EMBUREY	BOWLED	HOGG	42
1.40	2.15	35	10	WILLIS	Cᵀ WRIGHT	HOGG	12
1.59	(2.15)	16	11	HENDRICK	NOT OUT		3
				* CAPTAIN † WICKET-KEEPER	EXTRAS	b 1 lb 16 w 2 nb 4	23

TOTAL (OFF 142.6 OVERS IN 703 MINUTES) **360**

BOWLER	O	M	R	W	nb/w
HOGG	27⁶	7	59	3	2/-
HURST	37	9	97	4	1/2
CARLSON	27	8	41	2	-
YARDLEY	20	6	60	0	2/-
HIGGS	28	4	75	1	-
BORDER	3	2	5	0	-
Extras			23		
	142.6	36	360	10	

HRS	OVERS	RUNS
1	12	22
2	12	22
3	12	35
4	12	21
5	12	30
6	10	47
7	13	27
8	15	34
9	13	29
10	13	30
11	12	38

RUNS	MINS	OVERS	LAST 50 (in mins)
50	128	25.6	128
100	237	47.4	109
150	322	63.6	85
200	410	80.6	88
250	505	103.6	95
300	603	124.5	98
350	692	141.1	89

2ND NEW BALL taken at 2.01 pm on 3rd DAY
- ENGLAND 161-6 after 65.3 overs.
3RD NEW BALL taken at 12.21 pm on 4th DAY
- ENGLAND 324-7 after 130.6 overs.

WKT	TOTAL	6s	4s	BALLS	NOTES ON DISMISSAL
4	106	·	2	212	Followed ball which left him – 1st slip catch, high to his right.
1	31	·	·	65	Shuffled across stumps – missed ball which kept low.
2	57	·	2	50	Mishooked bouncer – skier to mid-wicket.
3	97	·	2	74	Pushed forward and outside line of ball which hit off stump.
6	132	·	3	54	Missed pull at long-hop.
5	130	·	1	29	Edged off-drive hard to 3rd slip.
7	267	·	5	203	Edged leg glance – leg-side catch.
8	336	·	6	300	Edged leg glance at slower ball – leg-side catch. EQUALLED HIS HIGHEST F-C SCORE
9	347	·	4	132	Late on yorker. Highest score in Tests.
10	360	·	1	18	Edged attempt at vast off side hit.
-	-	·	·	10	-

0^6 26^4 1,147 balls (including 5 no balls)

12 OVERS	1 BALLS/HOUR
2·52	RUNS/OVER
31	RUNS/100 BALLS

TEA: 26-0
BOYCOTT 17* (62b, 70 min)
BREARLEY 7* (50b, 70 min)
OFF 14 OVERS IN 70 MINUTES

STUMPS: 82-2
(2ND DAY)
BOYCOTT 38* (151b, 189 min)
GOOCH 11* (39b, 46 min)
OFF 38 OVERS IN 189 MINUTES

LUNCH: 134-6
MILLER 0* (2b, 8 min)
TAYLOR 2* (4b, 2 min)
OFF 61 OVERS IN 309 MINUTES

TEA: 213-6
MILLER 31* (78b, 128 min)
TAYLOR 46* (120b, 122 min)
OFF 85 OVERS IN 429 MINUTES

STUMPS: 272-7
(3RD DAY)
TAYLOR 69* (211b, 244 min)
EMBUREY 0* (9b, 13 min)
OFF 113 OVERS IN 551 MINUTES

LUNCH: 336-8
EMBUREY 33* (114b, 130 min)
OFF 137 OVERS IN 668 MINUTES

WKT	PARTNERSHIP		RUNS	MINS
1st	Boycott	Brearley	31	82
2nd	Boycott	Randall	26	57
3rd	Boycott	Gooch	40	85
4th	Boycott	Gower	9	33
5th	Gower	Botham	24	30
6th	Gower	Miller	2	4
7th	Miller	Taylor	135†	229
8th	Miller	Emburey	69	130
9th	Emburey	Willis	11	17
10th	Willis	Hendrick	13	16

† RECORD ENGLAND 7TH WICKET P'SHIP AT ADELAIDE
360

123

41 Brearley lbw b Carlson 9 – Carlson, supported by a chorus from Border, Darling, and fellow debutant Wright, claims his first Test wicket.

AUSTRALIA v ENGLAND — 5th Test
at Adelaide

2ND DAY TIME	BOWLERS (O'CONNELL) CATHEDRAL END — BOWLER	O.	(BAILHACHE) R. TORRENS END — BOWLER	O.	BATSMEN SCOREBOARD LEFT — SCORING	BALLS	6s/4s	SCOREBOARD RIGHT — SCORING	BALLS	6s/4s	ENGLAND 2ND INNINGS NOTES	O.	RUNS	W.	L BAT	R BAT	EXTRAS
					BREARLEY (Helmet/Cap)	6		BOYCOTT (cap)	2								
2.32	HOGG	1			....:.x.	6		.B.	2		Ⓑ M1	1	1				1
37			HURST	1				x. .2...x.	10			2	3			2	
42	"	2			7 1	7		....	17			3	4		1		
48			"	2	......2.	15						4	6		3		
53	"	3						.....P 2↑ 4	25	1		5	10			6	
58	3-1-5-0 (1)		"	3	L P	23					Toohey sub for Hogg M2 (2 overs)	6					
3.04	CARLSON	1			.....	28		..1 1E	28			7	11			7	
08			"	4	.	29		....x 3 1E	35			8	14			10	
13	"	2	4-1-7-0 (-)		...	32		.↑.: 1E LB 2.	40		•Appeal ct wkt (LB)	9	17			12	2
18			HOGG	4				...3 2....	48			10	19			14	
23	"	3			L P	40					M3	11					
27	3-1-3-0 (-)		"	5	..	42		...↑.. 1 3	54		1 HR →	12	22			17	
33	YARDLEY	1						.P.....P	62		M4	13					
38	1-1-0-0 (-)		"	6	8 2......L 2	50	–		62	1	BREARLEY on '3' for 46' Short run last 2 balls	14	26	–	7	17	2
3.42	TEA										M4 NB/-			T E A		
4.01	CARLSON	4						EP	70		M5	15					
04			HOGG	7	...-....: 3LB	58					M6 (3LB)	16	29				5
10	"	5			L 2 L ..2..W	65	–					16/7	31	1	9	17	5
13					RANDALL (cap)										0		
15	"	5			.	1						17					
16			"	8				↑.....4	78			18	32			18	
21	"	6						....	86		M7	19					
25			"	9	..x.. 7 1	6		↑...	89		Toohey sub for HIGGS (2 overs)	20	33		1		
32	"	7			......: 7	14						21	34		2		
35			"	10	⊙4.↑!.. 1↑3 ↑↑2 1.1	22	1	S 1	90		(NB) NB/1	22	41		7	19	6
42			"	8	4 1	23		8 .1	97			23	43		8	20	
47			HURST	5	E 1	30		.	98		2HR →	24	44		9		
52	"	9			7s ..1	33		.7 2...	103			25	47		10	22	
56	9-3-11-1 (-)		"	6	..x.. ↑8 4..	41	2					26	51		14		
5.01 04	DRINKS HIGGS	1			...P.	48		1 1	104			27	52			23	
08			"	7	3 ↑7 1W 50	50	2	↑.1 ↑7 6 ..3 1	109			27/7	57	2	15	27	6
12					GOOCH (Helmet/Cap)										0		
14			"	7	2 2	1						28	59		2		
15	"	2						......3 4	117	2		29	63			31	
19			"	8	P E 3LB	7		.-	119		(3LB) M8	30	66				9
24	"	3			2 7 4..1	11	1	....	123			31	71		7		
28			"	9	...-..P.	19					M9	32					
33	"	4	9-3-19-1 (1)					....3 2.	131			33	73			33	
5.37	4-0-12-0 (2)		HOGG	11	....:..↑.	27	1		131	2	M10 NB/1	34	73	2	7	33	9

AUSTRALIA v ENGLAND — 5th Test

at Adelaide

2nd DAY TIME	BOWLERS (O'Connell) CATHEDRAL END BOWLER	O.	(Bailhache) R.TORRENS END BOWLER	O.	BATSMEN SCOREBOARD LEFT SCORING	BALLS	6s/4s	SCOREBOARD RIGHT SCORING	BALLS	6s/4s	NOTES	END-OF-OVER TOTALS O.	RUNS	W.	'L' BAT	'R' BAT	EXTRAS
					GOOCH	27	1	BOYCOTT	131	2	M10 NB/1	34	73	2	7	33	9
5.43	HIGGS	5			7 1E 21 ..x	32		4 8 .1	134			35	78		10	35	
47			HOGG	12	..	34		....1 9	140		3 HR →	36	79			36	
52	"	6	12-3-23-0 (2)		....1 7	39		4 .1 8	143			37	82		11	38	
57	6-0-20-0 (2)		YARDLEY	2		39	1	....	151	2	M11 NB/1	38	82	2	11	38	9
6.00	STUMPS		(2ND DAY)												STUMPS		
3RD DAY 11.00	CARLSON	10			......3 7	47					ATTENDANCE (3rd) 13,965	39	85		14		
04			HOGG	13	....	55					very hot – no wind M12	40					
09	"	11			..	57		.L ...1 4	157			41	86			39	
13			"	14				.. 8 .2	165			42	88			41	
18	"	12			....	65					M13	43					
22			"	15	8 .4 1..	70	2	..6 ..1	168			44	93		18	42	
27	"	13				72		.L 6 ...1	174			45	94			43	
31			"	16				..O 9 .2....	183		(NB) NB/2 Toohey sub for HOGG 11-38 to 12-32	46	97			45	10
38	"	14	16-4-32-0 (3)		YE x ±W	74	2					46	97	3	18	45	10
39	DRINKS				GOWER Helmet cap (LHB)										0		
43	"	14			.....E	6					M14	47					
45			HURST	10	....	10		...3 4	187		4 HR →	48	100			48	
51	"	15						L	195		M15	49					
55			"	11	..1 .....1 3	16		2LB↑ ..	197		(2LB)	50	103		1		12
12.00	"	16			9 .1 ...3	20		...1 4	201		YALLOP off – 1 ball. (To persuade HOGG to return.)	51	105			2	49
05			"	12				P↑ .↑.↑	209		W M16	52	106				13
10	"	17			....	28					M17	53					
15			"	13				.. E W	212	2		53	106	4	2	49	13
16	DRINKS							BOTHAM Helmet cap			• strained right knee					0	
20	"		"	13				...↑1 7	5			54	107			1	
23	"	18			.1 4	30		Y 8 1	11			55	109			3	2
27			"	14	8 3 4..4.1 9	35	2	...1 4	14			56	118		12		
32	"	19			9 6 2.1	38		..4.. 4	19	1	HOGG back	57	125		15	6	
37	19-7-27-2 (1)		"	15	....	46					M18	58					
42	HIGGS	7			...7 4	50	3	...1 4	23			59	130		19	7	
46			"	16				...↑1 E W	29	1		59	130	5	19	7	13
50								MILLER Helmet cap								0	
52			"	16				..	2		M19 5 HR →	60					
54	"	8	16-6-33-3 (3)		..2 7 W	54	3					60	132	6	21	0	13
56					TAYLOR Helmet -cap										0		
58	8-0-29-1 (3)	8	"		E 1E ..2	4	–		2	–		61	134	6	2	0	13
1.00	LUNCH										M19 NB/2			LUNCH			

126

AUSTRALIA v ENGLAND — 5th Test

at Adelaide

3RD DAY TIME	BOWLERS (O'Connell) CATHEDRAL END — BOWLER	O.	(Bailhache) R. TORRENS END — BOWLER	O.	BATSMEN SCOREBOARD LEFT — SCORING	BALLS	6s/4s	SCOREBOARD RIGHT — SCORING	BALLS	6s/4s	ENGLAND 2ND INNINGS — NOTES	O.	RUNS	W.	L BAT	R BAT	EXTRAS
					TAYLOR	4	-	MILLER	2	-	M 19 NB/2	61	134	6	2	0	13
1.40			HURST	17	8·2·6	6		··7·4··3 PEI	8	1		62	143		4	7	
46	HIGGS	·9			3·4····	11	1	·· LB	11		LB	63	148		8		14
50			"	18				·····44 18+7!	19	3		64	156			15	
55	"	10			5·3	13		2····· 1E	25			65	161		11	17	
59	10-0-38-1 (4)		"	19	····1 ↑·9	19		··	27		NEW BALL/2 ↑ taken at 2·01 pm	66	162		12		
2.05	HOGG	17			···:3 YE 1E	27						67	165		15		
10			"	20	2·1 8 7 8 1	30		?4··1 9	32		2LB	68	172		19	18	16
16	"	18			···2·3	35		····	35			69	175		22		
21 24	DRINKS 18-4-38-0 (3)		"	21	···+1 P 7S	41		··L	37		W 6HR→	70	177		23		17
31	CARLSON	20	21-6-57-3 (6)		·1·1 L 1E	44		····1	42			71	178		24		
35			HOGG	19	········L	52					M20	72					
40	"	21			↑···	55		··2·1 8 6	47		Toohey sub for DARLING	73	181			21	
44	"		"	20	·······	61		·1 8	49		50 p'ship in 67 min.	74	182			22	
50	"	22			·····	65		···3 7	53			75	185			25	
54	22-7-34-2 (1)		"	21	EYL·1·21 29	71		·1 7	55			76	189		27	26	
59 3.02	DRINKS YARDLEY	3	21-5-43-0 (3)		·········	79					DARLING back. M21	77					
06			CARLSON	23	·2····· 9	86		1 2	56			78	192		29	27	
10	"	4			2·8·	88		·····3 P 9E	62			79	197		31	30	
16			"	24				·········	70		M22	80					
20	"	5			·····3 4	94		P··	72			81	200		34		
24			"	25	····1	99		··L	75			82	201		35		
27	"	6	25-8-28-2 (1)		2··1 1E 7	105		··	77		7HR→	83	204		38		
31			HIGGS	11	·2··· 1E P	113						84	206		40		
36	7-3-18-0 (1)	7	11-0-40-1 (4)		····4··2 4 2	120	2	1 6	78	3	M22 NB/2	85	213	6	46	31	17
3.40	TEA										TEA						
4.00			HIGGS	12	···1	123		····1 4	83			86	214			32	
03	YARDLEY	8			·1	124		·1·1 P x 7	90			87	215			33	
07	"		"	13	···1	127		····1 8	95			88	216			34	
10	"	9			·1	128		····1 7	102			89	217			35	
14			"	14	LB	129		·1 2·4· 2E 8 3	109	4	LB	90	225			42	18
17	"	10			····1 67 41	136	3	·1	110		TAYLOR'S 50: 142 min 4 all-run	91	230		51		
22			"	15	········1 x P	144					M 23	92					
25	"	11						···:O PP	119		NB NB/3 M24	93	231				19
30			"	16	········1	152					M 25	94					
33	"	12						·········	127		M 26	95					
37			"	17	1·6	153		·····4 4	134		100 P'SHIP: 158 min	96	233		52	43	
40 43	DRINKS	13			·1	154		····41 78	141	5	Toohey sub for WOOD (1 over)	97	238			48	
48			"	18	········1	159		·········	149		M 27 8HR→	98					
4.50	14-5-34-0 (3)	14	18-3-51-1 (5)		·1 ···	159	3	··3 9	152	5	MILLER'S 50: 180 min M 27 NB/3	99	242	6	53	51	19

AUSTRALIA v ENGLAND — 5th Test
at Adelaide

ENGLAND 2ND INNINGS

3RD DAY TIME	BOWLER (Cathedral End)	O.	BOWLER (R. Torrens End)	O.	SCORING (Left)	BALLS	6s/4s	SCORING (Right)	BALLS	6s/4s	NOTES	O.	RUNS	W.	'L'BAT	'R'BAT	EXTRAS
					TAYLOR	159	3	MILLER	152	5	M 27 NB/3	99	242	6	53	51	19
4.54			HIGGS	19	.	160		2	159		°Dropped slip (BORDER)	100	243			52	
58	YARDLEY	15	19-3-52-1 (5)		..	162		P...8	165			101	244			53	
5.02	15-5-35-0 (3)		HURST	22				LP.6....2	173			102	246			55	
09	HIGGS	20			9.3	164		x	179			103	249		56		
13			"	23	↑....↑LB	170		..	181		RECORD ENGLAND 7TH WCT P'SHIP at (LB) ADELAIDE M28	104	250				20
18		"	21		x8.1	176		9.3	183			105	254		57	58	
21 / 25	DRINKS		"	24	......6.1	182		8.1	185			106	256		58	59	
30	"	22			7 7	184		3 4.2	191			107	261		60	62	
33	22-3-64-1 (5)		"	25	66.7 3.1	187		xL	196		°Ran 4 - 1 short	108	265		64		
39	BORDER	1			....	195					M 29	109					
43			"	26				8↑E 2..W	203	5	.	109/7	267	7	64	64	20
47								EMBUREY	Helmet cap							0	
49			"	26				..	1			110					
50	"	2	26-7-67-4 (6)		..•	203					°Stumping appeal M30 9/HR→	111					
54			YARDLEY	16				....	9		M 31	112					
58	3-2-5-0 (1)	3	16-6-35-0 (3)		...3.4.7..1	211	4		9	-	M 31 NB/3	113	272	7	69	0	20
6.02	STUMPS		(3RD DAY)													STUMPS	
4TH DAY 11.01			HURST	27	x.8..	219					ATTENDANCE (4th) 10,508	114	274		71		
06	CARLSON	26			.1	221		1E .1	15		Hot - slight breeze.	115	276		72	1	
10			"	28	....	229					M 32	116					
15	"	27			....	233		...9.1	19			117	277			2	
19	27-8-41-2 (1)		"	29	P...LB	239		2.1 9.1	21		(LB)	118	280			4	21
24	HIGGS	23			....	245		P8.1	23			119	281			5	
28			"	30	5.3	247		8.1 ...19.1	29			120	286		75	7	
33	"	24			'			L	37		M 33	121					
36			"	31	....	255					M 34	122					
40 / 43½	DRINKS "	25	31-9-76-4 (6)					1E P..2....	45		°Missed sweep - ball hit his 'visor'.	123	288			9	
47			YARDLEY	17	6.1	256		64 44.	52	2	°4 all-run 10/HR→ °Dropped slip (BORDER)	124	297		76	17	
52¼	"	26			6.1	257		P8 ..2...	59			125	300		77	19	
55			"	18	P8 2.⊙..P6 4	266	5				(NB) NB/4	126	307		83		22
12.00	"	27			...P..	271		P7.1	62			127	308			20	
03			"	19	..8.2..	276		4 6.21	65			128	313		85	23	
08	"	28						....8.4...	73	3	50 p'ship in 81 min	129	317			27	
12	28-4-75-1 (6)		"	20	7 6.41	279	6	LP.....	78			130	322		90		
17	HOGG	22	20-6-60-0 (7)		.8 2...t.	287					†NEW BALL/3 taken at 12.21pm	131	324		92		
23 / 26	DRINKS		HURST	32	7S① .	289		7...75.1	85		NB/5	132	327		93	29	
32	"	23						P........	93		M 35	133					
37			"	33	5S.1	291		t...6x2.	99			134	330		94	31	
12.42	24-6-47-0 (3)	24	33-9-82-4 (6)		3S ..	295	6	...8.1	103	3	M 35 NB/5	135	332	7	95	32	22

AUSTRALIA v ENGLAND

at Adelaide

5th Test

4TH DAY TIME	BOWLERS (O'CONNELL) CATHEDRAL END BOWLER	O.	(BAILHACHE) R.TORRENS END BOWLER	O.	BATSMEN SCOREBOARD LEFT SCORING	BALLS	6s/4s	SCOREBOARD RIGHT SCORING	BALLS	6s/4s	ENGLAND 2ND INNINGS NOTES	O.	RUNS	W.	L BAT	R BAT	EXTRAS
					TAYLOR	295	6	EMBUREY	103	3	M35 NB/5	135	332	7	95	32	22
12.48			HURST	34	7 2.↑	299		x..7	107		11 HR →	136	335		97	33	
53	HOGG	25	34-9-85-4(6)		E W	300	6	......L LB	114	3	(LB) M36 NB/5	137	336	8	97	33	23
	25-7-47-1 (3)																
12.58 LUNCH					WILLIS	NO CAP					last bam from short run-up				LUNCH		
1.40			HURST	35	1E 2....	5		P..9	117			138	339		2	34	
45	HOGG	26			.	6		6 8 L 9b 2.4...1	124	4	• Leg-side chance to wk • Hit in chest.	139	346			41	
51	"		"	36	..	8		x...7	130			140	347			42	
56	"	27						Yx W	132	4		140²	347	9	2	42	23
57								HENDRICK	NO CAP							0	
59	"	27			4 .1	10		P7 ...1	4		• Dropped gully (YARDLEY)	141	349		3	1	
2.04			"	37	2 1E x4 42.1	14	1	...1 2•	8		Wood misjudged bounce - hit on jaw.	142	357		10	2	
11	27.6-7-59-3(4)	28	37-9-97-4(7)		E 5 x E .2.W	18	1	x 8 .1	10	-	(mid-off) TOOHEY sub. • Dropped DARLING (dp straight)	142⁶	360	10	12	3	23
2.15	ENGLAND ALL OUT										M 36 NB/5		ALL	OUT			
	BATTING TIME: 703 MINUTES							1,147 balls									

AUSTRALIA REQUIRE 366 RUNS TO WIN IN A MINIMUM OF 553 MINUTES

42 and 43 A record partnership – Bob Taylor *(left)* and Geoff Miller in action during England's highest seventh-wicket partnership at Adelaide. Hughes gives a cameo of a day in the life of a short-leg.

AUSTRALIA 2nd Innings

Requiring **366** runs to win in a minimum of **553** minutes

IN	OUT	MINS	No.	BATSMAN	HOW OUT	BOWLER	RUNS
2.27	3.30	63	1	WOOD	RUN OUT [BOYCOTT]		9
2.27	3.16	49	2	DARLING	BOWLED	BOTHAM	18
3.18	12.00	208	3	HUGHES	Cᵗ GOWER	HENDRICK	46
3.32	11.48	182	4	YALLOP *	BOWLED	HENDRICK	36
11.50	12.20	30	5	BORDER	BOWLED	WILLIS	1
12.02	1.53	74	6	CARLSON	Cᵗ GOWER	HENDRICK	21
12.24	12.25	1	7	YARDLEY	Cᵗ BREARLEY	WILLIS	0
12.27	12.43	16	8	WRIGHT †	Cᵗ EMBUREY	MILLER	0
12.45	12.55	10	9	HOGG	BOWLED	MILLER	2
12.57	(2.04)	30	10	HIGGS	NOT OUT		3
1.55	2.04	9	11	HURST	BOWLED	WILLIS	13

* CAPTAIN   † WICKET-KEEPER

EXTRAS	b -	lb 1	w -	nb 10	11

TOTAL (OFF **67** OVERS IN **345** MINUTES) **160**

BOWLER	O	M	R	W	nb
WILLIS	12	3	41	3	11
HENDRICK	14	6	19	3	-
BOTHAM	14	4	37	1	-
MILLER	18	3	36	2	-
EMBUREY	9	5	16	0	1
Extras/Run out			11	1	
	67	21	160	10	

HRS	OVERS	RUNS
1	10	36
2	11	24
3	14	19
4	15	35
5	10	12

RUNS	MINS	OVERS	LAST 50 (in mins)
50	97	16.1	97
100	214	44.5	117
150	339	66.1	125

2ᴺᴰ NEW BALL TAKEN AT 1.52pm on 5ᵗʰ DAY
- AUSTRALIA 147-8 AFTER 65.2 OVERS.

WKT	TOTAL	6⁵	4⁵	BALLS	NOTES ON DISMISSAL
2	36	.	.	41	Attempted single to mid-on who threw down bowler's stumps.
1	31	.	2	37	Bowled behind legs attempting leg glance.
4	120	-1⁵⁶	4	176	Edged square drive low to point's left - superb catch.
3	115	.	3	176	Misjudged line - offered no stroke to ball which hit off stump.
5	121	.	.	19	Played inside line of ball which left him and hit off stump.
9	147	.	2	51	Turned shortish ball off legs to forward square leg. Good catch.
6	121	.	.	2	Edged off-drive waist-high to 1st slip.
7	124	.	.	16	Edged off-break via pad to forward short-leg.
8	130	.	.	7	Pushed forward - beaten by off-break - bowled through 'gate'.
-	-	.	.	10	-
10	160	.	2	13	Drove over yorker.

0⁶⁵ 13⁴ 548 balls (Including 12 no balls)

11 OVERS 5 BALLS/HOUR
2.39 RUNS/OVER
29 RUNS/100 BALLS

TEA: 44-2   HUGHES 13* (23b, 25 min)   YALLOP 0* (8b, 11 min)
OFF 13 OVERS IN 76 MINUTES

STUMPS: 82-2 (4TH DAY)   HUGHES 30* (126b, 148 min)   YALLOP 16* (126b, 134 min)
OFF 40 OVERS IN 199 MINUTES

LUNCH: 131-8   CARLSON 8* (34b, 61½ min)   HIGGS 0* (7b, 6½ min)
OFF 63 OVERS IN 322 MINUTES

ENGLAND WON BY 205 RUNS
at 2.05 p.m. on the fifth (last) day —
to take a 4-1 lead in the six-match rubber.

MAN OF THE MATCH: I.T. BOTHAM

TOTAL MATCH ATTENDANCE: 70,936

WKT	PARTNERSHIP		RUNS	MINS
1ˢᵗ	Wood	Darling	31	49
2ⁿᵈ	Wood	Hughes	5	12
3ʳᵈ	Hughes	Yallop	79	182
4ᵗʰ	Hughes	Border	5	10
5ᵗʰ	Border	Carlson	1	18
6ᵗʰ	Carlson	Yardley	0	1
7ᵗʰ	Carlson	Wright	3	16
8ᵗʰ	Carlson	Hogg	6	10
9ᵗʰ	Carlson	Higgs	17	19
10ᵗʰ	Higgs	Hurst	13	9

160

AUSTRALIA v ENGLAND — 5th Test

at Adelaide

AUSTRALIA 2ND INNINGS

4TH DAY TIME	BOWLERS (O'CONNELL) CATHEDRAL END — BOWLER	O.	(BAILHACHE) R.TORRENS END — BOWLER	O.	BATSMEN SCOREBOARD LEFT — SCORING	BALLS	6s/4s	SCOREBOARD RIGHT — SCORING	BALLS	6s/4s	NOTES	O.	RUNS	W.	'L' BAT	'R' BAT	EXTRAS
					WOOD cap (LHB)			DARLING Helmet-cap									
2.27			WILLIS	1	··×·⁹1	4		··⊙⊙··ᴾᴾᴾ	6		NB NB NB/½	1	3		1		2
34	HENDRICK	1			·³ˢ1	6		·····ᴾ·	12			2	4		2		
38	"		"	2	×·²1 ·⊙··	12		··⁷	15		NB NB/3	3	7		3	1	3
45	"	2			··⁵³	15		····⁷1	20			4	11		6	2	
50	"		"	3	··⁷1 ⁷ˢ⊙	19		⁺⁸↑ ⊙4··⊙1 ⁺⁸↑	26	1	● Ro chance (DARLING) Gower throw. NB/4'S	5	19		8	7	4
58	"	3	3-0-10-0 (1)		········1	27					M1	6					
3.03			BOTHAM	1	ᴾ³⁵1	30		·³·4·8 1 ⁺⁸	31	2		7	26		9	13	
08	"	4			······⁻1	36		·⁶1	33		● Emburey injured hand stopping cut (Gully)	8	27			14	
14	4-1-6-0 (—)		"	2	⎫			²²×× 22·W	37	2	— LEVER sub. (2 overs)	8	31	1	9	18	4
16					⎬			HUGHES cap ⁵ˢ4ˢ								0	
18			"	2	⎭ ·⁰×·1	39		²₀5	1	1/—	● 3 + 2 overthrows (GOOCH) ● Appeal at wkt (leg-side)	9	36			5	
23	MILLER	1						·····ᴾ·	9		● Appeal ct slip (GOOCH) M2 1HR→	10					
28	"		"	3	ᴾ Rᴏ	41	—				Treatment for WOOD (plaster on face) (2 min)	10²	36	2	9	5	4
30					YALLOP Helmet-cap (LHB)						(Batsmen crossed)				0		
32			"	3				·⁷·4·³1	15	1/2		11	44			13	
36	"	2			········	8					M3	12					
39	2-2-0-0 (—)		"	4		8	—	·········1	23	1/3	M4 NB/5	13	44	2	0	13	4
3.43	TEA		4-1-24-1 (3)								TEA						
4.00	HENDRICK	5			········×	16					M5	14					
06			WILLIS	4	···⊙·⁰·⊙⊙↑	35					NB NB NB NB⁶/7&9	15	48				8
15	"	6			··⁶1	19		·····	40		'M6 YALLOP 27'on b'.	16	49		1		
21	"		"	5	·⊙·⁷ˢ1	23		··×···	45		NB NB/10	17	51		2		9
27	"	7			·ᴸ···ᴱ	31					M7	18					
33			"	6	··⁹1	34		⁹ᴱ·⁷2·1 ··	50			19	55		3	16	
39	"	8	6-1-15-0 (1)		····⁷4···	42	1					20	59		7		
44	8-3-11-0 (1)		BOTHAM	5	···××↑·1	49		⁵1	51		2HR→	21	60			17	
49	MILLER	3			·²1	50		·⁹1 ·····	58			22	62		8	18	
52			"	6	×·ᴸ⁹1 ··	56		·⁷ˢ1	60			23	64		9	19	
58	"	4			·²1	57		····⁷1 ·	67			24	66		10	20	
5.01 04	DRINKS		"	7	×ᴸ···⁹1	64		··	68			25	67		11		
09½	"	5			···⁷1 ·	69		··⁶1	71			26	69		12	21	
13			"	8	↑··ᴸ1	76		²1	72			27	70			22	
18	"	6	8-1-29-1 (3)		·····1	81		⁸ᴱ··1	75			28	71			23	
23			EMBUREY	1				··········	83		BOTHAM off (LEVER sub) (1 over) M8	29					
26	"	7			····⁷1	88		⁶1	84			30	73		13	24	
29			"	2				·········	92		M9	31					
33	"	8			ᴾ⁸1	90		······	98			32	74		14		
36			"	3	ᴾ·1	98					M10	33					
5.40	9-2-13-0 (—)	9	3-3-0-0 (—)		···1	101	1	·⁶·2⁷·1	103	1/2	M10 NB/10	34	77	2	14	27	9

132

AUSTRALIA v ENGLAND — 5th Test

at Adelaide

4TH DAY TIME	BOWLER (O'CONNELL) CATHEDRAL END	O.	BOWLER (BAILHACHE) R.TORRENS END	O.	SCOREBOARD LEFT — SCORING	BALLS	6s/4s	SCOREBOARD RIGHT — SCORING	BALLS	5s/4s	NOTES	O.	RUNS	W.	'L' BAT	'R' BAT	EXTRAS
					YALLOP	101	1	HUGHES	103	1/2	M10 NB/10	34	77	2	14	27	9
5·43			EMBUREY	4				7 2·······	111		3HR→	35	79			29	
45½	MILLER	10			·······L	109					Round wkt to LHB M11	36					
50			"	5				·······	119		M12	37					
53	"	11			E·7 ·1	112		·····	124			38	80		15		
56			"	6	········	120					M13	39					
59	12-3-16-0(-)	12	6-5-2-0(-)		P··9 ·1	126	1	4 ·1 ·	126	1/2	M13 NB/10	40	82	2	16	30	9
6·03	STUMPS		(4TH DAY)									STUMPS					
5TH DAY 11·00			EMBUREY	7	···8 ·1	130		☉····	131		(NB) NB/11	41	84		17		10
04	MILLER	13			····3 P·	136		·3 ·1	133		50 p'ship in 140 min	42	86		18	31	
08	"		"	8	···3 ·1	141		·8 ··	136		ATTENDANCE (5th) 4,102	43	88		19	32	
11	"	14			···2°	149					• In air over gully	44	90		21		
14			"	9	873 ·243	153	2	8 ··	140		Hot; slight breeze.	45	101		30	34	
18	"	15	9-5-16-0(1)		··4 ·1	156		6° ·4 ·1 ·4	145	1/3	• Ro appeal (Brearley "mid-on) threw down wkt	46	107		31	39	
23	15-3-26-0(1)		HENDRICK	9	2 P 2 x 4·· ·1 ···	163	3	7 ·1	146			47	113		36	40	
29	BOTHAM	9						····· x x	154		M14	48					
34			"	10	x····· x	171					M15	49					
38	"	10			···	175		LB ···1	158		(LB) M16 4HR→	50	114				11
42 / 45 DRINKS			"	11	W	176	3	···8	162			50	115	3	36	41	11
48					BORDER cap (LHB)										0		
50			"	11	L ·1··	3						51					
52	"	11						·4·····1	170	1/4		52	120			46	
57			"	12				x···· E W	176	1/4		52	120	4	0	46	11
12·00								CARLSON Helmet cap								0	
02			"	12				··	2		M17	53					
05½	"	12			····P9 ·1	10		x ·1	3		Round wkt to LHB.	54	121		1		
09			"	13	····x	18					M18	55					
14½	"	13	13-6-18-2(2)					↑·······	11		M19	56					
20			WILLIS	7	x W	19	-					56	121	5	1	0	11
20½ DRINKS					YARDLEY Helmet cap										0		
24			"	7	E ±W	2	-					56	121	6	0	0	11
25					WRIGHT cap										0		
27			"	7	·····	5					M20	57					
31	"	14						···4 2····	19			58	123			2	
35	14-4-37-1(4/1)		"	8	x·x	13					M21	59					
40	MILLER	16			EP ··W	16	-	8 ·1	20			59	124	7	0	3	11
43					HOGG Helmet-cap										0		
45	"	16			·7 2··	4					HOGG removed helmet when facing Miller 5HR→	60	126		2		
47			"	9	x ·:·	6		↑·····4 ·3	26			61	129			6	
12·53	16.5-3-30-2(?)	17	9-3-18-2(1)		x W	7	-	···1 2	30	-	M21 NB/11 Out at 12.55pm	61	130	8	2	7	11

133

AUSTRALIA v ENGLAND — 5th Test

at Adelaide

5TH DAY TIME	BOWLERS (O'CONNELL) CATHEDRAL END — BOWLER	O.	(BAILHACHE) R.TORRENS END — BOWLER	O.	BATSMEN SCOREBOARD LEFT — SCORING	BALLS	6s/4s	SCOREBOARD RIGHT — SCORING	BALLS	6s/4s	AUSTRALIA 2ND INNINGS — NOTES	O.	RUNS	W.	L BAT	R BAT	EXTRAS
					HIGGS	cap		CARLSON 30		-	M 21 NB/11	61⁵	130	8	0	7	11
12.57	MILLER	17			...	3						62					
58	17-3-30-2 (1)		WILLIS	10	.ᴸ..	7	-	...³1	34	-		63	131	8	0	8	11
			10-3-19-2 (1)														
1.03½	LUNCH												LUNCH				
1.41	MILLER	18						L:...4.2³ᴱ	42	1		64	137			14	
44	18-3-36-2 (2)		WILLIS	11	x²3			.4³.⸫³	47	2		65	147			3	21
51	HENDRICK	14			.	10		..ᴸ.⁷W	51	2	† NEW BALL TAKEN at 1.52pm	65⁴	147	9	3	21	11
53								HURST	cap							0	
55	"	14						xx.¹ᴱ1	4			66	148			1	
57	14-6-19-3 (2)		" 12-3-41-3 (4)	12		10	-	3x²2.②ᴱ³³W44	13	2	NB/12	67	160	10	3	13	11
2.04	AUSTRALIA ALL OUT										M 21 NB/12		ALL OUT				
	BATTING TIME: 345 MINUTES										548 balls						
	ENGLAND WON BY 205 RUNS AND ENSURED VICTORY IN THE RUBBER.																

44 The ball that broke Mailey's record – Bryan Charlton captures Rodney Hogg bowling the ball which dismissed Willis, his 37th wicket of the rubber.

AUSTRALIA v ENGLAND

at Adelaide

45, 46 and 47: Ian Botham, 'Man of the Match' – *(top left)* Driving Hurst during his first innings 74;
(top right) Displaying his Benson and Hedges Award and cheque; *(bottom)* Giving umpire Max O'Connell
his first duck of the season, aided by Kim Hughes during the rest day visit to Yalumba vinery in the
Barossa Valley.

THE SIXTH TEST AT SYDNEY

The final humiliation of Yallop's inexperienced team was mercifully completed with a day and a half to spare. With the rubber already decided, this match was inevitably superfluous but it did allow England, smarting from a recent 2–1 defeat in the one-day internationals, to inflict the first-ever 5–1 hiding on their opposition. With those limited-overs games now an established part of the Australian tour it would seem prudent to return to a five-match rubber of Tests. Certainly the pitiful attendance at this match confirmed that the Sydney public, like its pitches, was sated with cricket of varying hues.

After Australia had won their fifth toss and recorded their 10th run out of the rubber, Graham Yallop played his finest innings. Shaking off his usual inhibitions, he showed the form which has won him such a reputation at State level. His agile footwork and confident strokeplay bore no relation to much of his batting in the earlier Tests. Assessed by the only realistic means of measuring the length of an innings, his hundred off 186 balls, was the fastest of the rubber. Gower had needed eight more balls but 26 fewer minutes to reach his century at Perth. Yallop's 121 represented 61.1 per cent of his team's total. Only four other batsmen, led by Charles Bannerman's 67.3 per cent in the very first innings of all, have contributed a higher proportion of a completed Test innings. By a strange coincidence Yallop and his fellow captain, Brearley, each scored their 1,000th run in Test cricket in this match.

Even the splendid Yallop could not prevent Australia from recording their

eighth total under 200. Once again Hendrick bowled superbly but Botham took the wickets on a pitch which looked ideal for batting. It started to turn in England's innings, the most notable feature of which was a splendid partnership of 67 in 58 minutes between Gooch and Gower. Graham Gooch had been in danger of losing his place after the Fourth Test but Tolchard's fractured cheekbone and Radley's inability to cope with Australian pitches had ensured his retention. Now, in his final innings of the rubber, he showed the form that English crowds have grown to expect. Having reached 18 for the seventh time in the rubber he managed to maintain his concentration, eschew a variety of rash strokes developed in the limited-overs game, and move confidently beyond his first 50 in 15 innings against Australia.

By the time that Australia began their final innings the pitch had become a spin bowler's paradise. After another magnificent spell from Hendrick, who has yet to find the luck but not the ability to take five wickets in an innings of a Test match, Miller and Emburey, assisted in varying degrees by their victims, completed the final rout. It was the fifth successive innings in which Australia had failed to total 200.

The final innings began some eight minutes late after the England captain and manager had, quite correctly, objected to the umpires allowing Australia's spinners an old ball at the start of the innings. Before the tour was ended, fittingly by a boundary from the victorious Brearley, Hogg (amazing everyone – especially his captain who once had to go off in search of him – by remaining on the field for an entire innings) showed that a sense of humour lurks beneath his austere image. He produced an unplayable problem for incoming batsman Randall by dropping his final delivery of a record-breaking initial series, a not-obviously artificial snake, on a perfect length.

AUSTRALIA 1st Innings v ENGLAND

at Sydney Cricket Ground on February 10, 11, 12, 14, 1979

IN	OUT	MINS	No.	BATSMAN	HOW OUT	BOWLER	RUNS
11.00	11.30	30	1	WOOD	Cᵀ BOTHAM	HENDRICK	15
11.00	11.18	18	2	HILDITCH	RUN OUT [GOOCH → EMBUREY]		3
11.20	12.59	99	3	HUGHES	Cᵀ BOTHAM	WILLIS	16
11.32	4.59	267	4	YALLOP *	Cᵀ GOWER	BOTHAM	121
1.41	2.27	46	5	TOOHEY	Cᵀ TAYLOR	BOTHAM	8
2.29	2.35	6	6	CARLSON	Cᵀ GOOCH	BOTHAM	2
2.37	2.51	14	7	YARDLEY	BOWLED	EMBUREY	7
2.53	3.02	9	8	WRIGHT †	Sᵀ TAYLOR	EMBUREY	3
3.04	4.09	47	9	HOGG	Cᵀ EMBUREY	MILLER	9
4.11	(5.03)	52	10	HIGGS	NOT OUT		9
5.02	5.03	1	11	HURST	BOWLED	BOTHAM	0

* CAPTAIN   † WICKET-KEEPER   EXTRAS   b - 1b 3   w - nb 2   5

DEBUTS: A.M.J. HILDITCH
and umpires A.R. CRAFTER, D.G. WESER.

TOTAL   (OFF 60.7 OVERS IN 303 MINUTES)   198

BOWLER	O	M	R	W	nb		HRS	OVERS	RUNS		RUNS	MINS	OVERS	LAST 50 (in mins)
WILLIS	11	4	48	1	3	1	11	22		50	92	16.3	92
HENDRICK	12	2	21	1	-	2	11.1	45		100	162	30.4	70
BOTHAM	9.7	1	57	4	1	3	11.7	42		150	231	43.7	69
EMBUREY	18	3	48	2	-	4	12	48					
MILLER	9	3	13	1	-	5	14.6	41					
BOYCOTT	1	0	6	0	-								
Extras/Run Out			5	1									
	60.7	13	198	10									

Toss: AUSTRALIA

WKT	TOTAL	6s	4s	BALLS	NOTES ON DISMISSAL
2	19	·	2	25	Edged off-drive low to 2nd slip's right. (Superb right-handed, diving catch.)
1	18	·	·	8	Failed to regain ground after 3rd slip (Gooch) returned to short leg.
3	67	·	2	86	Edged defensive push low to 2nd slip's left (two-handed catch).
9	198	·	13	212	Pulled half-volley to mid-wicket.
4	101	·	·	37	Edged off-drive to 'keeper.
5	109	·	·	5	Fended bouncer to 3rd slip's right — simple catch.
6	116	·	1	15	Misjudged line of off-break which hit leg-stump. (No stroke)
7	124	·	·	11	Went down wicket and missed drive - beaten by flight.
8	159	·	1	46	Edged off-break to short square-leg.
·	·	·	1	45	-
10	198	·	·	1	Missed ball which hit off bail - out first ball.

0⁶ 20⁴ 491 balls (including 4 no balls)

12 OVERS 0 BALLS/HOUR
3·25 RUNS/OVER
40 RUNS/100 BALLS

LUNCH: 67-3 YALLOP 29* (61b, 87') OFF 22·1 OVERS IN 119 MINS

TEA: 157-7 YALLOP 90* (154b, 208') HOGG 8* (31b, 38') OFF 46 OVERS IN 240 MINUTES

WKT	PARTNERSHIP		RUNS	MINS
1st	Wood	Hilditch	18	18
2nd	Wood	Hughes	1	10
3rd	Hughes	Yallop	48	87
4th	Yallop	Toohey	34	46
5th	Yallop	Carlson	8	6
6th	Yallop	Yardley	7	14
7th	Yallop	Wright	8	9
8th	Yallop	Hogg	35	47
9th	Yallop	Higgs	39	48
10th	Higgs	Hurst	0	1

198

AUSTRALIA v ENGLAND — 6th Test
at Sydney

1ST DAY TIME	BOWLERS Paddington End BOWLER	O.	Randwick End BOWLER	O.	BATSMEN Scoreboard Left SCORING	BALLS	6s/4s	Scoreboard Right SCORING	BALLS	6s/4s	NOTES	AUSTRALIA 1ST INNINGS End-of-over totals O.	RUNS	W.	'L' BAT	'R' BAT	EXTRAS
					WOOD (cap) (LHB)			HILDITCH (cap)			Fairly hot; humid						
11·00	WILLIS	1			·4·241 (8 8 25)	6	2	·2 (↑8)	2	2	ATTENDANCE (1st): 8,601	1	13		11	2	
06			HENDRICK	1	P x	14					M1	2					
11	"	2			·22· (48)	18		···1 (8)	6		Round wkt to LHB	3	18		15	3	
17			"	2	⌉			RO ··	8	–		3²	18	1	15	3	–
18					⌐			HUGHES (cap)								0	
20			"	2	····· ⌋	23		1 (8)	1			4	19			1	
24	"	3			·			↑x x	9		M2	5					
29			"	3	·W (E)	25	2					5²	19	2	15	1	–
30					YALLOP (Helmet/cap)(LHB)											0	
32			"	3	··1 (8)	3		···1	12			6	20			1	
36	"	4			·······1 (↑ ↑)	11					M3	7					
42			"	4				·x··x x··1 (9)	20			8	21			2	
47	"	5						·········0 (L)	29		NB NB/1 M4	9	22				1
53	5-3-18-0 (2)		"	5	·········L	19					M5	10					
57½	BOTHAM	1						·········	37		M6 1HR→	11					
12·01½ 04	DRINKS		"	6	····· (1E)	25		·· x	39		* Edged just short of GOOCH (3rd slip)	12	23			2	
09	"	2			44·x·4··1 (1E 1 x 2 LB)	32	3	··	40		LB	13	36		14		2
15			"	7	4····1 (4 L 7)	38	4	··	42			14	41		19		
20	"	3	7-2-9-1 (1)		···1 (6 ↑)	41		4···1 (7)	47	1		15	47		20	7	
26			EMBUREY	1				·······1 (6)	55			16	48			8	
30	"	4			·1 (8)	42		·1 8 ·····	62			17	50		21	9	
35	4-1-20-0 (4)		"	2	·1 (2)	44		4····· (8)	68	2		18	55		22	13	
38	WILLIS	6			21 (6 75)	46		··0·x·· (L)	75		NB NB/2	19	59		25		3
44			"	3	·1 (8 7)	51		·1 (L 7 LB)	78		LB	20	63		27	14	4
48	"	7	3-0-9-0 (1)		···1 (8 circled)	56		·1 (75 ·!)	82		NB/3	21	65		28	15	
55			MILLER	1	··1 (8)	61		··1 (8)	85		Round wkt to LHB	22	67		29	16	
58	7-1-3-23-1 (2)	8	1-0-2-0 (–)			61	4	W (E)	86	2		22¹	67	3	29	16	4
12·59	LUNCH							TOOHEY (cap)			M6 NB/3	LUNCH					
1·41	WILLIS	8						······· (E)	7		M7	23				0	
45			HENDRICK	8	····1 (7)	66		·x·	10			24	68		30		
51	"	9			3 (5)	67		·x 75	17			25	72		33	1	
57			"	9	····1 (6S)	73		·!· (LB 7)	19		LB	26	75		34	2	5
2·02	"	10			21 (78)	75		2·1 2··1 (79 7)	25			27	83		37	7	
07	10-4-35-1 (2)		"	10	·1	77		······	31			28	84		38		
13	BOTHAM	5	10-2-13-1 (1)		1··2·4·1 (4· 2 5)	85	5				↑ Round wkt	29	90		44		
19			EMBUREY	4	··1 (P 4S)	88		1 (8) ····1	36		Round wkt to LHB	30	92		45	8	
22	"	6			·422··1 (3 73 x 2)	95	6	W (E)	37	–	YALLOP'S 50: 130 min	31	101	4	54	8	5
27	6-1-35-1 (6)							CARLSON (Helmet/cap)								0	
29			5-0-17-0 (2)	5	···4·2 (7 2)	103	7	–		–	M7 NB/3	32	107	4	60	0	5

140

AUSTRALIA v ENGLAND — 6th Test

at Sydney

1st DAY TIME	BOWLERS (WESER) PADDINGTON END	O.	(CRAFTER) RANDWICK END	O.	BATSMEN SCOREBOARD LEFT SCORING	BALLS	6s/4s	SCOREBOARD RIGHT SCORING	BALLS	6s/4s	NOTES	O.	RUNS	W.	'L' BAT	'R' BAT	EXTRAS
					YALLOP	103	7	CARLSON	–	–	M7 NB/3	32	107	4	60	0	5
2.33	BOTHAM	7						8 2··W	5	–		32⁵	109	5	60	2	5
35								YARDLEY Helmet-cap								0	
37	"	7						L···	3			33					
39			EMBUREY	6	········	111					M8 3HR→	34					
41 44	DRINKS "	8			···	114		↑↑··· 1E 3 4⃝3	9	1	NB/4	35	116			7	
49			"	7				6 ·····x	15	1	* No chance – sent back after backing up (BREARLEY)	35⁶	116	6	60	7	5
51								WRIGHT (cap)								0	
53			"	7				··P	2		M9	36					
55	"	9			4··1 5 2 x	120	8	4 6s 21	4			37	124		65	3	
3.00	9-1-52-2 (8)		"	8				······x W	11	–		37⁷	124	7	65	3	5
02								HOGG Helmet								0	
04			"	8				·	1		M10	38					
05	HENDRICK	11			····44 21	127		·	2			39	127		68		
11			"	9	·····8 1	133		·P	4			40	128		69		
14	"	12			···9 1	137		↑··4	8	1		41	133		70	4	
20	12-2-21-1 (2)		"	10	·3 1	139		·P·P	14			42	134		71		
24	WILLIS	11			17782 24421	144	10	·	17		Round wkt to LHB	43	147		84		
31	11-4-48-1 (4)		"	11	4·· 3 3	146		····P·1 3	23			44	154		88	7	
35	MILLER	2			··5 1	149		·P·····	28		Yallop removed helmet. Miller round wkt to LHB.	45	155		89		
39	2-0-3-0 (–)		12-3-28-2 (2)	12	4·1 ···	154	10	P·8 ·1	31	1	M10 4HR→ NB/4	46	157	7	90	8	5
3.42	TEA															T E A	
4.00	MILLER	3						PP··P·P	39		* Leg bye disallowed M11	47					
04			EMBUREY	13	·6 1 ·····	161		8E	40		British Airways aircraft circled ground.	48	159		91	9	
07½	"	4						Y P P P EP ———W	46	1		48⁶	159	8	91	9	5
09	"							HIGGS (cap)								0	
11	"	4						··	2		M12	49					
13			"	14	6 48 1 22··	166		··1 2E	5			50	165		96	1	
17	"	5						·········	13		M13	51					
21			"	15	···5 1	170		····	17			52	166		97		
24	"	6			······6 1	177		·	18			53	167		98		
27			"	16	·····6 1	183		··P·	20			54	·168		99		
31	"	7			··3 3 1	186		1E 2····	25		YALLOP's 100 in 240'	55	171		100	3	
36			"	17	·····56 41	193	11	·	26			56	176		105		
40	"	8			4 6s ·21	196		·····	31		* Dropped wide-mid-off (BREARLEY) – skier, running	57	179		108		
44			"	18	E X···74 ·41	204	12				* shot took him to 1,001 runs in TESTS.	58	184		113		
47	"	9	18-3-48-2 (4)		·25 21	207		·····	36			59	187		116		
51	9-3-13-1 (–)		BOYCOTT	1	·8 7 4	210	13	E X·9 ·1	41		* stumping appeal	60	193		121	4	
55	BOTHAM	10	1-0-6-0 (1)		·7 x W	212	13	1E X·1 4·1	45	1	5HR→	60⁶	198	9	121	9	5
59	DRINKS				HURST (cap)											0	
5.02½	9-7-1-57-4 (9)	10			x W	1	–		45	1	M13 NB/4	60⁷	198	10	0	9	5
5.03	AUSTRALIA ALL OUT				BATTING TIME: 303 MINUTES			491 balls					ALL OUT				

AUSTRALIA 1st INNINGS

END-OF-OVER TOTALS

ENGLAND 1st Innings
In reply to AUSTRALIA'S 198 all out

IN	OUT	MINS	No.	BATSMAN	HOW OUT	BOWLER	RUNS
5.14	11.41	91	1	BOYCOTT	Ct HILDITCH	HURST	19
5.14	2.10	200	2	BREARLEY *	Ct TOOHEY	HIGGS	46
11.46	12.00	14	3	RANDALL	LBW	HOGG	7
12.02	3.10	148	4	GOOCH	St WRIGHT	HIGGS	74
2.12	11.53	141	5	GOWER	Ct WRIGHT	HIGGS	65
3.13	11.27	54	6	BOTHAM	Ct CARLSON	YARDLEY	23
11.29	12.58	89	7	MILLER	LBW	HURST	18
11.55	(3.17)	160	8	TAYLOR †	NOT OUT		36
1.40	2.00	20	9	EMBUREY	Ct HILDITCH	HURST	0
2.02	3.12	70	10	WILLIS	BOWLED	HIGGS	10
3.14	3.17	3	11	HENDRICK	Ct AND BOWLED	YARDLEY	0
* CAPTAIN † WICKET-KEEPER				EXTRAS	b 3 lb 5 w - nb 2		10

TOTAL (OFF 103 OVERS IN 505 MINUTES) **308**

BOWLER	O	M	R	W	nb		HRS	OVERS	RUNS		RUNS	MINS	OVERS	LAST 50 (in mins)
HOGG	18	6	42	1	-		1	12	26		50	116	20.7	116
HURST	20	4	58	3	1		2	10	30		100	176	34.5	60
YARDLEY	25	2	105	2	1		3	14	45		150	227	44.7	51
CARLSON	10	1	24	0	1		4	12	58		200	282	56.2	55
HIGGS	30	8	69	4	-		5	13	63		250	349	70.7	67
							6	12	34		300	485	98.5	136
Extras			10				7	13	21					
	103	21	308	10			8	11	19					

2ND NEW BALL TAKEN AT 12.39 pm on 3RD DAY
- ENGLAND 265-6 after 80.4 overs

142

WKT	TOTAL	6s	4s	BALLS	NOTES ON DISMISSAL
1	37	·	1	80	Edged backfoot defensive stroke low to 2nd slip.
3	115	·	3	148	Checked cover-drive - leg break took thick edge to cover (falling).
2	46	·	1	9	Played back and missed ball which kept low and came back.
4	182	1	7	136	Beaten by flight and turn - missed drive.
6	247	·	6	111	Edged googly which turned and bounced sharply.
5	233	·	2	53	Drove half-volley to mid-off (head-high, two-handed catch).
7	270	·	2	84	Beaten by 'breakback'.
·	·	·	2	118	-
8	280	·	·	18	'Hung out' bat at short off-side ball; edged to 2nd slip.
9	306	·	·	63	Missed sweep at leg-break.
10	308	·	·	7	Mistimed straight hit.

1^6 24^4 827 balls (Including 3 no balls)

12 OVERS 2 BALLS/HOUR
2·99 RUNS/OVER
37 RUNS/100 BALLS

STUMPS: 24-0
(1ST DAY)
BOYCOTT 6* (39b, 50')
BREARLEY 18* (41b, 50')
OFF 10 OVERS IN 50 MINUTES

LUNCH: 98-2
BREARLEY 41* (122b, 170')
GOOCH 29* (55b, 58')
OFF 33 OVERS IN 170 MINUTES

TEA: 216-4
GOWER 47* (71b, 88')
BOTHAM 17* (22b, 27')
OFF 58 OVERS IN 290 MINUTES

STORM DURING TEA INTERVAL PREVENTED FURTHER PLAY
STUMPS (2ND DAY) 216-4 [120 MINUTES LOST 2ND DAY]

LUNCH: 270-7
TAYLOR 10* (51b, 63')
OFF 83.6 OVERS IN 408 MINUTES

TEA INTERVAL TAKEN AT END OF INNINGS

WKT	PARTNERSHIP		RUNS	MINS
1st	Boycott	Brearley	37	91
2nd	Brearley	Randall	9	14
3rd	Brearley	Gooch	69	88
4th	Gooch	Gower	67	58
5th	Gower	Botham	51	54
6th	Gower	Miller	14	24
7th	Miller	Taylor	23	63
8th	Taylor	Emburey	10	20
9th	Taylor	Willis	26	70
10th	Taylor	Hendrick	2	3

308

AUSTRALIA v ENGLAND — 6th Test

at Sydney

ENGLAND 1ST INNINGS

TIME	BOWLER (PADDINGTON END)	O.	BOWLER (RANDWICK END)	O.	SCOREBOARD LEFT SCORING	BALLS	6s/4s	SCOREBOARD RIGHT SCORING	BALLS	6s/4s	NOTES	O.	RUNS	W.	'L' BAT	'R' BAT	EXTRAS
					BOYCOTT (cap)			BREARLEY (Helmet cap)									
5.14	HOGG	1			....	8					M1	1					
19			HURST	1	³4......	15	1	7...	1			2	5		4	1	
26	"	2						ˣ....	9		M2	3					
31			"	2	......↑	23					M3	4					
36	"	3						......³	17			5	6			2	
41			"	3	.	24		.....² 1	24			6	7			3	
46	"	4	3-1-6-0 (1)		......	30		⁶.3	26			7	10			6	
51	4-2-4-0 (-)		YARDLEY	1				...ᵉ4.ˣ..	34	1	• Dropped slip (HUGHES)	8	14			10	
55	HURST	4			7.P.↑.ˣ 1	37		9 1	35		BOYCOTT on '4' for 26'	9	16		5	11	
59½	4-1-8-0 (1)		2-0-12-0 (2)	2	⁸.1	39	1	¹.3 ⁸4....	41	2	M3 NB/-	10	24	-	6	18	-
6.04	STUMPS		(1ST DAY)													STUMPS	
2ND DAY 11.00	HOGG	5			...ˣ⁷ˢ1	44		...	44		ATTENDANCE (2nd): 8,187	11	25		7		
06			HURST	5	⁷ˢ1	45		......ᴾ	51		Hot; humid; no cloud 1 HR→	12	26		8		
11	"	6			..⁵2	53						13	28		10		
18			"	6				....	59		M4	14					
23	"	7			....ᴾ²3	59		.ᶠ	61			15	31		13		
29	7-2-10-0 (-)		"	7	²2..↑..¹	67						16	34	-	16		
35	CARLSON	1			²2.1	73		..	63			17	37		19		
39	1-0-3-0 (-)		"	8	..ˣ..ᴱ W	80	1					17⁷	37	1	19	18	-
41	DRINKS (11.42½)				RANDALL (cap)										0		
46			"	8	³2.↑	2					NB¹1	18	39		2		
48	HOGG	8			..⁷4	5	1	⁷ˢ....1	68		BREARLEY on 18 for 54'	19	44		6	19	
54			"	9	..²1	8		ᴸᴮ..	73		(LB)	20	46		7		1
59½	"	9	9-2-15-1 (1)		ᴸW	9	1					20¹	46	2	7	19	1
12.00					GOOCH (Helmet cap)										0		
02	"	9			⁷1 ⁵1	3		.ᴾ⁸.ᶠ⁵3	77			21	52		2	23	
08	9-2-21-1 (1)		YARDLEY	3				.⁷²2..	85		2 HR→	22	56			27	
12	CARLSON	2			....	11					M5	23					
17			"	4	......	18		²3	86			24	59			30	
20 23	DRINKS "	3						³2.⊙....	95		(NB) •Ro attempt NB 2	25	62			32	2
27			"	5	¹2..²2...	26						26	66		6		
32	"	4			......	33		9 1	96			27	67			33	
35			"	6	⁷2...	37		.ᴾ⁸1	100			28	70		8	34	
40	"	5			⁶1	38		......⁷1	107			29	72		9	35	
44			"	7	¹.4⁴.⁴³3	43	2	...	110			30	83		20		
48	"	6			⁸2..⁷1	47		....	114			31	88		25		
52			"	8	³↑.4......	55	3				†Round wkt.	32	92		29		
57	7-1-19-0 (1)	7	8-0-41-0 (5)			55	3	↑..⁴⁸4²...	122	3	50 p'ship in 57min BREARLEY 1000 RUNS IN TESTS WHEN 37	33	98	2	29	41	2
1.00	LUNCH										M5 NB/2			LUNCH			

144

AUSTRALIA v ENGLAND

6th Test

at Sydney

2ND DAY	BOWLERS				BATSMEN						ENGLAND 1ST INNINGS					
	(WESER) PADDINGTON END		(CRAFTER) RANDWICK END		SCOREBOARD LEFT			SCOREBOARD RIGHT			NOTES	END-OF-OVER TOTALS					
TIME	BOWLER	O.	BOWLER	O.	SCORING	BALLS	6s/4s	SCORING	BALLS	6s/4s		O.	RUNS	W.	'L' BAT	'R' BAT	EXTRAS
LUNCH					GOOCH	55	3	BREARLEY	122	3	Gooch in straw hat M5 NB/2	33	98	2	29	41	2
1.40			HIGGS	1	....	63					M6	34					
44	HOGG	10			.. 7/1	64		... 7S/1 ...	129			35	100		30	42	
49	"		"	2	... 1E	68		....	133		3HR→	36	101		31		
52	"	11			.3 4	70		8 4 9 ..2.2	139			37	108		34	46	
59			"	3	....3/1	75		...	142		BORDER sub for HOGG (one over)	38	109		35		
2.02	"	12			Y.4.2/81	81	4	...	144			39	114		40		
08	12-2-35-1 (2)		"	4	...4/4	85		...3W	148	3		40	115	3	41	46	2
10								GOWER	Helmet cap	(LHB)						0	
12	HURST	10			..8/4 1 ...	92	5	1	1			41	121		46	1	
17			"	5	..	94		...7 4 4 443	7	2		42	132			12	
22 / 24	DRINKS "	11			..↑87/41	98	6	..4 2/1 4	11	3	Round wkt to LHB GOOCH'S 50 : 105 min	43	142		51	17	
30			"	6	...7	102		...P	15			44	143		52		
34	"	12			6..6 3	105		..7.x 3	20		* over mid-wkt's head (Toohey)	45	150		56	20	
39	12-2-38-1 (4)		"	7	....	113					M 7	46					
42	YARDLEY	9			4.E/	118	7	.E 1	23		Round wkt	47	155		60	21	
48			"	8	3/3	119		L.. 3S P.	30		Gower hatless 4HR→	48	159		63	22	
52	"	10			8 4 7/1 6...2	126	1/7	7/1	31		50 p'ship in 43 min.	49	169		72	23	
57			"	9				....8 1E/4.2	39	4	Difficult driving chance to slip (HUGHES)	50	175			29	
3.00 / 04	DRINKS "	11			.6 2B ...	134					2B * Superb stop by bowler	51	179		74		4
08			"	10	.W	136	1/7	7 4/21	41		Round wkt to LHB.	51	182	4	74	32	4
10					BOTHAM	NO cap									0		
13			"	10	1E PP/2...	4						52	184		2		
15	"	12						..3 2	49		Gower in sunhat. overcast - thunder near.	53	187			35	
18			"	11	x. 1E ./.3	9		8 . 7/1..1	52		* Top edge over slip	54	192		5	37	
23	"	13			.LB 9/.4	14	1	4/.1 LB	55		LB LB	55	199		9	38	6
28			"	12				....	63		M8	56					
31	"	14			2.4 7/.4.1.2.	21	2	3/3	64			57	209		16	41	
36	14-0-76-0 (8/1)		13-3-42-2 (4)	13	7/1	22	2	..7 4 L46/4...11	71	5	* Appeal ct wkt	58	216	4	17	47	6
3.40	TEA										M8 NB/2				TEA		
3.43	RAIN STORM										Rain ceased at 4.15p				RAIN		
5.00	PLAY ABANDONED - STUMPS (2ND DAY)										Both batsmen wearing helmet caps.				STUMPS		
3RD DAY 11.00	CARLSON	8			.....LB	27		.6/.1	74		LB Very warm; very humid.	59	218			48	7
05			HIGGS	14	.......9/..2	35					no cloud. Both bowlers round wkt to LHB.	60	220		19		
08	"	9						.....2/..2	82		GOWER'S 50 in 99' 5HR→	61	222			50	
12			"	15	...8/.1	41		P 9E/.3	84		* Technical chance to wkt.	62	226		20	53	
16	"	10			../.1	43		...2/1 ..	90		ATTENDANCE (3RD): 4,159	63	228		21	54	
20	10-1-24-0 (1)		"	16	4/2.....P	51						64	230		23		
24	YARDLEY	15	16-3-50-2 (4)		.W	53	2	4/.3	92	5	50 p'ship in 53 min.	64	233	5	23	57	7
27	14.4-0-79-1 (8/1)										M8 NB/2						

145

AUSTRALIA v ENGLAND — 6th Test

at Sydney

3RD DAY TIME	BOWLERS (WESER) PADDINGTON	O.	(CRAFTER) RANDWICK END	O.	BATSMEN SCOREBOARD LEFT MILLER	BALLS	6s/4s	SCOREBOARD RIGHT GOWER	BALLS	6s/4s	ENGLAND 1ST INNINGS NOTES	O.	RUNS	W.	'L' BAT	'R' BAT	EXTRAS
					Helmet/cap				92	5	M8 NB/2	64	233	5	0	57	7
11.29	YARDLEY	15			· · · E · 4	4					Both bowlers round wkt to LHB.	65					
31			HIGGS	17	· · 1 IE	6		1 · · · · L 98	98			66	235		1	58	
35	"	16			· · · · · · · · · 14	14					• Appeal ct wkt (legside) M9	67					
39			"	18				· 2 · · · · · P 106	106			68	237			60	
42 45	DRINKS "	17			· · · · 6 · · E 22	22	1				Miller wearing sunhat	69	241		5		
50			"	19	1 IE 23	23		1 · · · 4 W 111	111	6	Gower wearing sunhat	69	247	6	6	65	7
53								TAYLOR Sun hat								0	
55			"	19				· · E · 2	2			70					
56	"	18			· · · P P 8 · 29	29		9 · 3 4	4			71	251		7	3	
12.00			"	20				· · · · · · · · 12	12		M 10	72					
03	"	19			1 · · 1 35 · 2 · 1 35	35		· 8 · 1 14	14		6 HR →	73	256		11	4	
09			"	21	· · · 4 41	41		· 1 IE 16	16			74	258		12	5	
12	"	20						· · · · · · · 8 · 2 24	24			75	260			7	
15			"	22	· · · E 8 · 1 47	47		· · 26	26			76	261		13		
18	"	21			P · · · · · · · · 55	55					M 11	77					
22 25	DRINKS "							· · 1E 2 · · · · 34	34			78	263			9	
28	"	22			P P · · · 8 · 62	62		· · 35	35			79	264		14		
32	22-2-95-1(9/1)			24	· · · · · · · 70	70					M12 Both batsmen & helmet caps.	80					
36	HOGG	13	24-5-65-3(5)		· 1 · x 75	75		L B 38	38		(B) M13 ↑NEW BALL/2 taken at 12.39 pm	81	265				8
43			HURST	13				· · · L L · · 46	46		M 14	82					
48	"	14			· · · · 1 · · · 83	83	2					83	269		18		
54	14-3-39-1(3)		" 13·6-3-39-2(4)	14	W 84	84	2	Y · P 8 · · 1 51	51	—	M14 NB/2	83	270	7	18	10	8
12·58	LUNCH				EMBUREY Helmet-cap											LUNCH	
1·40			HURST	14	· LB 1	1		· 52	52		(LB)	84	271		0		9
42	HOGG	15			x · · · · · · · 9	9					M15	85					
47			"	15				· · 2 · · 7 1·9 2·2 60	60		7HR →	86	277			16	
52	"	16			· · · · · · · 17	17					M16	87					
58			"	16	E W 18	18	—	· · 2 3 63	63			87	280	8	0	19	9
2·00					WILLIS No cap										0		
02			"	16	· · 2 1 3	3		· 1 · 1 64	64			88	282		1	20	
05	"	17						↑ · · · · · · · 72	72		Round wkt (3 balls) M17	89					
11			"	17	· · x 2 1 6	6		L L · · 7 · 4 77	77	1	• Dropped gully (YARDLEY)	90	287		2	24	
16	"	18	17-3-55-3(5)		3 · · ↑2 · 1 10	10		· 9 2 · · 1 81	81		• Over ship's head	91	290		4	25	
22 25	DRINKS 18-6-42-1(3)		HIGGS	25	E · · · · 1 IE 17	17		· 82	82		• Over ship's head	92	291		5		
29	HURST	18			2 · 18	18		· · · · · · · · 89	89		• Appeal ct wkt	93	292		6		
35	"			26	· · · 3 2 · · · 26	26						94	294		8		
38	"	19			8 · 1 27	27		· · · · 1 · ↑ 96	96		Round wkt to WILLIS	95	296		9	26	
43½			"	27	E · · · · · · · 35	35					M 18	96					
47	20-4-68-3(5)	20	27-6-68-3(5)		35	35	—	· · · · · · · · 104	104	1	M 19 NB/2 8HR•	97	296	8	9	26	9

146

AUSTRALIA v ENGLAND

at Sydney

3RD DAY	BOWLERS				BATSMEN						ENGLAND 1ST INNINGS						
	(WESER) PADDINGTON	END	(CRAFTER) RANDWICK	END	SCOREBOARD LEFT			SCOREBOARD RIGHT			NOTES	END - OF - OVER TOTALS					
TIME	BOWLER	O.	BOWLER	O.	SCORING	BALLS	6s 4s	SCORING	BALLS	6s 4s		O.	RUNS	W.	'L' BAT	'R' BAT	EXTRAS
					WILLIS	35	–	TAYLOR	104	1	M 19 NB/2	97	296	8	9	26	9
2.52			HIGGS	28	....	43					M 20	98					
55	YARDLEY	23			..	45		2 x 8 3 ·2 · · 4 1	110	2		99	303			33	
59			"	29	. . . .	52		3 1	111			100	304			34	
3.02 05	DRINKS	24			7 ·· 1	55		P 3s · · · 1	116		Taylor wearing sunhat.	101	306		10	35	
09			"	30	.... W	63	–				M 21	102	306	9	10	35	9
12					HENDRICK	NO CAP					"				0		
14	25-2-105-2 (b/1)	25	30-8-69-4 (5)		P 5 · · · O · · W	7	–	5 · 1	118	2	(NB) NB/3	103	308	10	0	36	10
3.17	ENGLAND ALL OUT										M 21 NB/3	ALL		OUT			
	ENGLAND'S LEAD : 110										827 balls	BATTING TIME : 505 MIN					

49 Randall lbw b Hogg 7 – The hero of the previous Test on this ground becomes Hogg's 41st and final victim of the rubber.

AUSTRALIA 2nd Innings

110 runs behind on 1st Innings

IN	OUT	MINS	No.	BATSMAN	HOW OUT	BOWLER	RUNS
3.39	5.15	96	1	WOOD	Cᵗ WILLIS	MILLER	29
3.39	3.58	19	2	HILDITCH	Cᵗ TAYLOR	HENDRICK	1
4.00	4.26	26	3	HUGHES	Cᵗ GOOCH	EMBUREY	7
4.29	11.17	107	4	YALLOP *	Cᵗ TAYLOR	MILLER	17
5.17	5.20	3	5	TOOHEY	Cᵗ GOOCH	EMBUREY	0
5.22	5.23	1	6	CARLSON	Cᵗ BOTHAM	EMBUREY	0
5.25	(1.43)	160	7	YARDLEY	NOT OUT		61
11.19	12.14	55	8	WRIGHT †	Cᵗ BOYCOTT	MILLER	5
12.17	12.41	24	9	HOGG	BOWLED	MILLER	7
12.43	12.48	5	10	HIGGS	Cᵗ BOTHAM	EMBUREY	2
12.50	1.43	16	11	HURST	Cᵗ AND BOWLED	MILLER	4
* CAPTAIN † WICKET-KEEPER				EXTRAS	b 3 lb 6 w – nb 1		10

TOTAL (OFF 61.1 OVERS IN 266 MINUTES) **143**

BOWLER	O	M	R	W	nb
WILLIS	3	0	15	0	1
HENDRICK	7	3	22	1	-
EMBUREY	24	4	52	4	-
MILLER	27.1	6	44	5	-
Extras			10		
	61.1	13	143	10	

HRS	OVERS	RUNS
1	11	34
2	15	26
3	16	39
4	13	31

RUNS	MINS	OVERS	LAST 50 (in mins)
50	106	22.7	106
100	185	43.1	79

WKT	TOTAL	6s	4s	BALLS	NOTES ON DISMISSAL
3	48	·	3	78	Edged lofted drive – skier to wide mid-off (running catch).
1	8	·	·	17	Edged late outswinger to 'keeper – low catch.
2	28	·	1	16	Edged off-break to backward short leg.
6	82	·	·	120	Edged leg-break to 'keeper (also given 'out' 'stumped').
4	48	·	·	2	Edged off-break to backward short leg – falling catch.
5	48	·	·	2	Pushed off-break to forward short leg
-	-	·	3	147	-
7	114	·	·	62	Swept off-break to backward square leg.
8	130	·	·	25	Hit across flighted off-break.
9	136	·	·	4	Edged off-break via pad to short square leg.
10	143	·	1	17	Mistimed drive.

0⁶ 8⁴ 490 balls (Including 1 no ball)

13   OVERS 6 BALLS/HOUR
2·34   RUNS/OVER
29   RUNS/100 BALLS

STUMPS : 70 - 5   YALLOP 13* (99b, 91')
(3RD DAY)   YARDLEY 16* (35b, 35')
          OFF 31 OVERS IN 141 MINUTES

LUNCH : 143 - 9   YARDLEY 61* (139b, 157')
                   HURST   4* (16b, 13')
          OFF 60 OVERS IN 263 MINUTES

WKT	PARTNERSHIP		RUNS	MINS
1st	Wood	Hilditch	8	19
2nd	Wood	Hughes	20	26
3rd	Wood	Yallop	20	46
4th	Yallop	Toohey	0	3
5th	Yallop	Carlson	0	1
6th	Yallop	Yardley	34	51
7th	Yardley	Wright	32	55
8th	Yardley	Hogg	16	24
9th	Yardley	Higgs	6	5
10th	Yardley	Hurst	7	16

143

50 Bob Taylor, Test allrounder – Hilditch and Wright witness the Taylor sweep. Suddenly the world's best wicket-keeper discovered that he could play long innings at the highest level.

51 Yardley b Emburey 7 – Deceived by his own kind, Yardley offers no stroke to a vast offbreak but in the second innings he overcame all the pitch's irregularities.

AUSTRALIA v ENGLAND — 6th Test

at Sydney

3RD DAY TIME	PADDINGTON END (CRAFTER) BOWLER	O.	RANDWICK END (WESER) BOWLER	O.	SCOREBOARD LEFT SCORING	BALLS	6s/4s	SCOREBOARD RIGHT SCORING	BALLS	6s/4s	AUSTRALIA 2ND INNINGS NOTES	O.	RUNS	W.	L BAT	R BAT	EXTRAS
					WOOD cap	cap	(LHB)	HILDITCH cap	cap							
3.39	WILLIS	1			·· ⁴ ₃	3		··· ↑ ⁷ ₁	5			1	4		3		1
44			HENDRICK	1				········ x	13		*Brilliant stop and return by Gooch (EMBREY)	2					
50	"	2			···· ⁹ ₄ P	11	1				M1 Background sounds of	3	8		7		
56			"	2				··· E W	17		Rod Stewart concert rehearsal in neighbouring showground	3⁴	8	1	7	1	–
58								HUGHES cap	cap							0	
4.00			"	2				····	4		M2	4					
02	"	3			·····○ ⁷ ₁	18		⁸⁸ ₄₂	6	1	Round wkt (NB) NB 1	5	16		8	6	1
09	3-0-15-0 (2)		"	3	⁵ ⁹ ₁ ·4·4·1	24	3	·· x	8			6	25		17		
14	EMBUREY	1	3-2-9-1 (2)		·········	32					LEVER sub for HENDRICK M3	7					
19			MILLER	1	·· ⁸ ₁	35		⁶₁ ····	13		Round wkt to LHB	8	27		18	7	
24	"	2			³₁	36		·· E W	16	1	* Half chance to sh.leg (BOTHAM)	8⁴	28	2	19	7	1
26								YALLOP Helmet-cap	cap							0	
29	"	2			·	37		·· ² ₃	3		Round wkt to LHB	9	31			3	
32			"	2				³₂ x P	11			10	33			5	
35	"	3			⁸₁ ·	39		······	17		1HR →	11	34		20		
38			"	3	···· x ² ₁	46		·	18			12	35		21		
41	"	4			L ·· ⁸ ₁	52		··	20		Yallop batting without helmet-cap	13	36		22		
44			"	4	² ₁ ·	54		P·	26			14	37		23		
47	"	5			⁷₁	55		L ·	33			15	38		24		
50			"	5	········ ⁷ ₁	63						16	39		25		
53	"	6			⁸₁ ··	66		E· ² ··· ₃	38		* Near slip + gully	17	43		26	8	
56			"	6	···· P ⁸ ₂	71		P LB	41			18	46		28		2
5.00	"	7			·	72		···· ² ₁	48		Yallop wearing cap	19	47			9	
03			"	7				····· EP	56		M4	20					
07	"	8			² ₁ ·	74		······	62			21	48		29		
11 / 14	DRINKS		"	8	··· W	78	3					21⁴	48	3	29	9	2
15					TOOHEY cap	cap					(Batsmen crossed)					0	
17			"	8				····	66		M5	22					
19	"	9			· E W	2	–					22²	48	4	0	9	2
20					CARLSON cap	cap										0	
22	"	9			E· E W	2	–					22⁴	48	5	0	9	2
23					YARDLEY cap	cap										0	
25	"	9			·· ² ₃	3		·	67			23	51		3		
27			"	9	·· ⁸ ₁	6		·····	72			24	52		4		
31	"	10			P· ⁵ ₃	10		····	76			25	55		7		
34			"	10	··· ⁴ ₁ ³⁴ ₁	16		² ₁ ⁶₁	78		2HR →	26	60		10	11	
40	"	11			·· ² ₂ ⁵ ₁ ··	23		⁵₁	79			27	64		13	12	
44			"	11				·········	87		M6	28					
5.47	12-1-26-3 (-)	12	11-3-15-1 (-)		⁵₁ ³₁	26	–	··· ⁷ ₁ ·	92	–	M6 NB/1	29	67	5	15	13	2

151

AUSTRALIA v ENGLAND　　　6th Test

at Sydney

AUSTRALIA 2ND INNINGS

	BOWLERS (CRAFTER) PADDINGTON END		(WESER) RANDWICK END		BATSMEN SCOREBOARD LEFT			SCOREBOARD RIGHT			NOTES	END-OF-OVER TOTALS O.	RUNS	W.	'L' BAT	'R' BAT	EXTRAS
TIME	BOWLER	O.	BOWLER	O.	SCORING	BALLS	6s/4s	SCORING	BALLS	6s/4s		O.					
					YARDLEY	26	-	YALLOP	92	-	M6 NB'1	29	67	5	15	13	2
5.51			MILLER	12	4·1	27		·······	99			30	68			16	
56	EMBUREY	13	12-3-16-1(-)		LP ·····2LB	35	-	·······	99	-	M7 NB'1 (2LB)	31	70	5	16	13	4
6.00	STUMPS		(3RD DAY)		cap			no cap					STUMPS				
4TH DAY 11.00			MILLER	13	·2 3	37		····· 5	105		Cool; heavy cloud; humid. Rando to RHB	32	73		18	14	
05	EMBUREY	14			·······	44		3 1	106		Round wkt to LHB	33	74			15	
09			·	14	·	45		···· Y 6 1	113		Round wkt.	34	75			16	
12	"	15			·· 1E 4 2·4	50	1	4s 1·	116		*Brearley threw down stumps – RO appeal	35	82		24	17	
16			·	15	)			x E W	120	-	ATTENDANCE (4th) 2,003	35·4	82	6	24	17	4
17								WRIGHT	cap							0	
19			·	15	)			PP	4		M8	36					
21	"	16			8 1	51		PP ···	11			37	83		25		
24			"	16	EP ·····2 LP2	59					Round wkt	38	85		27		
28	·	17			·· 3 ·4··	64	2	P8 ·1	14			39	90		31		1
32			·	17				P L P P P	22		M9	40					
35	·	18			6 1	65		·· P · P	29		*Appeal ct sh.leg.	41	91		32		
38			·	18	3LB PP ·2 9	71		3B ·x	31		(3LB)(3B) 3HR→	42	99		34		10
42½	"	19						P	39		M10	43					
45			·	19	8 1	72		·· Y	46			44	100		35		
48	·	20			8 x 3 8 2····1 1	79		8 1	47		Round wkt M11	45	105		39	2	
52	20-3-46-3(2)		"	20	·····.	87					*Hendrick hit on leg (backward sh.leg)	46					
56	HENDRICK	4						Y ·······	55		*Hit on right ear (sweeping) M12	47					
12.01 03½	DRINKS ·	21			4 1 ··9·1	91		1E ·3 ··	59		*Edged past slip (GOOCH) AVOIDED INNINGS DEFEAT	48	110		41	5	
07½	·	5			EP 5 P ·4·	99	3					49	114		45		
13	5-3-13-1(3)		"	22	)			8 ··W	62	-		49·3	114	7	45	5	10
14								HOGG	no cap							0	
17			"	22	) ····	103		9E 3·	1		*Nearly played on	50	117			3	
20	EMBUREY	21			··	105		P · 4	7			51	118			4	
23	21-3-47-3(2)		"	23	8 1	106		···· P8 1·	14			52	120		46	5	
26	HENDRICK	6			5 x F7 1 ·3	111		2E ·1 x	17		YARDLEY'S 50: 125'	53	125		50	6	
32			"	24	··· 8	115		· P Y	21			54	126		51		
35	"	7			3 x 2 2·.1 ↑1	120		·· 2 1	24		4HR→	55	130		54	7	
40	7-3-22-1(3)		·	25	)			x W	25	-		55·1	130	8	54	7	10
41					)			HIGGS	cap							0	
43			·	25	·· P4 ·3	124		EP 9E ·2·	3		*Ran 3 – 1 short	56	135		57	2	
47	EMBUREY	22	)		EP 4 1	126		EP W	4	-		56·3	136	9	58	2	10
48								HURST	cap							0	
50	"	22						PP. PP	5			57					
52			·	26	2 P 1E E· ·2·1	134					*Nearly played on.	58	138		60		
12.56	23-3-52-4(3)	23	26-6-43-4(-)			134	3	3 P PP ·4····	13	1	M12 NB/1	59	142	9	60	4	10

152

AUSTRALIA v ENGLAND

at Sydney

4TH DAY TIME	BOWLERS (CRAFTER) PADDINGTON END BOWLER	O.	(WESER) RANDWICK END BOWLER	O.	BATSMEN SCOREBOARD LEFT SCORING	BALLS	6s 4s	SCOREBOARD RIGHT SCORING	BALLS	6s 4s	AUSTRALIA 2ND INNINGS NOTES	END-OF-OVER TOTALS O.	RUNS	W.	'L' BAT	'R' BAT	EXTRAS
					YARDLEY	134	3	HURST	13	1	M12 NB/1	59	142	9	60	4	10
12.59			MILLER	27	5 . 4 . 4̇	139	3	. ᴾY	16	1		60	143	9	61	4	10
1.03	LUNCH		27·6·44·4 (-)										LUNCH				
1.40	EMBUREY	24			3 . . . . . . ᴾ	147					M13	61					
43	24·4·52·4(3)		MILLER	28		147	3	5̇ W	17	1	M13 NB/1	61¹	143	10	61	4	10
1.43	AUSTRALIA ALL OUT		27·1·6·44·5(-)								490 balls		ALL	OUT			
	ENGLAND REQUIRE 34 RUNS IN A MINIMUM OF 579 MINUTES																
	BATTING TIME : 266 MINUTES																

52 and 53 Two rare moments – *Left:* Becapped and serious, Boycott bowls his first ball in a Test in Australia since 1970. *Right:* Another problem for the Sydney curator! England need three runs for victory and trust Randall to discover a snake in the grass.

ENGLAND 2nd Innings
Requiring 34 runs to win in a minimum of 579 minutes

IN	OUT	MINS	No.	BATSMAN	HOW OUT	BOWLER	RUNS
2.01	2.36	35	1	BOYCOTT	C^t HUGHES	HIGGS	13
2.01	(2.40)	39	2	BREARLEY *	NOT OUT		20
2.38	(2.40)	2	3	RANDALL	NOT OUT		O
			4	GOOCH			
			5	GOWER			
			6	BOTHAM			
			7	MILLER	DID NOT BAT		
			8	TAYLOR †			
			9	EMBUREY			
			10	WILLIS			
			11	HENDRICK			
* CAPTAIN † WICKET-KEEPER				EXTRAS	b - 1b - w - nb 2		2

TOTAL   (FOR 1 WICKET)   35

(OFF 10·2 OVERS IN 39 MINUTES)

BOWLER	O	M	R	W	nb	HRS	OVERS	RUNS		RUNS	MINS	OVERS	LAST 50 (in mins)
YARDLEY	5·2	O	21	O	2								
HIGGS	5	1	12	1	-								
Extras			2										
	10·2	1	35	1									

WKT	TOTAL	6^s	4^s	BALLS	NOTES ON DISMISSAL
1	31	·	·	52	Top-edged cut at leg-break to cover-point.
-	·	·	2	30	- (Made winning hit – boundary off Yardley)
-	·	·	·	2	-

0^6 2^4 84 balls (including 2 no balls)

15 OVERS 6 BALLS/HOUR
3.41   RUNS/OVER
42   RUNS/100 BALLS

ENGLAND WON BY 9 WICKETS
at 2.40 p.m. on the fourth day
and won five Tests in a rubber in Australia
for the first time.

MAN OF THE MATCH : G.N. YALLOP

TOTAL MATCH ATTENDANCE : 22,950

TIME LOST : 120 MINUTES

WKT	PARTNERSHIP		RUNS	MINS
1st	Boycott	Brearley	31	35
2nd	Brearley	Randall	4*	2
			35	

AUSTRALIA v ENGLAND
at Sydney

4TH DAY TIME	BOWLERS (CRAFTER) PADDINGTON END BOWLER	O.	(WESER) RANDWICK END BOWLER	O.	BATSMEN SCOREBOARD LEFT SCORING	BALLS	6s/4s	SCOREBOARD RIGHT SCORING	BALLS	6s/4s	ENGLAND 2ND INNINGS NOTES	O.	RUNS	W.	L BAT	R BAT	EXTRAS
					BOYCOTT cap			BREARLEY cap			Old ball used - in spite of England's objection.						
2.01	YARDLEY	1			.2 ·8PP ·8P	8					* Appeal ct fwd sh leg	1	2		2		
05			HIGGS	1	x......	15		7/	1			2	3			1	
08	"	2			E. P. P3 .2.	22		2/1	2			3	6		4	2	
12			"	2	·4·2....	10						4	12			8	
16	"	3			.3 1E2.	26		...3	14		* Between wk & slip (Childitch)	5	20		9	11	
20			"	3	P3.3	28		8.1 P EP...	20			6	24		12	12	
23	"	4			PP8.P8S 1	34		..	22		* Nearly played on	7	25		13		
27			"	4	PP....LY	42					M1	8					
30	"	5			PPP..O.O.	51		3/3	23		NB NB NB/x2	9	30			15	2
34			"	5	E3 W	52	–	x....1	28			9.6	31	1	13	16	2
36			RANDALL cap		..	2					RANDALL dropped rubber snake on				0		
38			"	5							pitch - handed it to umpire Crafter.	10					
39	5.2-0-21-0 (i)	6	5-1-12-1 (i)		..	2	–	.4	30	2	M1 NB/2	10.2	35	1	0	20	2
2.40	ENGLAND WON BY 9 WICKETS										84 balls						
	BATTING TIME: 39 MINUTES																

54 and 55 Both captains scored their thousandth Test run in this match – *Left:* Graham Yallop, 'Man of the Match' in the Sixth Test. His 121 was the fastest century of the rubber and represented 61 per cent of the first innings total. *Right:* Mike Brearley made his three highest scores of the rubber at Sydney. His strategic skill brought an historic victory in the Fourth Test.

STATISTICAL SURVEY OF THE RUBBER

ENGLAND – BATTING

	Tests	Innings	Not Outs	Highest Score	Runs	Average	Minutes	Balls	Runs per 100 Balls	100	50	Sixes	Fours
D. I. Gower	6	11	1	102	420	42.00	1,121	880	48	1	1	–	38
D. W. Randall	6	12	2	150	385	38.50	1,299	1,074	36	1	2	1	35
I. T. Botham	6	10	0	74	291	29.10	827	657	44	–	2	2	29
C. M. Old	1	1	1	29*	29	–	113	102	28	–	–	–	2
R. W. Taylor	6	10	2	97	208	26.00	989	831	25	–	1	–	11
G. Miller	6	10	0	64	234	23.40	961	790	30	–	1	–	20
G. A. Gooch	6	11	0	74	246	22.36	942	764	32	–	1	1	22
G. Boycott	6	12	0	77	263	21.91	1,448	1,163	23	–	1	–	6
J. M. Brearley	6	12	1	53	184	16.72	875	712	26	–	1	–	10
J. K. Lever	1	2	0	14	24	12.00	105	94	26	–	–	–	–
J. E. Emburey	4	7	1	42	67	11.16	306	268	25	–	–	–	5
R. G. D. Willis	6	10	2	24	88	11.00	422	294	30	–	–	1	5
M. Hendrick	5	9	4	10	34	6.80	118	126	27	–	–	–	3
P. H. Edmonds	1	1	0	1	1	1.00	15	9	11	–	–	–	–
TOTALS	66	118	14	(150)	2,474	23.78	9,541	7,764	32	2	10	5	186

AUSTRALIA – BATTING

	Tests	Innings	Not Outs	Highest Score	Runs	Average	Minutes	Balls	Runs per 100 Balls	100	50	Sixes	Fours
A. R. Border	3	6	2	60*	146	36.50	510	482	30	–	1	–	18
G. N. Yallop	6	12	0	121	391	32.58	1,305	1,191	33	2	–	–	34
K. J. Hughes	6	12	0	129	345	28.75	1,346	1,162	30	1	–	3	29†
G. M. Wood	6	12	0	100	344	28.66	1,393	980	35	1	1	–	18
W. M. Darling	4	8	0	91	221	27.62	729	536	41	–	1	1	17
B. Yardley	4	8	1	61*	148	21.14	440	412	36	–	1	–	12
P. M. Toohey	5	10	1	81*	149	16.55	505	399	37	–	1	–	8
G. J. Cosier	2	4	0	47	52	13.00	146	101	51	–	–	–	4
J. A. Maclean	4	8	1	33*	79	11.28	447	357	22	–	–	–	5
K. J. Wright	2	4	0	29	37	9.25	156	158	23	–	–	–	2
R. M. Hogg	6	12	0	36	95	7.91	318	303	31	–	–	–	10
J. D. Higgs	5	10	4	16	46	7.66	273	212	22	–	–	–	1
P. H. Carlson	2	4	0	21	23	5.75	89	63	37	–	–	–	2
G. Dymock	3	6	1	11	28	5.60	221	200	14	–	–	–	1
A. G. Hurst	6	12	2	17*	44	4.40	118	116	38	–	–	–	5
T. J. Laughlin	1	2	0	5	7	3.50	21	11	64	–	–	–	–
A. M. J. Hilditch	1	2	0	3	4	2.00	37	25	16	–	–	–	–
TOTALS	66	132	12	(129)	2,159	17.99	8,054	6,708	32	4	5	4	166

COMPARATIVE SCORING RATES

ENGLAND: 34.33 runs per 100 balls (2,665 runs, including 191 extras, off 7,764 balls)
AUSTRALIA: 34.30 runs per 100 balls (2,301 runs, including 142 extras, off 6,708 balls)

ENGLAND – BOWLING

	Overs	Maidens	Runs	Wickets	Average	Best Analysis	5 Wickets in Innings	10 Wickets in Match	Balls per Wicket	Runs per 100 Balls	No Balls	Wides
J. K. Lever	15.1	2	48	5	9.60	4–28	–	–	24	40	–	–
G. Miller	177.1	54	346	23	15.04	5–44	1	–	62	24	–	–
M. Hendrick	145	30	299	19	15.73	3–19	–	–	61	26	6	–
J. E. Emburey	144.4	49	306	16	19.12	4–46	–	–	72	26	1	–
C. M. Old	26.7	2	84	4	21.00	2–24	–	–	54	39	11	–
R. G. D. Willis	140.3	23	461	20	23.05	5–44	1	–	56	41	51	4
I. T. Botham	158.4	25	567	23	24.65	4–42	–	–	55	45	19	1
P. H. Edmonds	13	2	27	0	–	–	–	–	–	26	–	–
G. A. Gooch	6	1	15	0	–	–	–	–	–	31	–	–
G. Boycott	1	0	6	0	–	–	–	–	–	75	–	–
TOTALS	827.4	188	2,159	110	19.62	(5–44)	2	–	60	33	88	5

AUSTRALIA – BOWLING

	Overs	Maidens	Runs	Wickets	Average	Best Analysis	5 Wickets in Innings	10 Wickets in Match	Balls per Wicket	Runs per 100 Balls	No Balls	Wides
R. M. Hogg	217.4	60	527	41	12.85	6–74	5	2	42	30	36	4
A. G. Hurst	204.2	44	577	25	23.08	5–28	1	–	65	35	8	5
J. D. Higgs	196.6	47	468	19	24.63	5–148	1	–	83	30	–	–
G. Dymock	114.1	19	269	7	38.42	3–38	–	–	130	29	31	1
P. H. Carlson	46	10	99	2	49.50	2–41	–	–	184	27	1	–
A. R. Border	31	13	50	1	50.00	1–31	–	–	248	20	–	–
B. Yardley	113.2	12	389	7	55.57	3–41	–	–	129	43	9	1
T. J. Laughlin	25	6	60	0	–	–	–	–	–	30	–	–
G. J. Cosier	12	3	35	0	–	–	–	–	–	36	–	–
TOTALS	959.7	214	2,474	102	24.25	(6–74)	7	2	75	32	85	11

COMPARATIVE BOWLING RATES

ENGLAND: 12 overs 0 balls per hour (827.4 overs in 4,139 minutes)
AUSTRALIA: 11 overs 7 balls per hour (959.7 overs in 4,870 minutes)

FIELDING

ENGLAND (68 caught, 2 stumped)
20 – Taylor (18 caught, 2 stumped)
11 – Botham
9 – Gooch
6 – Emburey
5 – Brearley
4 – Gower, Randall
3 – Hendrick, Willis
2 – Boycott
1 – Edmonds, Miller, substitute

AUSTRALIA (69 caught, 1 stumped)
18 – Maclean
8 – Wright (7 caught, 1 stumped)
6 – Wood
5 – Hughes, Toohey
4 – Darling, Yardley
3 – Border, Yallop
2 – Carlson, Cosier, Hilditch, Laughlin
1 – Hurst

EXTRAS

England conceded 142 extras in the rubber: 19 byes, 47 leg byes, 5 wides and 71 no balls. Australia conceded 191 extras: 52 byes, 62 leg byes, 11 wides and 66 no balls. There were 173 calls of 'no ball' during the six Tests, 88 of them against England bowlers.

TIME LOST DURING THE RUBBER: 4 HOURS 54 MINUTES

The time – in minutes – was lost as follows:

Day	Brisbane	Perth	Melbourne	Sydney (4th)	Adelaide	Sydney (6th)
1	26	–	–	–	–	–
2	36	–	–	–	–	120
3	25	–	–	–	–	–
4	–	87	–	–	–	–
5	–	–	–	–	–	–
TOTALS	87	87	–	–	–	120

For the benefit of club scorers and those who just like scoring for themselves, I have designed a special scoring sheet. It combines the method I have described on two facing, looseleaf pages which can accommodate a 100-overs innings. They fit into a specially designed, green rexine-covered board binder with gold blocking and three brass interscrews. A sample sheet and price details will be sent on application with a stamped self-addressed envelope (at least 9in by 4in, please) to Bill Frindall, 19 Chessing Court, Fortis Green, London N2.